Compassion

Compassion

*Loving Our Neighbor
in an Age of Globalization*

MAUREEN H. O'CONNELL

ORBIS BOOKS

Maryknoll, New York 10545

Published by Orbis Books, Maryknoll, New York 10545–0308.
Manufactured in the United States of America.
Manuscript editing and typesetting by Joan Weber Laflamme.

Unless otherwise noted, Bible quotations are taken from *The New Oxford Annotated Bible with Apocrypha*, 3rd ed., ed. Michael D. Coogan, Marc Z. Brettler, Carol A. Newsom, and Pheme Perkins (New York: Oxford University Press, 2007).

Queries regarding rights and permissions should be addressed to: Orbis Books, P.O. Box 308, Maryknoll, New York 10545–0308.

Library of Congress Cataloging-in-Publication Data

O'Connell, Maureen H.
    Compassion : loving our neighbor in an age of globalization / Maureen H. O'Connell.
        p. cm.
    Includes bibliographical references and index.
    ISBN 978–1–57075–845–4
    1. Compassion. 2. Political theology. 3. Compassion—Religious aspects—Christianity. 4. United States—Race relations. 5. Whites—United States—Attitudes. 6. Globalization. I. Title.
    BJ1475.O26 2009
    241'.677—dc22

                                                                    2009006872

For my parents,
George and Kathleen O'Connell

Contents

Acknowledgments

Anais Nin says that "we write to taste life twice." That has been in the case in this project, since in thinking and writing about compassion I have tasted more deeply my experiences with underprivileged persons and savored more keenly the insights of many colleagues and friends I have encountered so far on my journey "down to Jericho."

Several communities supported me in writing this book. I am grateful to my colleagues in doctoral studies at Boston College who were with me as I struggled to answer nagging questions. I thank my faculty colleagues at Fordham University for their endorsement of my various theological endeavors since joining them in 2005 and for creating such a fruitful environment for theological scholarship and camaraderie. I am particularly blessed with my colleagues in theology at Fordham College Lincoln Center who have helped me make New York my home, and who remind me that often productivity requires time with good friends. I was also encouraged by my compatriots in the Ignatian Solidarity Network, particularly those from the New Orleans Province who shared their wisdom regarding Christian discipleship after Katrina. And I was sustained by the theological sisterhood of the New Voices Seminar, who invited me into an intellectual and spiritual space where young women theologians might imagine together our vision of our vocations, the academy, and the church.

I would not have achieved this milestone were it not for the guidance and, dare I say, compassion of several individuals. Lisa Sowle Cahill had persistent confidence in the viability of this inquiry and continues to support my voice as a woman and as a theologian. I am indebted to Kevin Burke, S.J., for his unwavering anticipation of my contribution to theology. M. Shawn Copeland's provocative understanding of theology as interruption has been a signpost for me, and I am grateful for her refusal to neglect the memory of forgotten persons in our nation's past and present. Terrence Tilley continues to make literal and figurative space for junior faculty at the "adults' table" in the theological academy. I am grateful for the gift of Kristin Heyer's friendship, as well as for her savvy editorial sense. She inspires me with the way she integrates her hunger and thirst for justice into her vocations as theologian, wife, mother of two, and dear friend. Laurie Cassidy, a flag bearer of political theology among the younger generation of theologians, continues to accompany me through the cathartic process of naming and taking theological responsibility for my whiteness and privilege. I thank her for her wisdom and patience. Roger Haight, S.J., helped me see my way from dissertation toward monograph, and James T. Keane, S.J., waded through endless split infinitives but never wavered in his endorsement of what I am trying to say here. I am grateful to Susan Perry for taking a risk with this manuscript and for shaping me as a theological writer. In the case of this project, one could say that she tasted life at least three times.

Finally, I owe a special thank you to my family who have shared in the many epiphanies and crises along my journey as a theologian. My brother Thomas and sister-in-law Christine never let me get too comfortable in the ivory tower. My sister and best friend, Corinne, has a heart always set aflame by real people who never seem to tire in their struggle for human dignity. She prophetically reminds me that even theological ideas have human consequences. And I thank my parents, George and Kathleen, who continue to nurture me, especially during my intermittent returns to their not-quite-empty nest. I owe them more than I can ever repay, but that is one of the unceasing lessons of unconditional love they continue to teach me.

Introduction

In this work I present a simple but urgent premise: dehumanizing suffering in our contemporary reality—both in distant places around the globe and in more familiar contexts within our nation and even our local communities—demands that North American Christians embrace compassion, or the capability to "suffer with another," as the definitive characteristic of our discipleship. Who more than we, Christian citizens of the world's wealthiest nation, possess the moral imperative, the material and human resources, and the luxury of freedom from want that are necessary to alleviate the unjust suffering in our world today? And at what other point in history, in this global age and in the midst of social disasters[1] and financial crises, has the urgency of human need been surpassed only by the human capability to meet it?

However, a variety of characteristics that are part of our privileged location make effective compassion a rarity in contemporary North American Christian discipleship. Individualism, materialism, consumerism, isolationism, racism, and protectionism—a litany of American cultural "isms" reinforced by the relatively recent phenomenon of globalization—dangerously perpetuate situations of unjust suffering. When coupled with the moral blindness of white or unearned privilege, they also negatively shape our abilities to respond effectively *and* affectively to those who struggle to survive. In short, we have lost sight of what it means to "suffer with" our neighbors at a time when compassion has never been more necessary or more possible.

The central thesis of this book is that privileged Christians need to reexamine the virtue of compassion exemplified by the Samaritan traveler on the road to Jericho in the Lukan parable. I intentionally use the term *privileged Christian* to refer to anyone who self-identifies with one of the travelers in the parable—the priest, the Levite, or the Samaritan—rather than the incapacitated person in the ditch. I contend that those of us able to encounter those who are suffering rather than deal with debilitating suffering ourselves, need to rediscover the central lessons of that story. We need to recapture what would have been radical ideas for first-century Jews living under political occupation, namely, that *neighbor* is a term that transcends all boundaries and that loving our neighbors makes significant demands on everyone who can manage a safe passage to Jericho.

But even more important is our need as twenty-first century Christians to understand the equally radical claims of that parable as we practice our faith in an equally oppressive age of empire. We must reinterpret what it means to love our suffering neighbor along the road to Jericho, when that road is now so dramatically influenced by the reality of globalization. Samaritanism in an age of globalization demands that we recognize the connection between our ability to travel comfortably, if not prosperously, on our way and others' *in*abilities to

1

even climb out of roadside ditches. It requires that we see the connection between our privilege and the under-development of others and between our inability to perceive injustices and others' perpetual experiences of them. It also
requires acknowledging that our moral imaginations have failed to understand
that a seemingly endless cycle of charity only calcifies social inequalities.

Samaritanism requires our humility in taking active responsibility for our
contributions to others' misfortunes and to do so in partnership with them. And
most important, it means that we must create new relationships among all travelers on the way down to Jericho.

I begin from the conviction that a renewal of Christian compassion responds
to the central imperatives of Christian social ethics: (1) we must sharpen our
abilities to perceive the social reality, (2) we must accurately interpret that reality from frequently overlooked perspectives, and (3) we must work actively to
transform it through an emphasis on empowerment and participation. In other
words, it is our responsibility to name the signs of the times, understand their
causes, and come up with effective responses.

Three theological sources motivate and orient my approach to compassion.
The first is the "see-judge-act" praxis of Catholic social teaching, perhaps most
clearly stated in 1961 by John XXIII in his social encyclical, *Mater et Magistra,*
which affirms and directs the social ministry of the Christian community (no.
236). Then, more than thirty-five years ago, the world's bishops articulated their
understanding of this praxis in *Justice in the World* when they proclaimed that
"action on behalf of justice and participation in the transformation of the world
fully appear to us as a constitutive dimension of the preaching of the Gospel"
(no. 6). This rich tradition reminds us that faith and theology are not merely
private and personal matters pertaining to isolated Christians. Faith and theology incorporate a collective public witness to the social implications of a
trinitarian and incarnate God who embodied radical ways of being human and
living in community, particularly in communities wrestling with unjust suffering. Our faith continually invites us to contribute to the unfolding process of a
more just creation.

Ignacio Ellacuría, the slain philosopher and rector of the Jesuit community at
the University of Central America in El Salvador, provides a second beacon.
Ellacuría encouraged theologians to "confront ourselves with real things in their
reality." Doing so requires "realizing the weight of reality" or actually situating
ourselves in a particular historical context, in this case the historical context of
globalization; "shouldering the weight of reality" or taking on the demands of
this reality, in this case the demands of the suffering majority of the world; and
"taking charge of the weight of reality" or a praxis of "doing something real" in
response to the reality.[2] Compassion, therefore, does not just alleviate suffering,
but rather transforms it.

Finally, I am compelled by M. Shawn Copeland's claim that truth-telling is
the main responsibility of theology, particularly in a post-9/11 world. She asserts that the theologian's vocation is to identify a critical interpretation of the
gospel that "repudiates the principles and powers of society and resists their

efforts to seduce its spirit-filled, prophetic, critical and creative impulse."[3] This orientation encourages me to consider critically the Christian tradition of compassion from the underside of history and to take seriously the demands of those on the margins. Compassion, therefore, is not comfortable and private but rather dangerous and political.

To these sources I add the wisdom of my own experience, given my historical, socioeconomic, and geographic location as a white, privileged, female North American. As one who participates knowingly and unknowingly in the processes of globalization and who does not experience social disasters but witnesses them from a safe distance, I attempt to do theology in partnership with those who do not share my privilege and to be attentive to their needs. I turn to compassion to do so.

OVERVIEW

My objective in this book is to suggest an alternative approach to compassion that responds to three urgent components of our contemporary reality: its massive unjust suffering, the phenomenon of globalization, and the social disasters fueled by radical social inequality.

In the first chapter I describe in greater detail the signs of the times for which I believe Christians are increasingly responsible: unjust suffering, the dehumanizing effects of globalization, and radical social inequality. Taking these realities seriously exposes a variety of flaws in our approaches to compassion. I explore compassion's simultaneous prevalence and ambiguity in the Christian tradition, as well as the problematic values and beliefs that shape it. I consider the dehumanizing potential of current expressions of compassion, most recently evident in individual and collective responses to the natural and social disasters that occurred at the turn of the new millennium. I also examine the limited and even erroneous understanding of compassion held by many Christian and secular ethicists.

In the second and third chapters I illuminate the features within philosophical and theological ethics that can contribute to a more useful definition of compassion. I examine the ways in which philosophers and theologians incorporate compassion into their political and moral systems, arguing that compassion is essential for personal *and* social transformation. In the second chapter I briefly review compassion's development in the philosophical tradition, paying particular attention to the ideas of the Stoic philosophers and those of the Enlightenment. In the third chapter I review the development of compassion in theological sources, particularly in biblical texts and in theories of virtue ethics. I also examine more contemporary scholarship that associates compassion with human development, including feminist and liberation theologies and the central documents of Catholic social teaching.

In the fourth chapter I turn to the insights of political philosopher Martha C. Nussbaum, who continually argues for the viability of philosophical inquiry in shaping public policy. Compassion increasingly lies at the heart of her diverse scholarship and human-development work. I illustrate how compassion supports her claims about the centrality of emotion in moral reasoning and development, and I explore her wariness of compassion's usefulness for theories of justice. I highlight Nussbaum's correctives for these erroneous judgments by lifting out intrinsic connections between compassion and her "capabilities approach" to human development.

In the fifth chapter I turn to the German political theologian Johann Baptist Metz and his contributions to articulating an approach to compassion in situations of massive unjust suffering. A great concern of Metz is compassion's tendency to dilute itself into a bourgeois experience that is ahistorical, privatized, and not sufficiently transformative. For Metz—and this is true of his theology in general—compassion should attend to dangerous and disruptive memories and narratives of suffering in order to be sufficiently political and socially transformative.

The sixth chapter integrates the transformative potential of compassion gleaned from the philosophical and theological traditions and from Nussbaum and Metz into what I propose as the central definition of compassion for North American Christians: loving our suffering neighbor in an age of globalization entails (1) the *ability to perceive* our connections to the causes of others' suffering; (2) the *willingness to interpret* contexts of injustice from the perspective of those who suffer; and (3) an *active commitment* to create new relationships with the capacity to transform the neighbor, ourselves and the social reality. Whether guided by Nussbaum's definition of compassion as an "upheaval" or Metz's as an "interruption," I argue that social change depends on a change in perception, evaluation, and action on the part of those whose lives are not consumed by a struggle for survival. Compassion is central to that process of change—for those above and below the threshold of flourishing, and for challenging what constitutes the "threshold of flourishing" itself.

I discuss the components, means, and results of transformation in light of Hurricane Katrina, perhaps the most massive human tragedy in our nation's history. The experience of Katrina demonstrates the flaws in our contemporary approaches to compassion as well as more authentic and transformative ways of suffering with our neighbor in the midst of social disaster.

In the seventh and final chapter I accept a challenge put forward by Martin Luther King, Jr., more than forty years ago that we think critically about why the road to Jericho is so dangerous for so many people. I propose political compassion as a tool for transforming the global Jericho road. I suggest that compassion might help us determine what kind of globalization we would like to experience and how we might direct it toward more humane and just ends. I identify four current models of global ethics—the "universal approach" of human rights, the "particular approach" of liberation ethics, the "discipleship" or responsibility approach, and the "love approach" of social charity—in light of the new terrain of this twenty-first century, which offers many challenges, including those of 9/11, Hurricane Katrina, and the pathology of white privilege. Compassion can be an effective moral disposition with the capacity to challenge privatized, individualized, and paternalistic responses to suffering at the hands of others.

THE GOOD SAMARITAN REPRISE

To some extent, my reconstruction of compassion interrupts and reinterprets the parable of the good Samaritan—the paradigmatic narrative of neighbor love in the Christian tradition. In our contemporary reality, defined by dehumanizing suffering, shaped by encounters with others that are increasingly defined by gross inequality and driven by an expanding global market economy, it is not enough for individual travelers to step into the ditch and offer emergency aid to the victims of humanly perpetrated violence. There are more victims than travelers, and the road to Jericho is paved with their labor and social deprivation. In addition, the distinction between innocent travelers and guilty robbers is increasingly blurred, and material resources alone cannot provide sufficient healing. We need a new approach to compassion.

Truly suffering with persons languishing in the ditch requires self-critical and collective consciousness on the part of Samaritans. It demands an individual and collective willingness to listen and to be transformed by the narratives of the victims in the ditch along with freedom to accept accountability for the conditions that caused their victimization. Compassion entails an active commitment to relationships that empower all travelers to reach their destinations. And compassion should be an endeavor with the potential to change the journey itself dramatically. Genuine and effective compassion is less concerned with emergency relief or philanthropic charity and more closely connected with development aid and social justice. Creating upheavals and interruptions in the world causes us to stop, to open our eyes, and to listen so that we might have a more accurate and effective vision of what might be and some knowledge as to how to move toward that new destination.

1

American Compassion in a Global Age

Convenient Samaritanism

In essence, Katrina was an American tsunami. . . . It was typical of the American spirit that, after the skies opened up, so did the hearts of our people. Indeed, the compassion shown by citizens offered the first ray of hope after those dark skies cleared. Pledges of help and money poured in from far and wide—corporate boardrooms and classrooms, celebrities and school children, large cities and small towns, and the churches and synagogues that literally threw open their doors to shelter the homeless from every faith and strata of society.[1]

It seems like it's almost in our DNA: We respond to the immediate crisis, but we don't think about systemic issues. . . . We'd rather give, feel good about it, and then it's over. It's a quick-fix mindset that's hard to overcome.[2]

These two statements offer a conflicting assessment of American compassion. In their reflections on Americans' response to Hurricane Katrina, former presidents Bush and Clinton commend our willingness to respond to those in need with "pledges of help and money" and claim this compassion as the very essence of the American spirit. When crisis strikes, we do not hesitate to respond by giving of our surplus and often do so in excessive amounts.

The second comment, on the other hand, made by a director of social ministries at an evangelical church in Texas, points to an unreflective immediacy to our compassion. When crisis strikes, Americans assuage our own discomfort at others' affliction with cathartic giving. Then we quickly move on with our lives. When we respond to others' affliction, we do not necessarily examine the social complexities of the crisis, come to know personally the people affected, or probe our connections to them or their suffering. Rather, we look at compassion as a quick fix, a band-aid, or a panacea in times of extreme need. We do not consider compassion an ongoing process, a persevering presence with those who suffer, or an opportunity for conversion in the midst of the many struggles of ordinary time. Ours is a compassion of convenience in times of crisis, rather than a compassion of commitment in the times in between.

6

It is no wonder that this is the case. At a time of color-coded terror alerts, voluntary white hyper-segregation, and militarized national borders, do we really want to leave our comfort zones of personal, economic, or national security in order to enter into the chaotic vulnerability of those in the ditch on the proverbial road to Jericho? If we are bombarded with hundreds of images of nameless suffering persons around the world, to the point of over-stimulation and saturation, do we really perceive them, understand the context of their affliction, or share their pain? When we mistakenly equate virtual connectivity with embodied relationality, instant messaging with conversation, and web browsing with conscience formation, do we really encounter those laid low by injustice—speaking with them, touching them, personally ministering to them, and being converted by them? If charity increasingly occurs through "buy-and-donate" retail gimmicks or "click-here-to-give" web links, do we detour from the routines of our consumerism to learn from people why the Jericho road is so dangerous for some to travel and how to redress collaboratively the threats to human dignity that so many face? When we seek justice through emailed petitions or online pledges, do we ever really go off-line in order to work with other travelers to ensure that those victimized by social injustice have access to long-term health care, decent education, affordable housing, or meaningful work?

Simply put, we need to ask ourselves how we love our suffering neighbors who are caught in social disasters in an age of globalization.

From the tragedies of ancient Greece to the language of "moral values" in the contemporary United States, human beings have long acknowledged the imperative to cultivate a sense of concern for those who suffer. In one way or another—whether as a virtue, a moral sentiment, a private expression of neighbor love, or a political platform—we uphold the ability to accompany others in their misfortune as integral to moral development on the individual and social scale. Consider, for example, iconic figures who experienced profound personal transformations as a result of unexpectedly deep encounters with those who suffer. Or consider the many political platforms or human development campaigns that turn to the experiences of suffering people to prick the collective human consciousness: Johnson's War on Poverty and King's civil rights movement in the 1960s, Bush's Compassionate Conservativism in the late 1980s, the international Jubilee 2000 campaign for debt relief and Bono's One Campaign at the turn of the millennium, or most recently, Barack Obama's Yes, We Can grassroots presidential campaign. In short, we recognize compassion as a necessary ingredient for personal and social change.

In particular, the Jewish people of the covenant and those who follow the way of Christ are called to participate in the transformative power of compassion. For example, the Book of Exodus clearly reveals that Yahweh's dramatic liberation of the Israelites from dehumanizing slavery in Egypt began with being moved by their suffering cries. "I have seen the affliction of my people who are in Egypt, and have heard their cry because of their taskmasters," Yahweh confesses to Moses. "I know their sufferings, and I have come down to deliver them out of the hand of the Egyptians, and to bring them up out of that land to a good and broad land, a land flowing with milk and honey" (Ex 3:7–9, New

Oxford Annotated Bible). Accounts of the healing miracles in the New Testament depict a Jesus who is similarly moved by the pain and suffering of those who cry out to him from roadsides and crowds throughout his travels in first-century Palestine. Just as Yahweh compassionately liberated the Israelites and established them as a new nation under a covenantal relationship, Jesus compassionately liberates those marginalized by physical and mental affliction and establishes a deeply relational "kin-dom" of God.[3] In both cases the well-being of the whole depends on the vitality of the least. These examples lead William Spohn to call compassion the "optic nerve" of Christian discipleship because it encourages us to see and respond to others' suffering as Jesus did.[4] Therefore, from Augustine's fourth-century sermons that identify compassion as "tribulations of the heart" to Pope Benedict XVI's twenty-first-century exhortation of "social charity" in his first social encyclical, the Christian tradition puts forward a variety of directives on how we might follow Christ and compassionately "do likewise" for those who suffer.

Despite compassion's prevalence, however, theologians and ethicists continue to debate its precise contours and its ultimate purpose. Both the philosophical and theological traditions offer a panoply of definitions of compassion. This lack of precision contributes to current ambiguity regarding compassion's social role and efficaciousness. For example, some scholars claim compassion is an erratic and unreliable sentiment, while others suggest it is an insightful and habituated virtue guided by prudence. Benedict XVI equates the love of compassion with charity in *Deus Caritas Est,* while Thomas Aquinas links it more closely with *misericordia* or mercy in his *Summa Theologica.* Liberation theologians rely on compassion to motivate relationality with more distant others through principles such as the preferential option for the poor or solidarity, while feminist theologians suggest its usefulness in mediating more immediate relationships among family and friends through an ethics of care. More contemporary philosophers such as John Rawls or even Charles Taylor inevitably rely on the ability to empathize with others as the foundation of social-contract theories, models of justice rooted in fairness, or for reflective civic engagement. These examples suggest that compassion's distinctiveness from responses such as mercy, solidarity, or empathy is often hard to articulate.

In a rather scathing review of compassion in Western philosophy and American political history, Clifford Orwin argues that lack of clarity about compassion, coupled with its uncritical use in a variety of political contexts, leads to misappropriation in both morality and politics. He claims that "compassion has become synonymous with sensitivity or openness. . . . It implies caring without judging, and acting morally while refraining from enacting one's own morals. . . . Compassion neatly splits the difference between Christian moralism and post-Christian moral relativism."[5] We need only consider that both George W. Bush and the Dali Lama call for compassion in tackling social problems to appreciate that compassion is susceptible to a variety of interpretations, some less than effective in "suffering with" others. In addition, in an age when moral values have become increasingly decisive issues in closely contested political elections, we would do well to reflect on Orwin's claim that "when the rhetoric of compassion must supplement it, democracy is in trouble."[6] And finally, we need only consider the sorry state of post-Katrina recovery in the poor neighborhoods and communities along the Gulf Coast to realize the practical ineffectiveness of our suffering with fellow Americans.

The point here is that we need to reconstruct compassion in order to address the problematic ambiguities in the Christian tradition regarding loving our suffering neighbors as well as the new ways in which human beings are related in an age of globalization. Two initial tasks are necessary. We need to understand fully *why* a new approach to suffering is necessary, and we need to consider *what* in our current expressions of Samaritanism needs to be changed.

DISPATCHES FROM THE ROAD TO JERICHO: WHY WE NEED COMPASSION MORE THAN EVER

Massive human suffering, the phenomenon of globalization, and radical social and economic inequality dictate the proverbial journey to Jericho for many. These three conditions of the Jericho road bring into sharp focus our increasing responsibility for the causes of others' suffering both at home and around the world. Each reinforces the need for compassionate first world travelers at a time when we seem least capable of suffering with others.

Suffering Reality

More than two-thirds of the world's population struggles for survival in the ditch along the road to flourishing, while the privileged minority continues its journey unaffected. Like the assaulted victim in Jesus' parable, these people are laid low by humanly perpetrated violence—the violence of extreme poverty, economic exclusion, social marginalization, and cultural amnesia. These persons experience what Wendy Farley calls a "radical suffering" that "pinches the spirit of the suffering, numbing it and diminishing its range." This suffering reduces their ability "to exercise freedom, to feel affection, to hope, to love God."[7] Radical suffering holds a particular power over persons—it strips them of their personal identity, denies their moral agency, stunts their capabilities to care for themselves and those they love, blinds them to alternative visions of the future, and traps them in a demoralizing and exhausting race against meaninglessness and death. Consider the following examples of dehumanizing suffering:

- The international aid organization, CARE, reports that every minute 21 children around the world die of malnutrition and preventable diseases.[8]
- CARE reports that 95 percent of the 40 million people affected with HIV/AIDS live in the developing world.[9]
- According to the World Bank, as of 2001, 46 percent of those in sub-Saharan Africa struggled to survive on less than $1 a day.[10]
- The One Campaign reports that one in seven persons (or 2.6 billion people) does not have access to clean water for drinking, cooking, and washing. As a result, every 15 seconds a child dies from an illness related to unsanitary water.[11]

- The average life expectancy in Haiti, the poorest country in the Western hemisphere, is 57; less than half of Haitians can read, and only 25 percent of the population has access to clean water.[12]

Ultimately, the pervasiveness of unjust suffering in the contemporary reality increases the urgency of more clearly understanding what it means to suffer with others. Authentic compassion makes demands of compassionate persons, resists the dehumanizing power of radical suffering, and focuses on full restoration of persons. It requires the ability to perceive the severity of dehumanizing suffering, to privilege the perspective of those who suffer in order to understand it, and then to resist the causes of that suffering through self-critical awareness of our connection to those causes. In short, in a time of tremendous suffering, when encounters among people are increasingly dictated by forces of a global market economy that unfairly privilege the minority at the expense of the majority, the suffering people of the world rightly demand that we respond to their suffering. What is more, in light of their radical suffering, our response ought to examine and transform the structures, institutions, and systems that generate wealth for some and deny basic human rights to others.

Globalization

We face new challenges in loving our many suffering neighbors in this new millennium. Globalization has dramatically changed the causes of unjust affliction and our means of responding to persons suffering from them. This second and perhaps most definitive characteristic of today's Jericho road is one of the most contested phenomena of human history. It brings with it a variety of competing definitions, epistemologies, and ways of evaluating human behavior. Consider just a small sampling of this variation, many offered by Christian social ethicists[13]:

- Max Stackhouse explains globalization as "a worldwide set of social, political, cultural, technological, ethical and ideological motifs, that are creating a worldwide civil society that stands beyond the capacity of any nation state to control." In his estimation, these emerging motifs in this new global society influence "every local context, all peoples, all social institutions and the ecology of the earth itself."[14]
- Anthony Giddens describes globalization as a complex set of political, technological, cultural, and economic processes that began with revolutions in communication technology in the 1960s. These processes have since created a variety of "upward pulls" (power is pulled away from the local toward the transnational), "downward pressures" (developments in world markets are often felt most acutely on the local level), and "sideways squeezes" (economic zones cross national boundaries, densely populated global cities are emerging). He contends that globalization now affects things "out there," such as "the world financial order," as well as things "in here" such as dynamics between the sexes and evolving family values.[15]
- Rebecca Todd Peters suggests four distinct theories of globalization, each of which stems from a different moral vision regarding the good life,

justice, and social responsibility: the neo-liberal approach, the development approach, the earth justice approach, and the postcolonial approach. She claims our perception of our reality influences our epistemological stance and shapes our evaluation of the means and ends of globalization.[16]

- Cynthia Moe-Lobeda observes that we most commonly consider globalization as a set of interrelated basic economic principles including a free and deregulated market that will benefit all consumers, "specialization according to comparative advantage" that will benefit those who engage in free trade, and competition that will ensure that equality. Many dispute the outcomes of these principles.[17]

- Robert Gillet identifies four characteristics of globalization: the progressive disempowerment and disenfranchisement of individuals and families, the increasing domination of corporations and financial institutions, the dangerous association of human flourishing with human consumption, and the sense that these features of human existence are unavoidable.[18] The challenge, in his estimation, is to resist the consolidation of economic, cultural, and social capital in the hands of an ever-shrinking minority.

- William Schweiker prefers to use the term *globality* or the phrase *many worlds* to explain the multicultural and pluralistic context in which we find ourselves. He suggests that "overhumanization" or the overwhelming sense that "human power is now given free reign to conquer and control life" has become the primary human experience in this time of many worlds.[19]

- John Coleman identifies four issues that globalization presents to the Christian tradition: insensitivity to human suffering, inattention to global sustainability, polarization within and among cultures, and the inability of the nation-state to meet basic needs.[20]

Given these characteristics, globalization makes it possible either to better love our neighbors or to more irrevocably reject them. For example, technology and systems of communication make it easier for us to perceive those afflicted by unjust suffering. But we can rely on this same technological connectivity to remain mere spectators of others' tragedies rather than moral agents who are responsible to others. In addition, transnational nongovernmental organizations have become the primary agents of social justice in many of the hardest to reach neighborhoods and communities on the globe. However, when these organizations merely work *for* these communities rather than *with* them, they perpetuate a paternalistic and disempowering relationality that does little to transform causes of injustice. Or consider the unparalleled ease and speed with which material goods and resources can be distributed to those in need. This blessing of our time, however, can reinforce the dangerous tendency of North Americans to equate loving the neighbor with donating material "stuff" to the neighbor rather than giving of our very selves.

With these challenges in mind, most ethicists agree that the critical question regarding globalization is not *whether or not* it ought to occur, but rather *what kind* of globalization we want to unfold. In other words, do we want a collection of economic, cultural, and social processes that promote unity as well as diversity by

bolstering intentional transnational relationships, or do we want to threaten that unity and diversity by unreflective acquiescence to the faceless power of the market economy? Do we want a phenomenon that makes us more acutely aware of our interdependence on others and the planet for our individual and corporate flourishing, or do we want a phenomenon that blinds us to the moral imperatives of this radical dependency because of a myopic obsession with individual consumerism? Do we want to come together voluntarily in order to seek a more just distribution of the earth's resources, or do we want to be "pulled" and "pushed" into conflicts over them? Do we want to be active moral agents who shape our future, or passive bystanders who merely accept what the invisible fist of globalization delivers? These are the pressing questions of globalization.

Rightly thinking about compassion—or the way in which we perceive, interpret, and respond to those in need along the side of the Jericho road—can assist us in making right choices about globalization. Consider the following three factors that enable compassionate persons to cultivate the kind of globalization that will empower more complete flourishing of all persons.

First, compassion takes seriously the suffering of others and in so doing uncovers the conscious and unconscious values that we rely on in order to perceive and to evaluate accurately what is going on in our reality. When viewed from the perspective of those who suffer, we realize that the social beliefs and values that shape our lifestyle choices, our interactions in a variety of public spheres, and our understandings of human flourishing are not all valid or morally viable. In other words, not all definitions and theories of globalization are accurate. For example, in an essay written immediately following the 9/11 terrorist attacks in the United States, liberation theologian Jon Sobrino and comparative theologian Felix Wilfred argue that those who flourish must be awakened by globalization's victims, who see a very different world "from the one which may be seen from the towers of trade centres and stock-exchanges." From the perspective of those who suffer, the promises of globalization are merely a "sweet illusion for the haves and the powerful of the world."[21] Sobrino argues that unless globalization is guided by the wisdom of the "have nots" and powerless of the world, wisdom that arises out of their experiences of suffering in the midst of globalization, its processes will accomplish little more than cultural homogenization and social exclusion.

Second, compassion reveals the damaging impact of globalization on all persons, not just those who struggle to survive. A sensitivity to others' suffering in the midst of these converging economic, political, and cultural processes heightens our awareness of the impact of these processes on us, middle-class North Americans who fuel the engines of globalization with our everyday consumerism. The psychological effects of globalization weigh heavily on those of us who live in the epicenter of its matrix of economic, political, and cultural structures.

For example, Peters depicts a sense of collective entrapment in the global economy when she notes that many of the "'first' world workers who lost their jobs to *maquiladoras* and 'free trade' zones also shop at Wal-Mart, drink Coca-Cola, and eat at McDonald's."[22] Or recall William Schweiker's observation about the moral paralysis and incoherence that accompany the experience of "overhumanization." Elliot and Lermert describe a "new individualism" that emerges through globalization. Its characteristics include "individual self-aggrandizement, desire for unrestrained individualism, instant gratification and insulated hedonism," all of which lead us to consider "life's possibilities and responsibilities in individualist terms—less as interwoven with cultural relations and social problems, and more as shaped by individual decisions, capacities and incapacities, personal achievements and failures."[23] In short, Cynthia Moe-Lobeda notes that many of us "are people of deep compassion and enormous heart" who may not want to contribute to situations of injustice; but whether insulated by privilege or overwhelmed by the magnitude of the problem, "we acquiesce."[24]

Compassion resists this paralyzing acquiescence. It makes us attentive to the webs of relationality that globalization generates. It enables compassionate persons to recognize our connections to others' suffering by virtue of our participation in structures and systems of institutional violence. It restores our moral agency by embracing rather than rejecting our inherent vulnerability. It relies on that vulnerability to spark the moral imagination that can break through the determinist logic around globalization. It frees us to envision different possibilities for more life-giving relationships in alternative structures and systems. If Peters is correct in suggesting that the choices of our everyday, middle-class North American consumerism fuel the engine of globalization, then we can also steer globalization with more intentional choices about loving our suffering neighbors.

And third, compassion can serve as an affective disposition and practice for a global approach to ethics. We have already discussed the need to incorporate different persons and different perspectives in reflecting on the kind of globalization we want. Compassion assists us with this by privileging the experiences, perspectives, and wisdom of people often denied access to this kind of critical reflection on globalization. In addition, we need an ethic that can balance the various tensions that arise within the complex web of relationships that globalization creates: between the local and the universal, between multiculturalism and cultural imperialism, between free-market capitalism and democratic capitalism, between third-world producers and first-world consumers, between empowerment and domination. For example, David Hollenbach wonders "how diverse forms of human association will help make good lives possible for human beings who have no choice but to live on the same earth together."[25] Compassion enables those who seek a global ethic to embrace the diverse particularities of cultures—religious practices, familial customs, and attitudes about women, for example—while simultaneously protecting those who suffer within them. Compassion makes this sensitivity possible through deep listening to those who suffer, a humble willingness to accompany them in their affliction, and a preserving commitment to address the causes of the injustice they experience. In addition, German theologian Hille Haker endorses compassion as a virtue for global justice because it enables first-world persons to overcome what she calls "cultural amnesia," which keeps us from acknowledging our responsibility for social suffering.[26] She connects compassion to justice through an emotive care or concern for the sufferer and a political concern with "raising up" the sufferer. To that end, compassion becomes an important complement to social justice theories.

In short, globalization presents a variety of complex moral issues that define the signs of our times. However, if we root, orient, and motivate the processes and relationships of globalization in compassion, we can harness its life-giving and life-enhancing attributes:

- When rooted in compassion, globalization does more than ensure that we have instantaneous access to images and accounts of human suffering around the world; it also becomes a way to perceive and to cultivate our connections to others in a variety of webs of relationality.

- When oriented toward compassion, globalization does more than provide economic, political, or cultural agency for *some*; it creates the opportunity for moral agency for *all* through increased capabilities for intentional relationality and collaborative reflection on the means and ends of these processes.

- When motivated by compassion, globalization does more than enable aid organizations to transcend a variety of barriers that at one time prevented resources from reaching those in need; it also empowers all persons to think critically about what it means to flourish and to distribute material and human resources accordingly.

Encountering Others in the Context of Radical Inequality

As followers of a tradition with an emphasis on loving God *and* neighbor, Christian disciples have always been called to encounter our vulnerable brothers and sisters who have been sidelined by injustices along that route. However, as Christian disciples in the world's only superpower, we find ourselves at a new crossroads along the Jericho road. Two distinctive characteristics of our encounters with others at this junction deserve our attention: the unprecedented inequality among the travelers, and the dangerous complicity of American Christians in the suffering of our brothers and sisters.

First, our encounters with others in our daily travels increasingly occur in the context of radical social, economic, and political inequality. Perhaps unlike any other time in Christian history, we come upon others whose journeys are dominated by the all-consuming task of navigating the social disaster of extreme poverty. If this sounds overstated, consider the following examples.

- The One Campaign reports that the world's fifty poorest countries control only 1 percent of the global economy. If these countries were to raise that level of participation by 1 percent, it would lift 128 million people out of extreme poverty.[27]

- The world's Highly Poor and Indebted Countries spend as much as 30 percent of their national budgets on servicing debt they owe to richer countries or international banks rather than on much-needed health care, education, and infrastructure, keeping these countries trapped in poverty.[28]

This inequality is not limited to the international context. Douglas Hicks notes that among the eight developed nations on the planet the United States "experiences the highest level of income inequality . . . surpassed only by the most unequal developing nations, including most Latin American nations, Thailand, and South Africa."[29] Consider, for example:

- The Congressional Budget Office reported that between 1979 and 2005 the income of the top 10 percent of wage earners more than doubled while people in the bottom 20 percent experienced only a 6 percent wage increase.[30]
- Almost 13 percent of Americans live below the poverty line of $19,000 per year for a family of four, a number that might include as many as 25 percent if that income line were only slightly adjusted.

The event of Hurricane Katrina, a social disaster we examine more closely in Chapter 6, revealed this radical inequality in many provocative ways. Consider a few quick examples:

- Of the 5.8 million people who lived in the areas affected by the storm, more than one in five, or one million, lived below the national poverty line of roughly $19,000 per year for a family of four.
- Twenty-eight percent of the citizens of New Orleans lived in tracts of what the Census Bureau calls "concentrated poverty," and 25 percent of its workers made less than $7.18 an hour.
- Mississippi and Louisiana, the two states most affected by the hurricane, boasted the highest and the second highest poverty rates in the nation (21.6 percent and 19.4 percent respectively, compared with the national average of 13 percent).

In order to unpack the distinct characteristics of our encounters with others, we can examine the differences between contemporary Christians and our first-century counterparts journeying down to Jericho in the parable of the Good Samaritan.

Unlike the priest and the Levite, who failed to acknowledge the victim of physical assault, we fail to acknowledge the *majority of the world's people* laid low by the structural violence of extreme poverty. For example, it is almost impossible to grasp the sheer magnitude of those struggling with extreme poverty. Three out of six people on the planet (or 3 billion) try to live on $2 a day, one in six (or 1 billion) eke out a living on $1 a day, and 800 million die each day in this struggle. Unlike the priest and the Levite, who had no direct culpability in this physical assault, we fail to minister to people *we directly and indirectly assault* through our participation in unjust systems, structures, and institutions. We wound these others with our everyday choices about what to wear, what to eat, what to do with our waste, how to heat our homes, how to spend our leisure time, and how to invest our savings. And unlike the priest and the Levite, who did not have the resources to address the structural injustices of the road to Jericho even if they had considered them, *we have the material and human resources to end extreme poverty*. We tragically fail to use them. Finally, unlike the priest and the Levite, who failed to see that the man in the ditch depended on their compassion in order to flourish, we fail to see that our *own flourishing depends on the compassion* we extend to those who suffer. We fail to realize that those to whom we minister can minister to us in return. Their vulnerability can penetrate our defensive invulnerability; their fundamental dependence on others can break through our isolating autonomy; their imagination can interrupt our market-driven logic; and their vision of the future can push us beyond our self-obsession with the present.

The point here is that, unlike travelers in previous centuries, the few of us capable of continuing our journey down to Jericho are guilty of three sins in addition to a failure to love our neighbors. We participate in structural violence that cripples the majority of the people on earth. We refuse to accept responsibility for our participation in this violence. And we fail to imagine ways we can use the world's resources that we hoard to transform structural injustices. Therefore, suffering people make claims on us based on our status as their neighbors, the central moral of the parable, and by virtue of our status as those who sustain rather than terminate the conditions of their affliction.

With the growing inequality among members of the human family, and keeping the humanly created and sustained causes of this inequality in mind, it becomes clear that would-be Samaritans need to engage in a critical examination of conscience in order to reverse these trends in social inequality. Henri Nouwen makes this point quite plainly: "No to racial injustice means a call to look at our own bigotry straight in the eye, and no to world hunger calls upon us to recognize our own lack of poverty."[31] In order to perceive, minister to, and restore the various persons we encounter on the road to Jericho, we must do these things for ourselves as well. We must more accurately perceive ourselves as culpable and capable moral agents. We must minister to our moral wounds as Christians of the First World: our isolating individualism, our paralyzing fear, and our demoralizing overhumanization. And we must think creatively about the flourishing we seek for ourselves and others.

In order to accomplish this task, however, we would do well to address the social sin of white privilege that shapes so many of our encounters with suffering others and that keeps us from the kind of self-reflection outlined above. White privilege is the collection of unearned social entitlements and assets that white persons unconsciously draw on in shaping our self-understanding, our moral values, and our frameworks of meanings or world views. It sustains racism or the structural and institutional systems that perpetuate inequitable distribution of resources, power, and social power based on socially constructed beliefs, attitudes, and dispositions toward others. White privilege also fuels the growing gap between rich and poor in our contemporary reality. Consider a few definitions of *whiteness* and *white privilege* that support this claim:

- Mary Elizabeth Hobgood notes that "whiteness is a major social structure that has developed historically to organize social space and individual experience" and that this structure "monopolizes power for whites" and "creates unearned advantages at the expense of others while denying dimensions of our relational capacities as human beings."[32]
- Sociologist Ruth Frankenberg notes that white pertains not only to skin pigment but also to a "location" or "stand point" for observing the social

reality. White people remain largely unaware that we stand in this location where power and dominance intersect, and where cultural, social, political, economic, and religious norms or prototypes are determined.[33]

- Peggy McIntosh, one of the first sociologists to use the term *white privilege,* describes it as "a right, advantage, or immunity granted to or enjoyed by white persons beyond the common advantage of all others." More figuratively, she considers it a "weightless invisible knapsack of special provisions, maps, passports, codebooks, visas, clothes, tools, and blank checks" that some "can cash in on."[34]

- Traci West explains white privilege in terms of entitlement and systemic investment. Whiteness is "normal," the "standard," or the "ideal" in American culture while other ethnicities are "abnormal," "substandard," or "less than ideal." As a result, white persons and their experiences are not subject to the ongoing critical qualification or evaluation that persons of other colors constantly endure. Since whiteness is valued differently, whiteness entitles people differently. Moreover, she notes that whites that collectively decide to invest in and protect whiteness by the way we distribute social goods and bads.[35] The tax code, our system of public education, the criminal justice system, and access to health care are all examples of systemic commitment to maintaining a status quo that benefits a few and burdens the majority.

- Both Traci West and Miguel A. De La Torre examine privilege in the context of denial. For example, West notes that whites regularly claim that racism is no longer a justice issue in post–civil rights America or argue that racism stems from individual actions and as such does not require ongoing critical social attention. Either way, privilege enables whites to deny the reality of racial injustice. This leaves the relationship between poverty and race, as well as the injustices of white privilege, dangerously unexplored. De La Torre notes that "the ethics advanced by the dominant culture appears to rationalize these present power structures, hence protecting and masking the political and economic interests of those whom the structures privilege."[36]

- Martin Luther King, Jr., implicitly explained white privilege in the context of fear. A year to the day before he was shot in 1968, King identified fear as the emotion that prevents people, particularly those who benefit from the status quo, from encountering one another. "It's possible that those men were scared," he said of the Levite and the priest who passed the Jew in the ditch on the road to Jericho. He notes that the fear-driven nature of their line of questioning—"If I help this man, what will happen to me?"—trapped these men in self-centeredness. A line of inquiry focused on the other—"If I do not stop to help this man, what will happen to him?"—may have liberated them from their fear and motivated them to respond.[37]

We can find concrete examples of the way that white privilege influences our encounters with suffering people in the social disaster of Hurricane Katrina. Recall former presidents Bush's and Clinton's commendation of Americans who "literally threw open their doors to shelter the homeless from every faith and strata of society" in the weeks and months after Katrina. While this is certainly an admirable response, a closer analysis of online postings for housing opportunities across the country reveals that many compassionate people expressed a preference for assisting white evacuees. Many black residents of the Gulf experienced homelessness twice—once at the hand of nature and then again at the hands of white Americans.[38] Therefore, whites and blacks of the Gulf Coast experienced the generosity of the American spirit quite differently. These expressed preferences to house white rather than black evacuees further widened the gap of inequality experienced by African Americans after Katrina.

Or consider the evidence of our systemic investment in whiteness in the ongoing plans for recovery of the Gulf Coast, particularly in the city of New Orleans. Many African American residents point to an overt effort on the part of federal, state, and local government officials to rebuild a "better" and therefore more white city by outsourcing redesign plans to private firms, by awarding contracts to predominately white bidders, by reclaiming the property of citizens who have yet to return home, by gentrifying traditionally black neighborhoods through escalating housing costs, and by demolishing much of the city's public housing. All of these factors discourage Katrina's largely non-white diaspora from returning to the city. While most white persons along the Gulf and throughout the country might not contribute directly to these decisions, we collectively benefit from them. Many of us see little to no increase in our home insurance premiums because companies refuse to pay for the damages caused by the storm, or because the homes of those who do not return have simply been razed. The white neighborhoods in the metropolitan New Orleans area, much like similar neighborhoods in other cities, remain safe because we incarcerate seven out of ten black men between the ages of eighteen and thirty-five. Our schools and their curricula remain segregated by race because we continue to fund our school districts through real-estate taxes, and we avoid difficult conversations regarding complicity in race simply by insisting that it is a non-issue.

Critical examination of media coverage of Katrina offers a powerful example of the denial that stems from white privilege. Ashley "Woody" Doane observes that in their reporting and analysis of the storm, the media emphasized poverty as a cause of the disaster rather than race. They tended to suggest government incompetence as the reason for the bungled response rather than race. And many commentators blamed the poor of New Orleans because they "waited for government help instead of saving themselves."[39] These commentators did not question the racist attitudes of their white neighbors. These attitudes sustained the dehumanizing social inequalities that literally trapped New Orleans' poorest citizens in their hyper-segregated neighborhoods.

And finally, fear paralyzes privileged travelers on the road to Jericho today, perhaps even more than in the lifetime of Martin Luther King, Jr. We fear becoming vulnerable—whether as individuals, as families, as communities, as cities, or even as a nation. This fear keeps us isolated from one another in disparate lifestyle enclaves. It also reinforces a divisive suspicion of others that enables us to perceive them as threats, to interpret their suffering as a ploy to take advantage of us, and to make responsibility for them someone else's concern. The new "prison industrial complex" in American culture provides undeniable evidence of the grip that this fearful suspicion has on our moral imaginations. The dramatic increase in the number of prisons, and incarcerated prisoners, as well as the booming personal-security market reflect our turn to "the use of policing, surveillance, imprisonment, and social control to address social and economic problems."[40] Fear motivated much of the immediate response to the social disaster of Katrina. For example, federal, state, and local governments made the restoration of law and order to the Gulf Coast a top priority, often at the expense of helping people in life-threatening situations. We prioritized security—of bodily integrity, of financial assets, of private or intellectual property, of neighborhoods, of national boarders—to the detriment of interdependence, mutual trust, and relationships with others.

All of these examples from the hurricane-stricken Gulf Coast illuminate the "color-blind" mentality most whites in America knowingly and unknowingly bring to our encounters with others. This blindness makes it impossible for us to see what West calls "the social and economic advantages that whites enjoy in the United States."[41] It is one of the most problematic items in McIntosh's "invisible knapsack," and it influences our encounters with others as we navigate the road to Jericho. When privileged persons deny the reality of racism, or deny the privileges we accrue by virtue of our whiteness, we also create obstacles to encountering others whose experience is not normative or whose perspective challenges our own. Because white privilege is both invisible and pervasive, it presents substantial challenges to contemporary understandings of compassion. Therefore, we need to articulate an approach to compassion through which the privileged can "learn about what kind of 'help' white people need in giving up privileges they enjoy at the expense of other people's exploitation."[42] In his examination of the damaging implications of our contemporary values on privileged and underprivileged people alike, John Kavanaugh provocatively notes that "it is none other than ourselves whom we must reflect upon, and, if necessary, seek to have changed."[43]

Concluding Remarks

Suffering, globalization, and encounters with others in the contexts of radical inequality all point to the pivotal role that compassion can play in social responsibility. In addition, these three signs of our times explain why we may need to reconsider the basic moral imperative in the parable of the Good Samaritan. Loving our suffering neighbor in a global age demands that we recognize that unjust suffering unites three-quarters of the world's population. It insists that we scrutinize our connections to this suffering, and in particular the ways in which our privilege acts to prevent us from doing so. And compassion seeks to liberate everyone from the potentially dehumanizing impact of globalization, whether physical or emotional. Consider a few contemporary expressions of compassion that offer possible starting points for this reconstruction:

- Oliver Davies suggests that compassion requires a "dispossessive intentionality," a willingness to know the self and then de-center the self through encounters with other selves.[44] He proposes that in these encounters compassion integrates the cognitive, affective, and volitional dimensions of the human.

- Steven Tudor contends that compassion entails a moral acknowledgment of the other, an acknowledgment that interrupts our own self-understanding when we perceive familiar others in a new light.[45] Therefore, compassion is as committed to "working upon *oneself*, one's own tendency toward the avoidance or blindness to the Others' suffering" as it is to addressing that suffering.[46] To that end he suggests that compassion can be understood as a perspective we bring to everyday interactions with others.

- Diana Fritz Cates claims that compassion can be understood primarily as a virtue best developed through encounters among friends or "other-selves" with tremendous potential for forming and transforming our character.[47]

- Henri Nouwen claims that compassion entails a confrontational element when encountering the idolatry, oppression, and exploitation that cause others' suffering, without which compassion "fades quickly into fruitless sentimental commiseration."[48]

Each of these contemporary contributions to the intellectual tradition of compassion is insightful. However, all fail to include a self-critical awareness of individual participation in dehumanizing suffering as well as a socially critical assessment of structural violence and injustice. This lack of critical consciousness may arise from values in Western culture that resist this type of reflection in moral life and civic engagement alike. We examine those values below in order to understand what we need to change about current expressions of Samaritanism.

CHALLENGES TO AUTHENTIC SAMARITANISM

Most Americans are "compassionate by proxy." Martin Luther King, Jr., used this term to describe a superficial suffering with others that demands little in terms of commitment of material resources or dedication of the self. Our tendency toward reactions that loosely approximate compassion arise from the central beliefs and values that ultimately shape the judgments we make about others' suffering. In our contemporary North American context, a variety of inaccurate beliefs and values—most of them rooted in concern for self rather than others—affect our judgment. At best they dangerously misdirect our attempts to suffer with others and at worst they prevent us from being compassionate at all. Again, Orwin offers a critical opinion when he notes that "where these other passions compete against each other rather than conspire with compassion, compassion has trouble making headway against them."[49] We can identify five particularly American values and beliefs with which compassion unsuccessfully competes in our contemporary context.

Individualism

Individualism affects our judgment about whether suffering is deserved. We tend to individualize the causes of human suffering, which in turn prevents us from considering the social causes of "individual" problems such as homelessness, addiction, urban violence, illegal immigration, and HIV/AIDS. This individualism creates categories of deserving and undeserving suffering persons. This judgment significantly affects our compassionate responses to these persons. We need only consider the discrepancy in foundational giving after 9/11 and Hurricane Katrina to appreciate the ways in which we are less willing to suffer with those we perceive as somehow responsible for their own affliction. *The Chronicle of Philanthropy,* for example, reports that private foundations pledged $557 million for hurricane-related needs, compared with more than $1 billion dedicated to 9/11–related efforts and charities.[50] Moreover, the value of individualism tends to affect the experience of compassion to the extent that suffering with another becomes a private, one-way, unreciprocated exchange. The American preference for online charity, the most popular means of responding to the East Asian tsunami in 2003 or Hurricane Katrina in 2005, underscores the magnitude of this privatization of compassion. While on-line giving successfully raised nearly $5 billion to assist those suffering from the impact of these natural disasters, philanthropic evaluator Charity Navigator indicted that more than 60 percent of those who gave had little confidence that their donation would reach those who needed it most. This kind of compassion by proxy requires little reflection or even personal investment on the part of compassionate persons. Furthermore, it did little to address the long-term needs of communities marginalized long before the disasters struck.

In addition, American individualism either places the onus for social change on society's least capable members or completely prevents them from participating in their own restoration. The sluggish reconstruction of New Orleans provides an outstanding example. Residents of the most impoverished parishes have either been left to fend for themselves in rebuilding their homes and neighborhoods, or they have been shut out of the redevelopment decision-making processes by more powerful private interests. We tend to justify their disempowerment by blaming them for not evacuating the city in the first place, for lifestyle choices that left them without a safety net, or for a deficient work ethic. Factors of race and class, which determined their vulnerability to Hurricane Katrina, now determine their capicity to participate in rebuilding. And marginalized persons have little control over these social factors.

Finally, the cultural emphasis on the rights, freedoms, and responsibilities of the American individual exonerates non-suffering people from our culpability in the causes of unjust suffering and therefore our responsibility to suffering persons. The classic "lift yourself up by your bootstrap" mentality that shapes the American collective consciousness enables many of us to continue on our journeys to Jericho without interruption. For example, many of us carry erroneous beliefs about race and class in our invisible knapsacks of white privilege. We falsely assume that all persons have access to special resources that help us navigate social disasters—whether "rainy day" funds, health and home insurance, social networks that extend beyond our immediate neighborhoods, the assistance of law enforcement, or the ear of government officials. These assumptions create a self-defensive rather than self-critical mentality that shapes our judgments about others in times of crisis. We confidently claim "if we can survive this, why can't they?" rather than critically examine "how is it that we can survive and they cannot?" The first line of thinking denies our implications in others' suffering, and the second begins to uncover collective efforts to consolidate and protect the privileges of whiteness. In short, in the context of American individualism we fail to recognize the impact of white privilege on the judgments we make about others' struggles in times of disaster, as well as the ways in which this fuels the disaster-enhancing social inequities that crippled so many along the Gulf Coast before the storm hit.

Autonomy

The social value of autonomy blinds potentially compassionate persons to the complex vulnerabilities that contribute to others' suffering. In addition, it creates erroneous judgments about the seriousness of many instances of social suffering. In assessing whether individuals are capable of recovering from certain setbacks or situations of suffering, we often assume that self-sufficiency or resiliency, two particularly American values that arise from autonomy, will carry them through adversity. For instance, in the case of responding to the more than 22 million Americans struggling with addiction or substance abuse, we often place the responsibility for recovery exclusively on the individual addict rather than the wider community of which that person is a member.[51] Assuming that the autonomous individual can "beat" his or her addiction absolves the community of our shared responsibilities in this endeavor: to provide meaningful and viable employment, to resist a culture that glorifies alcohol and drug abuse, to demand health-care coverage for rehabilitation treatment, and to integrate recovering addicts into the life of the community.

In addition, our focus on autonomy tends to individualize the causes of another's struggles rather than acknowledge any number of social, institutional, or systemic factors that contribute to his or her suffering and that also lie beyond the person's control. In the case of those wrestling with addiction, we are frequently less willing to suffer with people we assume have brought their suffering on themselves by the choice to abuse drugs or alcohol in the first place. In so doing, we fail to perceive the various social factors that often contribute to substance abuse, including mental illness and post-traumatic stress disorders, social and economic marginalization, lack of meaningful work, lack of social services, and the persistent insatiability perpetuated by a materialistic culture.

Finally, American understandings of autonomy as the freedom to exercise personal choice make us attentive to some injustices at the expense of others. For example, as Christian citizens in the world's quintessential democracy, we perceive threats to our autonomy as situations of grave danger. We readily support the types of human rights that protect ourselves and others against such

threats to our autonomy. These include freedoms of speech, religious preference, or political participation, for example. We need only to look to the moral
justifications for many U.S. military interventions around the world to acknowledge the importance that autonomous freedom plays in Americans' willingness
to respond to suffering others in distant places. However, the value of autonomy
also blinds us to other instances of suffering. When we become preoccupied
with freeing ourselves from others' claims on us, we frequently fail to recognize
the grave danger that unmet physical needs place on our capabilities as autonomous moral agents. Physician and human rights advocate Paul Farmer passionately points out that Americans do not value freedom from disease in the same
way that we value freedom from others who might thwart our ability to speak or
practice religion.[52] As a result, while we are willing to intervene on behalf of
others' political freedoms and rights, we are reluctant to bolster human rights
such as clothing, shelter, and bodily integrity.

Self-Sufficiency

A preoccupation with self-sufficiency inhibits non-suffering persons in making
compassion's judgment of "similar possibility," that is, the determination as to
whether a similar fate might befall us. Self-sufficiency prevents us from taking
seriously others' vulnerabilities because it condemns vulnerability, interdependence, or mutuality as social liabilities. In fact, a preoccupation with remaining
physically, emotionally, financially, and nationally invulnerable drives much of
American culture. We doggedly deny our lack of control over the circumstances
of our existence through everything from gene therapy and gated communities
to impenetrable automobiles and color-coded security alerts. We expend tremendous personal, national, and natural resources in a losing battle to remain
intractable to the limits of our human condition.

For example, the way we treat the most vulnerable members of our society,
particularly the elderly and those who care for them, reflects our cultural unwillingness to acknowledge the reality of our fragility, dependence on others, and
mortality. That some suggest we are in the midst of a "crisis of care" in this
country underscores our refusal to value dependency or caring for dependents.[53]
We disproportionately place responsibility for care of dependents on those grappling with economic vulnerability, especially women of color, and then fail to
adequately compensate them for their services. Not only are we unwilling to
respond to the vulnerable by becoming vulnerable ourselves, but we also fail to
adequately support those who do care for others.

Consumerism

Folding the American value of consumerism into this emphasis on self-sufficiency further compounds the limits of our compassion. Since we increasingly
equate human "being" with "having," we fail to appreciate that gifts of talent are
frequently more valuable and effective in interrupting structural injustices than
gifts of "treasure." The value of consumerism suggests that in order to suffer

with others we ought to provide material goods that we can purchase and that others can consume. Therefore, canned goods, coats, bottled water, and even cows, for example, trump more personally demanding and intangible resources such as physical presence, friendship, accompaniment, and moral imagination. These resources are equally necessary for ensuring the flourishing of all persons.

In addition, the "therapeutic" nature of much of American consumerism influences our philanthropy. Compassion can become a "do good to feel good" exercise with little concern for transforming suffering persons or the social injustices that define their realities. For example, during the six-week holiday season from Thanksgiving to Christmas, Americans "suffer with" the less fortunate at unprecedented levels. We donate food and toys, prepare meals, and make year-end philanthropic donations. However, given the lack of sustained giving throughout the year, these seasonal activities can easily become cathartic and tax-deductible expressions of compassion that ease the conscience of materialistic consumers. Moreover, psychologists note that this kind of unreflective and cyclical giving contributes to "compassion fatigue" or the inability to respond consistently to situations of unjust suffering that constantly bombard us.

This commoditized suffering with others solidifies the social barriers between the haves and the have-nots. It ultimately traps people in cycles of charity that perpetuate mutually exclusive relationships of givers and receivers of aid rather than foster mutually beneficial relationships of collaborators or partners in social justice. In other words, many good-hearted people depend on giving voluntarily of their surplus as the prevailing means of responding to others in need. In return, people in need become increasingly dependent on that voluntary charitable giving. In this disempowering cycle of charity, questions of *why* social inequity exists or whether there are more effective ways of responding to others in need may not be considered. The cycle of charity, while attempting to move from a "hand-out" to a "hand-up" mentality, fails to reach the important "hand-in-hand" stage of human interaction that acknowledges the equality, mutual interdependence, and collaboration necessary to respond effectively to others' needs. The cycle of charity allows the values of individualism, materialism, and personal security to go unchallenged, and as a result they continue to shape structures of violence and oppression.

American "Bourgeois" Christianity

Several expressions of Christianity germane to the American context negatively affect our ability to perceive and to take responsibility for our suffering neighbors. Johann Baptist Metz, one of the central resources for our eventual reconstruction of compassion, used the term *bourgeois* to describe the Christianity of his native Germany in the decades surrounding the Holocaust. Metz realized that Christianity after Auschwitz was not so much an opium for the have-nots, as Marx famously claimed, but rather an opium for "those who already have, those with secure possessions, the people in this world who already have abundant prospects and a rich future."[54] Metz explains that "bourgeois Christianity" endorses, reinforces, and perpetuates the comfort of those who benefit from the status quo. It also enables a series of self-exculpating deceptions regarding social sin because it primarily interprets the gospel message in light of the salvation of individual Christians apart from their social-historical realities. Bourgeois Christianity fosters an individual obsession with personal sin rather than collective concern with social suffering and an ecclesial commitment to doctrinal rigor rather than socially critical engagement in society. It cultivates what Metz would call a "merely believed in faith" that is ultimately self-referential rather than one that is actually practiced in solidarity with those who suffer.

Insofar as we can draw parallels between the experiences of everyday Germans of the World War II era and ordinary American Christians in the age of globalization when it comes to the holocausts that define our respective times, Metz's insights regarding bourgeois Christianity can help us identify the dangerous distortions in American Christianity that limit our Samaritanism. Metz provocatively asks comfortable, well-off, privileged Christians, "Do we share the sufferings of others, or do we just believe in this sharing, remaining under the cloak of a belief in 'sympathy' as apathetic as ever?"[55] We can easily ask this question of U.S. Christians.

The combination of the high rate of U.S. religiosity, which exceeds that of any other developed country, and our status as the world's most prosperous and powerful country makes our bourgeois approach to dealing with the "isms" of our cultural reality a deadly one for the majority of citizens of the globe. We are paralyzed by our own strain of this viral faith that insists on the compatibility of what Metz calls the practice of religion and the experience of life in society. This paralysis manifests itself in several ways. The findings of a recent study of generations of American Catholics by sociologist of religion James Davidson, for example, reveals that *assent* to central doctrinal beliefs—and not *practices* that reflect commitment to the faith—provides that social glue that holds American Catholics together.[56] Gloria Albrecht finds evidence of this disconnect in a zealous Christian engagement in divisive political debates about religiously rooted "family values" but a disinterested Christian disengagement from policies that actually value families.[57] In other words, we are more willing to support legislation with clear doctrinal moorings, such as abortion or same-sex marriage, than policies that seem to be doctrinally tangential, such as living-wage campaigns and health-care reform. In many ways ours is a discipleship of personal piety rather than public policy. This type of religiosity fosters an individualized approach to compassion and also fails to see compassion as a viable response to social calamities.

In addition, two mutually exclusive approaches to engaging faith in the American public square have emerged in this age of globalization, which is characterized by increasing religious pluralism and strident secularism. Each reflects elements of the bourgeois faith that Metz experienced in his World War II German context, and each presents challenges to authentic compassion. Alan Wolfe explored these two orientations in a survey of middle-class morality that he conducted in the 1990s. Wolfe interviewed ordinary Americans who "strive to earn enough money so that they feel that their economic fate is in their own hands but who also try to live by principles such as individual responsibility, the importance of family, obligations to others and a belief in something outside oneself."[58] On the one hand, nearly 60 percent of Wolfe's interviewees practice what he calls a "quiet faith" that views faith-based civic engagement or political activity as potentially intolerant, divisive, and distinctively un-American. Generally, quiet believers seem to fear imposing their personal beliefs on others or fear being accused of doing so by increasingly vocal secularists. As a result, many abide by the "eleventh" commandment: "Thou shalt not judge."[59] For quiet believers faith is a private and personal matter that is best kept separate from the public square.

Quiet believers are reluctant to use religious traditions and faith-based frameworks of meaning when evaluating social problems. In other words, in the spirit of tolerance or neighborliness quiet believers refuse to use the tenets of Christianity that make them distinct from others—the command to love neighbor or the dispositions of the Sermon on the Mount, for example—to evaluate the economy, immigration, or health-care reform. This reluctance to judge or make normative assessments of situations, and more particularly the hesitation to use religious frameworks when judging, is especially problematic when we consider the role that such assessments play in our responses to others' suffering. As we will see shortly, judging another's suffering as serious, undeserved, and somehow something we might experience ourselves frequently determines whether or not we will be moved by another's affliction. In short, if we are less likely to judge others or certain situations, we might also be less likely to respond to situations of injustice. In certain circumstances, therefore, the tolerance that arises from quiet faith is no longer a virtue. It actually becomes a vice that keeps quiet believers from accepting the responsibility we all have to others.

On the other hand, American bourgeois Christianity differs from that of our more secular European counterparts. We are a far more religious nation, given that 92 percent of us believe in God, 65 percent believe that the scripture is the word of God, more than half of us attend worship services regularly, and 40 percent of us want our government to be "more involved in morality."[60] U.S. Christians, on the whole, are more apt to "go public" with our faith in our increasingly multicultural public square. In his study Wolfe encountered at least 15 percent of middle Americans who fit the characteristics of "absolutists" and "strong believers." These believers adamantly and often vocally argue for the centrality of Christianity (exclusively) to America's founding, identity, and future. They contend that unless religion becomes "a more public force in American life, the country [will] slide into moral anarchy."[61]

While these Christians compensate for the quiet believers' reluctance to take faith public, they tend to do so in ways that reinforce the distinctions between the public and private spheres of life; they dangerously limit their public faith to issues pertaining to the private or personal sphere. Consider, for example, that American Christians surveyed during the 2000 and 2004 national elections reported that they tend to vote for candidates based largely on the rates of their personal worship and positions on moral values such as abortion, sexual orientation, and marriage.[62] Preliminary findings by the Pew Forum on Religion and Public Life suggest that this basic structure functioned in a similar way in 2008. We are less likely to recognize issues connected to our communal relationships on the local and national and global levels as moral values. In other words, issues such as the economy, health care, immigration, foreign policy, and military policy are less likely to galvanize us into political action. The increasingly vitriolic intersection between the religious and political spheres around private issues only reinforces the American perception that faith pertains only to personal and private matters, not to public or social problems.

Bourgeois Christianity manifests itself in contemporary spirituality. For example, in an extensive study with American youth across religious and secular traditions, Christian Smith and Melinda Lundquist Denton identify "moral therapeutic deism" as an emergent religiosity among young American Christians. By this they mean a sense that "God wants people to be good, nice, and fair to each other," and that "the central goal of life is to be happy and to feel good about one's self."[63] Certainly, this orientation has roots in what sociologists of religion have long identified as the "spiritual but not religious" marker of many Americans who are more likely to individualize their religious self-understandings and *seek* a personal relationship with the God of their understanding than to define those understandings in institutional terms and *dwell* within the boundaries of religious communities.[64] However, moral therapeutic deism dangerously reflects the bourgeois Christianity of Metz's day. It prioritizes a personal relationship with a God who is concerned primarily with the individual believer's material and spiritual well-being rather than with the salvation of the world. It cultivates individual practices of charity motivated by a desire for divine reward rather than transformative relationships of justice that seek the "kin-dom" of God in the here and now. And moral therapeutic deism separates individuals from their social context rather than reinforcing our inherently social nature. This approach to God begs a question that Metz asked of his fellow Christians after the Holocaust: "Do we believe in God, or do we believe in our faith in God, and in this perhaps really believe in ourselves, or in what we would like to be true about us?"[65]

This notion of a God who is concerned with the spiritual, emotional, and material well-being of believers is reinforced collectively by communities of worship that practice various derivations of the "Gospel of Prosperity"—or "Abundance," or "Health" or "Wealth"—all of which read a material literalism in Jesus' proclamation, "I come that you might have life and have it in abundance" (Jn 10:10). This movement has its roots in several distinctively American contributions to the Christian tradition. For example, the Social Gospel movement, first preached and practiced by Walter Rauschenbusch in the slums of New York City in the late nineteenth century, reawakened American Christians to the connection between the gospel and the lived reality of the poor. It is also a descendant of Pentecostalism, which began in earnest at the turn of the twentieth century in Los Angeles and has become the fastest-growing faith tradition with some 500 million members worldwide. Pentecostalism's charismatic spirit empowers believers to harness the transformative power of faith in their worship and in their everyday lives. The "Gospel of Abundance" is also fed by the celebrity status of evangelical preachers whose *New York Times* best sellers, such as *The Purpose-Driven Life, Before You Do: Making Good Decisions You Won't Regret*, and *The Prayer of Jabez: Breaking through to the Blessed Life*, reach far beyond their mega-church congregations in encouraging prosperity in the here and now.

While the "Gospel of Prosperity" rightly reflects the idea of the in-breaking of the "kin-dom," or the sense that the vision of the reign of God is not a distant but imminent reality, particularly for communities who historically have been told to await the good life in the next life, it can also reinforce the values of materialism and individualism that fuel many of the injustices of globalization. It perpetuates the sense that faith and Christian acts such as suffering with others can be commodified or monetarily assessed, as well as a neo-Calvinist percep-tion that both wealth and poverty are equally deserved because they depend on the moral choices each individual makes. And it suggests *flourishing* is best understood in terms of material wealth or propertied abundance rather than in simplicity and capability for self-gift or deep relationships with others.

In short, certain aspects of American Christianity perpetuate a bourgeois com-placency with the injustices inherent in the national status quo and justify atti-tudes and practices that privatize faith in a time of radical individualism and privatism. American bourgeois Christianity promotes individualism, perpetu-ates materialism, and tolerates disengaged apathy. As a result of these factors, we are more willing to believe in peace than to live peacefully, to believe in equality more than to treat others equally, to believe in the promises of abun-dance more than to work to create abundance for all, to believe in a friendly divine benefactor interested in our well-being more than to concern ourselves with justice for others. Ultimately, we believe in compassion more than we act compassionately.

Given the influence of individualism, autonomous self-sufficiency, therapeutic consumerism, and bourgeois Christianity on our approach to compassion, we need to retrieve and cultivate alternative values if we wish to avoid being "com-passionate by proxy." These alternatives include vulnerability and relationality, self-reflective social responsibility, and an appreciation for the nonmaterial as-pects of human flourishing. These neighbor-oriented values enable compassion-ate persons to identify more accurately and resist more effectively the structural causes of others' distress, many of which are sustained by the egocentric values we just examined.

Problematic Method

These misguided values give rise to an equally misguided method of compas-sion that can also weaken our Samaritanism. Several prevailing methods of com-passion emerge when we examine the American response to the various natural disasters of the new millennium, including charitable giving, emergency relief, and temporary aid. While donations certainly fund efforts to respond to the im-mediate symptoms of acute suffering in the wake of natural disasters—shelter and food, access to clean water, and medical attention—a financial response in the aftermath of natural disaster ignores or reinforces the conditions of "social disaster" which preceded and exacerbated the unjust suffering of the natural events. These conditions included extreme poverty, environmental degradation, overpopulated urban centers, and unequal distribution of emergency-preparedness resources. More needs to be said about our collective response to social disasters, and so we will explore this idea in greater detail in Chapter 6. But for now, we need to acknowledge our failure to be moved by the ongoing affliction of these kinds of social disasters as a significant flaw in our method of compassion.

In addition, this at-a-distance or online compassion targeted at "brand name" charities is frequently hampered by top-down bureaucracies that do not privilege the perspective of agencies on the ground, much less those affected by the tragedies. Through this kind of giving, we silence the voices of people most affected by suffering, and we lose the wisdom of their perspective. In fact, this kind of compassion relegates suffering persons to the position of victims who passively receive aid given to them. It fails to empower them as capable agents invested in their own restoration. And again, this approach to compassion pays less attention to rectifying the economic conditions and under-development that increases the vulnerability of whole populations to the natural disaster in the first place.

By relying exclusively on this method of disaster response we continue to resist the need to acknowledge and rectify North American Christians' participation in the structural causes of suffering—whether through our desire for cheap goods that stifles the economies in many of the nations affected by the tsunami in 2003 or the voluntary white segregation that creates pockets of concentrated poverty in urban areas such as New Orleans. The irony of compassionately giving our unwanted clothing back to the people of Indonesia who can barely sustain themselves on the wages they earned making it is easily lost in our contemporary consciousness. We also miss the irony of our desire to reconstruct individual homes along the Gulf Coast or in New Orleans without a similar commitment to deconstruct racism, white flight, and the depletion of natural resources. These ironies, however, are not lost on those we seek to assist. Perhaps more clearly than us, they experience the web of social sin that increasingly binds the human family in situations of injustice.

These specific examples of less-than-effective methodologies of compassion arise from a more general reluctance to incorporate compassion into human development strategies or even into principles such as solidarity or subsidiarity that foster justice on a global scale. Two factors contribute to this resistance. First, as we have already discussed, we tend to associate compassion with individual acts of charity rather than with collective commitments to social change. For example, in her important work on the roots of compassion in the teleological anthropology of Thomas Aquinas, Diana Fritz Cates suggests that our choice to feel for and with others is essential in order to strengthen human relationality. However, she argues that compassion begins by perfecting our concern for those closest to us before we can expand that sense of relationality to those who are more distant. This can reinforce a narrow relationality among those already isolated in self-selecting lifestyle enclaves that blinds us to suffering beyond our preferred circles of concern.

Even Benedict XVI's encyclical *Deus Caritas Est* emphasizes the individualized and charitable acts of the good Samaritan as the ideal of Christian love. He notes, "Christian charity is first of all the simple response to immediate needs and specific situations: feeding the hungry, clothing the naked, caring for and healing the sick, visiting those in prison, etc." (no. 31a). Here, he reinforces compassion as an individual and private expression of our participation in God's love. Moreover, by articulating that "the Church cannot and must not take upon herself the political battle to bring about the most just society possible" (no. 28a), Benedict XVI not only squarely places that responsibility on individual persons, but he also undermines the viability of compassion as a collective and socially transformative participation in God's love.

Second, despite its prevalence in individual Christian discipleship, compassion has never been among the central principles of Catholic social teaching that guide the people of God in engaging social questions regarding the state, society, and the world. For example, *Sollicitudo Rei Socialis*, John Paul II's paradigmatic encyclical on human development, recommends solidarity as the necessary Christian virtue for more complete approaches to human development. In fact, the pope distinguishes solidarity from what he calls "a feeling of vague compassion or shallow distress at the misfortunes of so many people." Unlike compassion, solidarity entails a "firm and persevering determination to commit oneself to the common good" (no. 38). Excluding compassion from Catholic strategies for human development fosters a dangerous short-sightedness that glosses over the casual connections between the radical suffering in our reality and the lifestyles of those who John Paul II would characterize as "super-developed." He fails to present compassion as essential for converting first-world Christians to the interruptive demands of the love commandment, and not simply as an expression of charitable love.

Therefore, building relationships with suffering persons in the process of responding to their afflictions might interrupt the cycle of charity that has become our main method of compassion. Or, said differently, this kind of compassion might break down the divisive and dehumanizing dynamics between victim and volunteer that dictate the way we respond to those in need. We need to shift our approach to "suffering with" our neighbor away from a limited focus on immediate or symptomatic relief and toward a more creative commitment to long-term development aid. Part of reconstructing compassion entails reconstructing the method we use to evaluate and respond to others' suffering. We turn to that constructive task now.

The Philosophy of Martha Nussbaum

Political philosopher Martha C. Nussbaum considers compassion the basic social emotion. It bridges the destructive gaps between persons that prevent us from perceiving and reacting to unjust suffering. It involves embracing the "upheavals" that compassion's evaluative judgments of the seriousness of the suffering, its deserved or undeserved nature, and the possibility that we might experience similar suffering—that is, judgments of seriousness, desert, and similar possibility—reveal. These upheavals include an uncomfortable awareness that most tragic situations have human causes, that material goods alone do not promise well-being, that emotions can be trustworthy sources of wisdom, and that autonomous individualism should not be the end goal of human development strategies. She encourages economically developed persons to accept our inherent vulnerabilities and to attune ourselves to the capabilities that all people, including ourselves, need to thrive. In short, she claims compassion as a central building block for social organization and human development theories that attempt to lift people above what she calls the "threshold of flourishing."

In addition, Nussbaum seeks to correct the social injustices that threaten the flourishing of so many of the world's people. However, in order to do so she increasingly concentrates her message of human development on the world's thriving populations. In other words, she acknowledges that social transformation of the marginalized necessarily requires personal and social transformation of those *within* the margins because we directly and indirectly determine the life-defining social, economic, and political boundaries for the rest of the world. We—and not those seeking development—fuel the engine of globalization, define thresholds of flourishing, determine poverty lines, control the criteria for strategic development grants, make online donations, determine who has access to the "knapsack of white privilege," and ultimately enjoy the luxury of responding to social disasters rather than experiencing them. Therefore, we have responsibilities as the benefactors of existing free trade policies, privatized health care, and poverty that is concentrated in neighborhoods other than our own. To that end Nussbaum seeks to expand our circles of concern, sharpen our perceptions and judgments, and motivate us to participate in her theory of justice. All of this requires a particular kind of compassion without which society falls apart. She notes that "there is reason to think that compassion gives public morality essential elements of ethical vision without which any public culture is dangerously rootless and hallow."[66]

Nussbaum can be a resourceful contributor to the a reconstruction of Christian notions of compassion in the United States, despite the fact that she rejects religious or theocentric frameworks as constructive foundations for philosophical thought.[67] She draws on personal experiences in making her argument against transcendent frameworks of meaning. As a young adult, she was a member of a Protestant congregation in suburban Mainline Philadelphia steeped in a transcendent and other-worldly eschatology. She recalls that "the harmony of Bryn Mawr was undisturbed" by the suffering reality of this world. "It seemed to me that Jesus encouraged complacency about poverty and indignity in this world, telling people that they could wait for the next to receive their due reward," she recollects. "I preferred the ideas of the Jews, that the Messiah should do his work for the downtrodden here and now."[68] Ultimately, a "this-worldly commitment to social justice" motivated her adult conversion to Judaism. She notes that "the combination of joy and relief I found in entering a community in which outrage at injustice was normal, propelled me strongly toward conversion."[69]

Nussbaum's self-identification as an "enlightened Jew" has led her to acknowledge the ethical viability of religious frameworks in everything from the primacy of individual conscience to an expansive philosophical humanism.[70] In more recent years she has drawn on core moral tenets of Judaism in her scholarship in the emotions, cosmopolitan citizenship, and the capabilities approach to human development. These include love of humanity, a desire for peace and justice, and the role of narrative and ritual in moral formation. For example, she now claims that "the acts of imagination and emotion that one performs when one participates in a ritual are intrinsically valuable acts, acts of expressive moral dedication, of fellowship, of longing for justice."[71]

Certainly, Nussbaum's wholesale dismissal of religious traditions as sources of ethical wisdom and action seems questionable, given that she affirms the compatibility of Judaism with her work in human rights and economic development.[72] However, Christian ethicists would do well to consider some of her objections to religious ethics. Most notable among these is her observation that insofar as religious traditions assign ultimate meaning and value to a world beyond the here and now, they dangerously devalue or dismiss this world and the people who struggle to survive in it. In addition, religious traditions often support attitudes and practices that render women highly vulnerable. These include exclusion from rites of worship, arranged marriage, female genital mutilation, corporal punishment, and domestic violence. The impact of religious traditions on women's well-being is particularly problematic when we consider that the contingencies of birth—gender, birth order, and geography—and not choice determine religious affiliation for the majority of the world's female population.[73] Ultimately, Nussbaum firmly believes that religion and the ethical systems connected to it are incapable of negotiating issues pertaining to the common humanity of persons within the finite reality, an agenda to which ethics and politics should attend, in her estimation.

Nevertheless, her work in uncovering the role of compassion in moral reasoning, personal moral development, and human social development is indispensable for the reconstructive task at hand.

The Theology of Johann Baptist Metz

Interestingly, Johann Baptist Metz, another resource for our reconstruction of compassion, also identifies the other-wordly orientation of Christianity as one of the great shortcomings of the Christian churches at the time of the Holocaust and today. He too turns to the Jewish tradition to correct this dangerous tendency and would agree with Nussbaum's assessment that "for a Jew the primary obligation is to act for the sake of justice and right in this world."[74] He claims that compassion "sends us to the front lines of social and cultural conflicts in today's world."[75] He further argues that no social revolution—particularly the type needed to break the deadly relationship between concentrated wealth and poverty—can be effective without converting the hearts of the comfortable and complacent. "This is the most radical and most challenging form of conversion and revolution. . . . And it is so because transforming situations in society never changes all that really needs to be changed."[76]

For Metz, compassion requires turning to face those who suffer, listening to their narratives of suffering, and bringing those narratives to the political sphere in active solidarity. Like Nussbaum, his biography shapes this orientation. Metz served as a teenager on the German front lines in the final months of World War II. Memories of those days continue to shape his self-understanding, his approach to God-talk, and the components of his theology. In fact, he uses these memories to examine critically the presuppositions of the comfortably bourgeois Bavarian Catholicism in which he was raised, presuppositions that continue to manifest themselves in the church and academy. One memory in particular stands out. Returning to his decimated regiment after delivering a dispatch, Metz can remember "nothing but a wordless cry" on discovering "only dead and empty faces" of his friends and comrades.[77] Nearly sixty years later, the memory of that anguished cry, as well as its continuous soundings around the globe, has served as the locus of his theological reflection.

Moreover, Metz insists that people of faith take suffering seriously and not dismiss it or explain it away. A faith that takes seriously the suffering of others is difficult, uncomfortable, and even self-incriminating. A theology that does the same is interruptive, radical, and dangerous. Ultimately, in Metz's estimation, few theologians engage in either. In fact, Metz charged Karl Rahner, his mentor and perhaps the most formidable theologian of the twentieth century, with failing to recognize the dangers of reducing "the heart of the Christian message and the practical exercise of faith to the decision of the individual standing apart from the world."[78] Certainly God-talk, his shortest definition of theology, stems from personal encounters with the divine. However, that conversation must not focus exclusively on the vertical relationship between disciple and the divine. Rather, it ought to be carried on collectively in the context of the often messy horizontal relationships that constitute communal life. Those currently excluded from that life in community ought to be dialogue partners. This creates a public rather than a private faith, and a political rather than a transcendent eschatology. He notes, "The central promises of the reign of God in the New Testament—freedom, peace, justice, reconciliation—cannot be made radically private affairs."[79] On this point, he and Nussbaum become ideal dialogue partners.

Finally, Metz insists that theology's central task is the ongoing "effort to formulate the eschatological message of Christianity in the conditions of present-day society."[80] These conditions have changed in Metz's lifetime, from the paralyzing silence of the German churches in the decades following the Holocaust to the destructive clamor of religious fundamentalism in the European Union. However, he has not wavered in his commitment to understanding the ongoing significance of the memory of the crucified and resurrected Christ, what he calls the *memoria passionis* and *memoria resurrectionis*, in the lives of disciples. Central to that memory is Christ's attention to those who suffer, Christ's own experiences of dehumanization and death, and the "kin-dom" his resurrection promises.

These memories of the cross and resurrection make Metz resourceful for our reconstruction of compassion. His concept of bourgeois Christianity unmasks many self-deceptions that influence faith and therefore compassion in the American context. With that in mind, he also challenges American Christians to perceive accurately and to articulate the memories of those who suffer in our own history and present reality. Finally, his argument for the political nature of compassion encourages us to enter into relationships with those on the margins.

Political Compassion

Nussbaum and Metz, although seemingly disparate conversation partners, actually propose that compassion ought to possess a self-critical element that helps us to see what is truly required of us to restore others to flourishing. When guided by Nussbaum's metaphorical definition of compassion as an "upheaval" or Metz's notion of compassion as an "interruption," we can begin to understand that social change depends on a change in perception, interpretation, and action on the part of those whose lives are not consumed by a struggle for survival. Compassion sparks the change in flourishing persons that leads to social change for those who are marginalized. Moreover, with Nussbaum's and Metz's insights in mind, we can begin to understand that compassion is not a private, one-way exchange between individuals. Rather, it becomes an experience of relational solidarity among groups of people that not only transforms those being compassionate but also those in need of compassion. It is in the context of this solidarity that compassionate perception and interpretation can more effectively transform travelers on the road to Jericho—and the road itself.

Simply put, Nussbaum and Metz merge in a compelling way on the topic of compassion. This congruence has great import for both political theology and social ethics. Through their contribution, compassion becomes self-critical rather than self-comforting, political rather than private, empowering rather than paternal, and an expression of justice rather than of charity.

Their work integrates compassion and flourishing, compassion and social justice, compassion and the "kin-dom" of God. Their ideas can assist North American Christians in turning to face, engage, and transform our reality. Integrating their ideas into the Christian tradition offers effective strategies for better loving our suffering neighbor in this global age. The kind of compassion we will reconstruct with their help entails:
- the *ability to perceive* our connections to the causes of others' suffering;
- the *willingness to interpret* contexts of injustice from the perspective of those who suffer; and
- an *active commitment* to create new relationships with the capacity to transform the neighbor, ourselves, and the social reality.

2

What Are They Saying about Compassion in Philosophical Ethics?

From Sophocles' heart-wrenching tragedies to John Rawls's detached veil of ignorance, the ability to be affected by another's distress has long been a cornerstone for individual moral living and a blueprint for social order. For centuries philosophers and theologians have incorporated a sense of "suffering with" another, compassion's most basic definition, into a variety of expressions of neighbor love, theories of emotion, political philosophies, and social-contract theories. And yet, despite this pervasiveness, it is difficult to find a detailed and consistent definition of compassion beyond that most basic sense of "suffering with" another. It seems as though compassion is a veritable chameleon in the philosophical and theological traditions, masquerading under the guise of various responses to affliction, such as sympathy, solidarity, charity, and mercy.

Consider, for example, the foundational definitions of *compassion, sympathy,* and *charity* that Laurence Blum provides in the *Westminster Dictionary of Christian Ethics*. He suggests that compassion is an "altruistic or other-regarding attitude with an emotional component" that presupposes sympathy and pity, and compels acts of beneficence.[1] Note that compassion is an affective disposition that motivates actions that fall under the open-ended category of beneficence. Sympathy, on the other hand, deals primarily with the "ability to understand and to share feelings of other human beings."[2] Notice that while sympathy is an affective disposition, it does not necessarily motivate moral agency. Finally, Blum defines *charity* as Christian "love of God and neighbor," a response that in secular contexts is synonymous with "active benevolence, beneficence, philanthropy, and mutual aid."[3] There is no reference here to affective dispositions or emotional states; rather, Blum emphasizes particular types of action on behalf of the neighbor.

Certainly, there are distinguishing characteristics among these three responses to our suffering neighbor. All three arise from concern for others in distress. But only compassion and sympathy emotionally move or affect us. And only compassion and charity physically move us toward an active response. Compassionate people are necessarily sympathetic and charitable because they are both moved by and toward another. But *sympathetic* people may not be compassionate or charitable because no action is required of them in their sympathy, and *charitable* people might not be compassionate or sympathetic because no emotion is required of them in their charity. Making these distinctions may seem to create unnecessary confusion, yet doing so reminds us that these responses to human suffering are not synonymous. A combination of emotion and action, or disposition and agency, or conviction and commitment seems to set compassion apart from the other responses to affliction.

However, it is often difficult to analyze the intangible subjectivities of compassion. For example, we have no definitive way to measure potentially compassionate agents' depth and authenticity of feeling, or the motivation for their action, or the outcomes they intend. Yet a close examination of these elements is absolutely crucial because, as we saw in the first chapter, not all compassionate responses are morally equivalent or practically viable. For example, compassion can easily slip into therapeutic sentimentality when we respond to another's situation out of feelings of guilt for our good fortune rather than out of feelings of anguish for others in their misfortune. The philanthropic rush of the holiday season offers an indisputable example of this. And a poorly motivated compassion can unintentionally perpetuate a paternalism that prevents real social change. For example, the person who donates online to the American Red Cross in order to meet material needs after a natural disaster differs from the person who accompanies victims in the recovery process in order to rectify the structural causes of their vulnerability. Disaster relief motivates the former response, while development aid motivates the latter. Less than genuine intentions can also erode compassion into a politicized ideology. "Lexus liberals" and "compassionate conservatives," for instance, often exemplify this kind of ambiguous compassion since both groups ultimately seek to preserve their own values and world view in their responses to situations of suffering rather than to restore marginalized people to the common good. Given these hard-to-pin-down variables, the search for compassion—not sympathy or charity—and authentic compassion at that—can seem fruitless.

However, in a more positive light, perhaps compassion's chameleon-like nature in the Christian tradition points to its historically contextual features rather than its problematic ambiguity. A perusal of the philosophical and theological tradition reveals that compassion is a dynamic and evolving means of responding to a dynamic and evolving social reality. In other words, as understandings of persons, moral development, flourishing, social order, and even suffering continue to emerge, so too do understandings of compassion. For example, Aristotle relied on *oiktos* or compassion in order to support his argument that human beings are not isolated individuals but rather social creatures who depend on relationships with one another to flourish. Centuries later Thomas Aquinas added a christological twist to this term and called it *misericordia*, a virtue that works in conjunction with charity and reminds us of our responsibility to the common good of all. Enlightenment philosophers such as Jean-Jacques Rousseau and Arthur Schopenhauer incorporate compassion as *pitié* or *Mitleid* in their endeavors to encourage a socially responsible social order. Compassion further evolves into solidarity in the thought of twentieth-century liberation theologians such as Jon Sobrino and Ignacio Ellacuría, who rely on radical relationality to resist the structural sins of neocolonialism.

Understandings of compassion can and should continue to evolve. The social conditions of our twenty-first century reality, which we examined in the last chapter, as well as the contemporary values and beliefs that shape our interior dispositions, demand as much. We have already begun to examine the impact of globalization on our twenty-first-century understandings of persons, flourishing, and human development, as well as the way these understandings shape our responses to others' suffering. In the following two chapters we track compassion's historical development—in the philosophical and theological traditions—in order to define more completely and develop a compassion for our global age. Two particular traits—compassion's viability for self-critical humility and for collective social transformation—will emerge.

We begin with resources of the philosophical tradition that present compassion as more than a mere reflexive sentiment, more than a self-referent assessment of another's misfortune, and more than an involuntary stirring of the heart on the occasion of another's suffering. Many philosophers point to compassion as an emotionally cognitive response to human vulnerability that informs and motivates our duties toward others, as well as our collective sensibilities about the social order. As such, it serves as an important disposition that once habituated can transform individuals and social structures.

COMPASSION AS AN EXPRESSION OF EMOTIVE REASONING

Compassion's emotional characteristics fuel great debate among those who historically have disputed its efficacy in guiding individual moral development and influencing social organization. Political philosophers have long deliberated about the viability of sentiments, feelings, and emotions in personal moral discernment and in public reasoning about the good life. In fact, much of our contemporary suspicion of compassion can be traced back to the somewhat critical stance of the Platonists, as well as Greek and Roman Stoics, toward the emotions or the "passions" *(pathe)*, as they called them. This philosophical heritage influenced the early Christian communities in and around Rome, particularly those under Pauline leadership. Foundational Christian scholars of the patristic period such as Origen, Tertullian, and Clement of Alexandria also inherited this suspicion of the emotions. Some current Christian approaches to the emotions in the moral life, particularly emotions such as compassion that deal with the unpredictable complexities of human suffering, can be traced to these sources. For example, our contemporary concerns about the irrationality and unpredictability of emotions, their involuntary and partial nature, and the vulnerability they create in otherwise reasonable, autonomous, and self-sufficient persons echo many of the concerns of Plato (428–348 B.C.), Stoic philosophers such as Zeno (334–262 B.C.), and Chrysippus (230–206), Seneca (1–62), and Marcus Aurelius (121–180). Since their insights continue to influence the ways we understand and use emotions such as compassion, we now turn to their contributions.

Plato

Plato's *Republic* offers a window into the Hellenistic distrust of the passions. *The Republic* is a "protreptic dialogue," a conversation between Socrates and two students that attempts not only to articulate a point but also to persuade passionately an audience of its veracity. In their exchange Plato examines the facets of individual and communal moral life by drawing analogies between rightly and wrongly ordered individuals and between just and unjust societies. Rightly ordered persons are indispensable for building a rightly ordered society. Through Socrates' conversation, Plato reveals his concern that emotions threaten that right ordering of individuals and societies.

For instance, Plato claims that the three parts of the soul—reason, passion, and desire—are influenced by different capacities: reason by wisdom, passion by ambition, and desire by avarice. The parts of the individual soul have counterparts in political organization—reason with kingship, passion with oligarchy, and desire with democracy. Plato argues that reason and the capacity for wisdom or "sight of the mind" best secure the goodness that both individuals and society are to seek, because wisdom keeps the passions and desires focused on more subordinate ends.[4] In other words, reason must rule over the passions and desires, or what he calls the "leaden weights which are grafted onto [our capacity for knowledge]." Otherwise, the passions, which Plato understands largely in terms of competition and ambition, possess the potential to become dictators within the individual and society, placing both "in a constant state of poverty and need."[5] Therefore, he deemed kingship, guided by reason, far more preferable to democracy, which is at the hands of our collective desires.

More specifically, in an argument against poetry as a means of informing our capacity to understand our reality, Plato also speaks to the dangers of unreasonable emotional responses to human suffering and tragedy. He proposes that unbridled grief at another's misfortunes "blocks our access to the very thing we need to have available to us in these circumstances," namely "the ability to think about the incident and, under the guidance of reason, to make the best possible use of one's situation, as one would in a game of dice when faced with how the dice have fallen."[6] Ultimately, Plato argues that passions such as pity only create fear. And fear enables either the passions or the desires to take control over an otherwise stable and reasonable individual or society. Emotions create partiality, instability, irrationality, unpredictability, and chaos. We can hear echoes of this in Clifford Orwin's claim that "where compassion is too powerful, justice is often its victim."[7]

Finally, Plato's lack of concern with the details or contingencies of human flourishing ground Orwin's claim that "no aspect of human life is worth bothering about a great deal."[8] Our main concern, rather, should be wisdom of the ultimate good, as the famous "Allegory of the Cave" in *The Republic* persuasively demonstrates. It is the light from the outside, and not our condition in the darkness of the cave or our emotional attachment to the shadows on the wall, that ought to capture our attention. This ambivalence about material flourishing undermines much of the motivation for emotions such as compassion. There is no call to be affected by the physicality of suffering, or flourishing, for that matter. In short, Plato had little need for emotions like compassion, and in fact urged reasonable people to resist them in the process of moral development.

The Stoics

Much like their Platonic predecessors, whose preoccupation with the immaterial and immutable animated their concern with the daylight beyond the cave rather than the fire-cast shadows that danced on its walls, the Stoics warned that the material world and the material things in it are of little moral significance. For them, happiness or *eudaimonia* can be found in the perfection of the human capacity for self-control, determination, and reason. In order to perfect reason, therefore, one detaches himself or herself from all things that are impermanent— possessions, goods, and body. Stoic philosophers understood the emotions as "passions" or beliefs with little foundation in knowledge that arise from attachments to the material world. They grouped these erroneous beliefs into four categories: desires or beliefs about goods in the future, fear or beliefs in future misfortune, pleasure or beliefs about goods of the present, and pain or beliefs about present misfortunes.[9]

Moreover, the Stoics suggested that passions threatened reason in three particular ways. First, once unleashed the passions can no more be controlled than a sprinter can make his legs abruptly stop, an analogy offered by the philosopher Chrysippus. They literally run away with us. Second, passions are a result of attachments to the material world that render us vulnerable or less self-sufficient. These might include concerns with tangible possessions such as personal property or our physical bodies, as well as intangible conditions such as physical health or power over others. Third, passions are not cognitive evaluations but mere knee-jerk opinions.[10] As such they do not involve critical reflection. Nancy Sherman nicely summarizes the moral motto of Stoic philosophy: "Untutored we live a life of emotion, cleaving to values other than virtue; as Stoics, our salvation is in learning how to detach from false goods."[11]

We can find many examples of philosophers of this frame of mind. For instance, in denying any relationship between the passions and happiness, Cicero notes that "once a man starts fearing that one of these supposedly 'good' possessions is going to vanish, it is out of the question for him to be happy any longer. For the happy man, as I see him, has to be safe, secure, inconquerable, impregnable: a man whose fears are not just insignificant but non-existent."[12] The secret to happiness, according to Cicero, is to remain like a calm sea "when there is not the smallest breeze" to ruffle it. Likewise, Seneca associates compassion with a "failing" or "weakness" of a mind willing to allow itself to become burdened or convoluted with the suffering of another person.

The Stoics embraced a dualistic world view, and the resulting tension between passion and reason, stability and irrationality, unpredictability and consistency pervades the Christian world view in nearly every century. This tension gave rise to the suspicion of the social efficacy of religious virtues or sentiments.[13] For example, scholars note the connection between the themes and structures of

Paul's letters to the early Christian communities in Philippi, Galatia, and Rome—the earliest accounts of the life of Christ and imperatives for Christian life—and the writings of the Stoic philosophers of his time, most notably Seneca. Engberg-Pedersen notes several similarities in the Stoic and Pauline processes of human development: a steadfast orientation toward an ultimate good (reason or God), an awareness of the obstacles created by the egocentric values of the world, a conversion away from the egotistical self toward an altruistic self who is attuned to the ultimate good and others, and finally, a commitment to public good.[14] The early Christian communities adopted Stoic ideas concerning materiality and reason into discussions of body and spirit. They translated the ideals of the transcendent moral good into a logos Christology, and a wariness about obstacles to the good such as bodily desires and passions into the doctrine of sin.

Interestingly, in her writings on the emotions, Martha Nussbaum claims that the introduction of Christian theology into philosophy marked a more positive turn in traditional philosophical thinking about emotions. Doctrines of original sin and grace challenged Platonic and later neo-Stoic confidence in the ability for individual persons to rely on reason alone to achieve immutable truth, or goodness, or happiness. Emotions in the Christian tradition were "seen as acknowledgments of neediness and a lack of self-sufficiency," which constantly reoriented individuals away from the concerns of this world and toward the divine. In short, emotions were not to be avoided but cultivated. Therefore, they were "restored to a place of value in the good human life" as a result of the integration of Christianity into Hellenistic philosophy.[15]

Ultimately, we can use the example of Plato's famous "Allegory of the Cave" to explore implications of this anti-emotion strand of the philosophical tradition on contemporary notions of compassion. The focus on individual perfection in Hellenistic and Roman contexts challenges the reasonableness and viability of emotions like compassion that motivate us to enter into the messiness and imperfections of human material existence. It encourages moral individuals to seek the source of light in the cave through self-sufficient and autonomous reason rather than to transform the cave through compassionate action. The Platonists and Stoics were concerned with a reasonable social order focused on a hierarchy of goods, and not necessarily with social justice focused on distribution of material resources or radical relationality among persons.

The focus on individual perfection also presents significant obstacles to cultivating wider social responsibility in our hyper-individualized, self-sufficient, and impenetrable American culture. Much of our North American consciousness reflects this Stoic suspicion of the emotions, particularly the vulnerability they create. In situations of conflict in our families and neighborhoods, or among nations, we are often reluctant to cultivate relationships that make the needs of others and our responsibilities to them more apparent out of concern that we may appear weak or unwavering in our resolve to achieve certain ultimate ends, or that others' needs will sidetrack us from meeting our own. We also question the resolve, rationality, and tenacity of leaders who are visibly moved by others' affliction. We do not trust decisions that we or others make in emotionally charged states. We recognize the detrimental impact of the emotion of fear in building broad and deep relationships in an increasingly multicultural and religiously plural society. The Platonic and Stoic roots of these suspicions are undeniable. These suspicions are also increasingly untenable, given the evolution of our ideas regarding persons, flourishing, and the social order.

It might seem that the Platonists and Stoics have little to offer to any retrieval of compassion, given their rather negative view of emotions. However, their thought does offer at least three contributions to the contemporary evolution of compassion. First, Plato underscores the necessity to perceive accurately our reality, given his insistence on the inherent capacity for "sight of the mind" or wisdom in achieving the good. While he might argue that the passions only obscure our vision, a point that Aristotle challenges, Plato does note that the struggle in moral education and living is not necessarily "the art of implanting sight" into the agent, but rather the effort to orient the agent's "sight of the mind" in the proper direction. This is clearly a task for compassion in our contemporary context.

In addition, the Stoics, particularly those of the Imperial period in Rome (Seneca and Cicero, for example), were concerned with integrating philosophical theory and practical living. Ethics, in other words, was their primary concern, and they approached the moral life as the challenging task to assess our impulses and passions, to determine the proper ways to control them, and to strive for consistency between impulse and action.[16] The Stoics implicitly acknowledge the power of the emotions in both the internal and external life of moral agents. Moral action stems from moral self-awareness. Therefore, they rightly suggest that we must continually evaluate the beliefs out of which the passions arise. This evaluation is particularly necessary in emotions that involve our beliefs about others, given the tremendous potential in our contemporary reality to operate with less-than-accurate views of others—whether through media stereotyping, selective attention, or voluntary ignorance. This points to the self-critical component of compassion that we will consider in the fourth chapter.

Finally, in their suspicions of the passions, the Stoics call our attention to their motivational, imaginative, and collective power, a resource that not all philosophers are willing to extirpate from human moral life. Contemporary feminist scholar Cheryl Hall says as much when she notes that in ancient philosophy, passion is a source of power, a source of our connections to others, and a source of our moral imagination.[17]

Aristotle

Ironically, Aristotle (384–322 B.C.) celebrated precisely the aspects of emotions that the Stoics condemned. He placed them at the heart of his discourses on *eudaimonia—On Rhetoric* and *Nichomachean Ethics*—precisely because of their partiality, involuntariness, and the vulnerability they create. Aristotle argues that emotions are not necessarily "over-hasty servants who run out before they have heard all their instructions, and then carry them out wrongly."[18] Unlike the appetites, which disregard reason completely, emotions "follow reason in a way" because they entail judgments about persons, situations, and their potential similarity to us.[19] These judgments are crucial for social living. Aristotle's preferences for emotions reflect his understanding of human persons as inherently social beings and his vision of *eudaimonia* as the ability to achieve our proper ends as individuals and as a community. They arise from his sense that a good society depends on distributive justice.

For example, in Aristotle's estimation, the partiality of our emotions calls attention to the particularities of human experience that a person of reason must address in order to act in a way that is consistent with his or her ultimate end. Central among these are the particularities of human relationships—with those closest to and most distant from us. We need relationships with others in order to flourish. In addition, the vulnerability that emotions reveal underscores the instrumental necessity of material goods in achieving happiness and in bolstering the inherent social nature of persons. We need certain "this-worldly" things—food, clothing, shelter, bodily integrity—in order to flourish, and a just society is one that distributes these material goods among its citizens. In addition, we need immaterial goods, particularly relationships with other people, if we are to flourish. Aristotle saw the emotions as proof of this.

The seeming involuntariness of emotions points to the complex relationship between the will and reason that must be rightly ordered in moral life. The will, the part of the soul attached to the desires, can work in conjunction with reason to order to identify expressions or experiences of flourishing most fitting to us. And the seeming irrationality of emotions highlights the capacity for human imagination and active engagement in our reality. Often, in order to achieve our ultimate ends as individuals and as a community, we need to think about how things might be rather than simply how they are.

Aristotle makes significant contributions to the evolution of compassion. First, the emotion of compassion entails a disposition toward suffering others, which awakens a valuable sense of vulnerability within the subject of compassion, meaning the compassionate person. For example, he deemed *eleos,* or pity, an emotion that comes closest to "suffering with another" in his repertoire of human experiences, to be an "appropriate expression of and response to our vulnerable and imperfect life" and one that plays a "salient role" in our moral development.[20] "Pity," he explains, "may be defined as a feeling of pain caused by the sight of some evil, destructive or painful, which befalls one who does not deserve it, and which we might expect to befall ourselves or some friend of ours, and moreover to befall us."[21] This ability to imagine another's misfortune, and the fear that it might "befall us" is the source of the vulnerability on which we can build human relationality. Therefore, Aristotle suggests that compassion requires "the thought that one's own possibilities are in significant ways shared with those of the person one contemplates."[22] In other words, perceiving the suffering of another fuses the horizons of otherwise separate and unfamiliar people. Nussbaum notes that Greek tragedies serve just this purpose. Tragedies connected those who suffer with those who do not precisely through this sense of similarity. Oliver Davies names this aspect of compassion an "epiphany of being" in which we viscerally know and experience our relational nature.[23]

In addition, in shaping our understanding of social connections among persons, this vulnerability can spur action on the part of individuals and groups to address and prevent suffering. For example, while Plato associates compassion with pity that sparks divisive and irrational fear, Aristotle connects pity with a cognitive experience of discovering a more unitive similarity among persons. As we will see in the following section, as a habituated disposition compassion empowers us to embrace our social natures as individuals and to cultivate practices that bolster our connectivity to others.

Aristotle's contributions to the tradition of compassion are ongoing, as will be evident in the fourth chapter where we evaluate Martha Nussbaum's Aristotelian approach to compassion. Two preliminary points, however, might be helpful at this point. First, Aristotle's emphasis upon vulnerability contradicts many of the predominant social values in contemporary North American culture, particularly individualism, self-sufficiency, and fear of those beyond our familiar lifestyle enclaves. As we will see more definitively in the next chapter, Aristotle's anthropology of vulnerability has the powerful potential to disrupt self-perceptions and world views that prevent frequent and accurate suffering with others.

In addition, Aristotle implicitly interprets the significance of suffering from the unsettling perspective of the suffering object of compassion. Not only are we as compassionate persons compelled to imagine the implications of the object's suffering in the context of our own lives, but we are also able to imagine what that suffering must entail in *another's* life. When we begin to see social injustice from this more vulnerable perspective, we become more capable of imagining new moral possibilities and solutions.

Immanuel Kant

The evolution of compassion as an emotion necessary for personal and social transformation continued during the Enlightenment period in the eighteenth century. The German philosopher Immanuel Kant (1724–1804), known more for his metaphysical approach to the role of reason in moral life and his emphasis on interior duty than external outcomes, surprisingly incorporates emotions into his moral system. Emotions help the moral agent to perceive duty presented in various situations and to follow that duty from a rightly ordered commitment to the moral law. Like the other philosophers we have considered, Kant's notion of persons, flourishing, and social order influences his approach to the emotions, particularly compassion.[24]

Throughout his life Kant attempted to articulate an epistemological middle way between those in the "empiricist" school of thought, who claimed that we gain knowledge through experience, such as John Locke and Francis Bacon, and those in the "rationalist" school, such as Descartes and Spinoza, who asserted that we best gain knowledge through observation of the natural world. Kant objected to both approaches to knowledge on anthropological grounds. The moral agent in both schools either passively receives knowledge through reflection on things that happen to him or her, or through reflection on things that happen in the natural world. Both approaches miss the sense that we shape and are shaped by both our experiences and the natural world. Therefore, he argued that persons are both sensual or shaped by experience and reasonable or capable of critically reflecting on those experiences. We are constituted by a desire for the good (the will) and an ability to know the good's claims on us (reason). Emotions play a role in both capacities.

Emotions alert us to inward states that can assist us in both knowing and committing ourselves to the good. This commitment is essential for moral living, which Kant equated with our duty to the universal moral law or "categorical imperative": treat all persons as an end in and of themselves, and never as a means to an end. The commitment of the will to the good, in Kant's estimation, was far more morally valuable than the resulting goods of any moral action. This moral system incorporates the emotions in order to shape the intention of the will or that aspect of us that motivates our internal commitment to the good that the categorical imperative puts forward. Therefore, we can use the emotions in cultivating virtues if we properly attend to them. In *Doctrine on the Virtues*, written nearly two decades after *Metaphysics of Morals* (1785), which many consider to be his foundational text, Kant explains that while moral action that arises from immediate inclinations might lack moral worth, not all inclinations in and of themselves are immediate. Some of these inclinations can be cultivated and shape virtues that master other inclinations.

In addition, Kant considers human flourishing in deontological rather than teleological terms. Said differently, goodness and happiness arise when we commit our wills to following the categorical imperative and not necessarily from the resulting consequences of those commitments. Certainly, his framework differs from Aristotle, who was concerned that people achieve their appropriate ends, evidenced by living a fully human life. But Kant is similar to Aristotle in that emotions are instrumental for this duty-based approach to flourishing. Emotions can convey a sense of moral interest in aspects of our reality that we might otherwise disregard. Kant ultimately parlays these moral interests into specific duties. The ability to identify these duties more clearly is necessary to live a moral life. For example, he encourages moral agents to seek out situations that might hone their sense of sympathy or compassion in order to help them shed light on the various duties that the will must seek. Moreover, Kant suggests that moral agents have a duty not to "avoid the pain of compassion" since "this feeling, though painful, nevertheless is one of the impulses placed in us by nature for effecting what the representation of duty might not accomplish by itself."[25]

And finally, emotions can help motivate Kantian duty, which is necessary for establishing a just society. A morally viable society is one in which persons are motivated by "good will" to comply with the categorical imperative for its own sake. Contemporary scholar Dana Radcliff echoes this idea from Kant. She does not deny the importance of commanded ethical behavior but she does suggest that we cannot continue to dismiss the emotive motivations behind such ethical duties as respect for persons or agapeic love. Rather, the affective disposition of compassion can supplement or complement the duty to love, not only when we fail in that duty through sin, but also when we fail to meet that duty effectively by ignoring the particularities of certain situations. Therefore, development of a compassionate disposition might be listed among our ethical duties "so that this emotional response will occur spontaneously and, if necessary, combine with one's abstract respect for persons, to motivate whatever actions duty demands."[26]

COMPASSION AS A VIRTUE FOR MORAL DEVELOPMENT

Compassion surfaces in another age-old philosophical debate regarding perhaps the most primary question in the field of ethics. Should moral agents be more concerned with *what we ought to do*, which evaluates the end results of our action and the duties that motivate it; or should we be more concerned with *who we want to become*, which evaluates how our actions shape our character? A variety of ethical theories stem from the former approach, including John Stewart Mill's utilitarianism, Kant's categorical imperative, the Roman Catholic moral principle of double effect, the UN Universal Declaration of Human Rights, and contemporary cost-benefit-analysis strategies for human development. Various expressions of virtue ethics—from Aristotle to Stanley Hauerwas—arise from the latter. This approach examines the dynamic relationship between our self-understandings as moral beings and our choices as moral agents, and the dispositions and intentional habits that link the two.

Plato and Aristotle were the first to engage in this debate about the primary moral question, and both agree that questions of character should be at the heart of ethical evaluation. In fact, their distinctive philosophical approaches actually intersect on the topic of the virtues. For example, both suggest that attention to virtue shifts our moral focus from what ought to be done in certain situations to who we want to become in the process of responding. They propose that virtues enable persons to achieve their fitting ends as persons, and that virtuous living perfects not only the individual but also contributes to the public good. Certainly, Plato's and Aristotle's virtue theories differed; nevertheless, in many ways the philosophical tradition has continued their centuries-old discussion about how best to cultivate and practice dispositions that form us as good persons and just societies.

The Christian moral tradition has only recently returned to the resources of virtue ethics, largely as a result of a revival of interest in the ethical writings of Thomas Aquinas (1224–75), who integrated of Aristotelian virtue theory into Christian moral theology in the thirteenth century.[27] Until the latter part of the twentieth century, most Christian ethical theories relied on a deontological or duty-based approach that reinforced the primacy of scripture, exemplified by Martin Luther's *Short Catechism*, the centrality of moral laws exemplified by Karl Barth's *Church Dogmatics*, and the responsibility to ecclesial authority exemplified by the moral teachings of Pope Pius IX. In addition, the Roman Catholic moral tradition, with its emphasis on auricular confession, moral casuistry, and intrinsically evil actions has tended to place the content and consequences of moral actions at the center of the moral life.

However, contemporary philosophical and theological scholars point to a renewed urgency in this debate between acts-based and virtue-based moral theory, given Alasdair MacIntyre's now-classic claim in *After Virtue* that moral relativism and emotivism dangerously dictate moral sensibilities in our post-modern age.[28] Aristotle's ancient insights into the role of virtue in achieving human flourishing and Aquinas's medieval claims that virtues can integrate our loving contemplation of God with active love of neighbor, now capture center stage in theories of moral development.[29]

The tradition of virtue ethics, both philosophical and theological, offers resources for considering compassion as a moral response that not only ministers to the suffering neighbor, but also sparks change within the moral agents who are habitually disposed to this kind of ministering. The potential for this kind of change is an aspect of compassion most easily overlooked in the North American consciousness. Yet the potential to transform those who suffer with others is absolutely necessary in order to love our neighbor authentically in an age of globalization when the power for much-needed social change lies in the hands of an unsuspecting and relatively comfortable few.

There are any number of features of virtue ethics that might be helpful in cultivating this kind of change within those who practice the virtue of compassion. For example, virtue ethics supports an optimistic focus on our capacity for good action rather than a negative focus on our inherent sinful condition. It empowers an innovative moral agency that seeks after the most appropriate response rather than a passive and restrictive adherence to moral laws or duties. And virtue ethics nourishes the imagination in order to envision what might be rather than fueling the superego that obsessively ruminates on things as they are. This kind of moral outlook and agency can certainly assist us in responding more effectively to the troubling dispatches from the road to Jericho we considered in the last chapter.

However, here we closely examine three features of virtue ethics that are of particular value in light of the challenges that globalization presents to us in loving our neighbors: historical consciousness, the integration of emotion and action, and the role of communal narrative or storytelling. Thinkers throughout the virtue ethics tradition who have developed these features can give us insights into how we might cultivate the kind of compassion that transforms us as well as those we seek to assist along the road to Jericho.

Compassion as a Historically Conscious Virtue

We can distinguish virtue ethics from other moral theories in the attention it pays to the situational details, contextual complexities, and personal particularities that shape our moral dispositions and choices. While these nuances might be considered a distraction in other moral theories, virtue ethics examines them for information that might lead us to the most fitting or appropriate response. Joseph Kotva explains that "virtue ethics moves the focus from rules and acts to agents and their contexts."[30] This makes virtue ethics a historically conscious approach to moral life. Said differently, virtue ethics focuses on the concrete situation rather than on abstract principles. It pays attention to the particularities of the actual persons involved rather than to metaphysical anthropology. It pulls people into relationships with one another in everyday circumstances rather than preoccupying them with a theoretical moral calculus reserved for special occasions of moral crisis. It is precisely as a historically conscious approach to moral development that virtue ethics can increase our level of moral self-awareness and our sense of accountability to others.

For example, Christian ethicist H. Richard Niebuhr (1894–1962) encouraged immersion in the complexity of moral situations by attending to specific details rather than extraction from them through appeals to abstract moral laws or detached moral duty. In his now classic *The Responsible Self* he suggests that our primary ethical question in any given situation ought to be "What is going on?" This kind of questioning reveals information that the theological question "How should I act?" or the deontological inquiry, "What are my obligations?" tend to miss, given their preoccupation with immediate action. Niebuhr's question requires critical reflection on as many aspects of the moral problem as possible, including its place in the wider social context, and our connection to both. Therefore, it also encourages self-critical awareness of the ways that we might be implicated in the situation and responsible to those affected by it. Niebuhr insisted that attention to this question raises an awareness that individual moral "selfhood" is possible in the context of intentional relationships with others. Moral living, therefore, requires that we habituate behaviors that accurately respond to the various demands of that relationality. Niebuhr purports that attending to what is going on in our reality increases the accuracy of our self-knowledge, our interpretation of reality, our understanding of God, and our accountability to others.

Compassion is potentially the most historically conscious of the virtues. When we ask ourselves what is going on in situations of dehumanizing suffering, we begin to discover the many layers of social injustices that give rise to these situations and perhaps our direct and indirect connections to these injustices. In addition, in order to answer Niebuhr's question properly, we must ask it of those who are suffering and deeply listen to their answers. As a result, we not only see the situation's complexities differently but also take the initial steps toward a relationship with these suffering persons. This increases our own vulnerability as well as our accountability to them, because they are no longer anonymous strangers to us but partners in responding to the situation at hand.

Consider, for example, the insights we might have received and relationships we might have created as a nation if we had followed Niebuhr's advice and asked ourselves what was going on in the wake of Hurricane Katrina, rather than rushing to be "compassionate by proxy." We might have discovered the various facets of concentrated poverty that literally trapped people in neighborhoods along the Gulf Coast before the storm hit. We might have realized the relationship between suburban sprawl and increased ecological vulnerability or decreased urban economic vitality. We might have connected the dots between voluntary white segregation and lack of racially integrated housing or public education. We might have deduced the difference between compassion that restores human flourishing and charity that ultimately threatens it. And perhaps we might have found friends in neighborhoods that had become so distant and separate from our own tightly knit communities.

Several thinkers in the tradition of virtue ethics implicitly and explicitly speak to the historically conscious aspects of virtues in general, and compassion in particular. Plato's discussion of the importance of "sight" in moral development, as well as the emphasis of Aristotle and Aquinas on the importance of the "who" and "what" we see in our pursuit of virtuous living, underscore the historical consciousness inherent in the virtue of compassion.

Plato

Although they share a general framework, Plato and Aristotle differed in their understanding of the end goal of virtue. Plato largely understands the virtues in a functional way—they are the dispositions of the rational component of the soul that allow persons to function properly as persons and not as other things. Part of what separates humans from other things, according to Plato, is our ability to distinguish among goods and to seek after the ultimate good. Virtue leads to the happiness of acting justly for its own sake, regardless of proximate goods or potential rewards. Therefore, Plato suggests justice, courage, and self-control as central virtues.

However, wisdom or the ability to perceive ultimate goodness is the highest virtue in Plato's estimation. "The sight of the character of goodness leads one to deduce what is responsible for everything that is right and fine, whatever the circumstances . . . and I think the sight of it is a prerequisite for intelligent conduct either of one's own private affairs or public business."[31] Plato's emphasis on accurate perception of ultimate goods provides a viable means to sift through the complexities of moral situations by reminding us to keep our sights set on ultimate goods. And this is an important contribution to our reconstruction of compassion. Consider, for example, William Spohn's suggestion that compassion is the "optic nerve" of the Christian vision. The right sightedness of wisdom can cure us of the various types of blindness that impair our moral vision.[32]

However, Plato's understanding of persons and flourishing influences his approach to the virtues and limits its viability for constructing a socially responsible compassion. For example, he considers virtue only in terms of the ways in which these dispositions and habits enable individual moral agents to achieve their respective ends as individuals. Even if we build a viable society along the way, this approach leads to an instrumental and individualized approach to the moral life. It fits seamlessly with the American values of individualism, productivity, and self-actualization that dangerously blind us to our connections and responsibilities to others. Moreover, it is not enough merely to perceive the other and respond for the sake of our moral development or for the sake of justice as an abstract principle that we seek. Rather, we need to perceive others as somehow connected to our own flourishing and respond for the sake of this mutuality. Aristotle and Aquinas offer corrective resources on this point.

Aristotle

In both Aristotle and Aquinas we can see that the virtue of compassion perfects what each philosopher designates as the primary virtue. For Aristotle, this is justice or giving others their due; for Aquinas, it is charity or the unitive love of God and neighbor. Compassion heightens our awareness of the situations of others, particularly those whom we might not otherwise perceive in the "background noise" of our daily routines or everyday moral decisions. It reminds us of what we owe them or of our responsibility to them in our response to God's love for us.

For example, Aristotle implicitly acknowledges the importance of Plato's emphasis on sight in rightly perceiving our proper ends. However, he questions Plato's narrow line of vision. In his approach to the virtues Aristotle underscores the necessity of perceiving others and material needs as essential rather than instrumental for a virtuous life. He defines virtues as dispositions toward our ultimate ends, informed by the contours of our specific contexts. He includes others—friends, fellow citizens, subordinates, and those who suffer injustice—in this contextual mix. Therefore, attention to others is what separates Aristotle's virtue theory from that of Plato: "And the best person is not the one who exercises virtue [only] toward himself, but the one who [also] exercises it in relation to another, since this is a difficult task."[33] According to Aristotle, justice is the greatest among the virtues because it focuses on our relationships with others. He notes that "justice is the only virtue that seems to be another person's good, because it is related to another; for it does what benefits another."[34]

Although they do not explicitly name it as such, perfecting this perception of others requires historical consciousness, which is an epistemological framework that compassion also sharpens. For example, Aristotle, and later Aquinas, suggests that the difficulty of virtuous living oriented toward justice or charity is the ability to determine the most fitting response for each separate moral agent, as well as the most fitting response given the complexities of the circumstances to which each moral agent attempts to respond. Aristotle calls this fitting response "the mean." By a focus on the mean, virtues become a dynamic capability to understand ourselves accurately, to perceive accurately the various details of our situation, and to act in a way that is consistent with our sense of who it is we wish to become in the process of this action. They are abilities to strive for that ultimate end in light of the specific conditions of our situations. According to Aristotle, humans are unique in our capability for practical reason, which channels our emotions and our intellectual evaluations of them toward an appropriate end. Kotva suggests that practical reason involves assessing "what is" and "what ought to be" and mapping a route that connect these two realities in incremental steps that avoid extremes.[35] All of these require historical consciousness.

Aquinas

Interestingly, the philosophical and theological traditions clearly merge on the topic of other-oriented virtues, particularly in the thought of medieval philosopher and theologian Thomas Aquinas. Aquinas mines Aristotle and integrates the idea of virtue into the moral life of Christian discipleship in a way that revolutionized moral thinking in an age of rigid confessional manuals and pre-occupation with evil acts that were to be avoided at all costs. Like Aristotle, who makes attention to others a priority through his focus on justice as the most important virtue for human happiness, Aquinas designates charity as the highest of the virtues because it empowers the moral agent to seek the greatest good—union with God—as well as to attend to our highest moral priority—loving the neighbor. Interestingly, Aquinas associates compassion with mercy, noting that mercy comes from *misericordia*, meaning a compassionate heart for another's unhappiness. He suggests that mercy is indeed a virtue because of its emotive origins in the sense appetite—the ability to feel the suffering and pain of an-other—as well as the necessity of reason in the intellectual appetite to discern the fitting response to this unhappy other.

Moreover, Aquinas suggests that "of all the virtues that relate to our neigh-bor, mercy is the greatest, even as its act surpasses all others. . . . The sum total of the Christian religion consists in mercy, as regards to external works."[36] Aquinas suggests that mercy complements charity in external works such as beneficence and almsgiving. It differs from charity in its object and level of perfection—mercy concerns itself with the imperfect suffering neighbor, while charity seeks the perfect love of God.

Just as Aristotle identifies the ability to attend to others as central to justice, Aquinas's understanding of mercy is pivotal both to understand what constitutes the common good and to accept the moral imperative to build it. Aquinas suggests that mercy begins with those closest to us in circles of family, civil society, and ecclesial communities. However, he warns that this partiality for friends should be trumped by the needs of others who have no one to assist them: "Suc-cor a stranger in extreme necessity, rather than one's own father, if he is not in such urgent need."[37] Therefore, to be of compassionate heart requires a histori-cal consciousness that is aware of those beyond one's immediate circle of con-cern and can evaluate different levels of need.

If Aristotle identifies attending to the circumstances of others as the most difficult expression of virtue, then compassion perfects our capability for his-torically conscious practical reason precisely because it attends to the most dif-ficult types of affliction—those in which we directly and indirectly participate. Moreover, identifying the mean of compassion necessarily requires that we dis-cover the perspective of the person in need in order to determine the most fitting response. This not only enables us to determine more accurately what is going on, but it also creates possibilities for transformative encounters with those who suffer. Compassion is an essential virtue because it takes seriously suffering and our responsibilities for those who suffer, both of which are easy to ignore in our contemporary context with its global complexities. Moreover, compassion per-fects our capacity for practical reason by encouraging the moral imagination in . our attempts to determine the path between what is and what might be. As we will see in the final chapter, practical reason informed by a disposition that at-tends to the suffering of others can serve as a central component of social ethics in an age of globalization.

Compassion as a Virtue That Integrates Emotion and Action

Virtues integrate internal dispositions into external actions. For example, in the *Nichomachean Ethics*, Aristotle concludes that virtues integrate feelings, capacities, and states of being. When intentionally habituated they lead us to *eudaimonia,* or flourishing, a condition of perfecting our respective natures. To that end Aquinas calls virtues a "perfection of a power" or the ordering of our lives toward a particular end.[38] Virtues depend on existing internal dispositions, but they perfect those dispositions through habituated action. In other words, they are not merely passive states but rather active commitments to perfecting certain powers—whether powers of the intellect, our appetites, or our capacities for relationships with others. For example, Diana Fritz Cates specifically notes that compassion is "an abiding state of character" or "intricate pattern of desires, beliefs and perceptions that disposes us, time and time again, to receive and respond in a characteristic way, to persons in pain."[39] Said differently, in order to be compassionate a moral agent must feel and act compassionately.

The integration of disposition and action in the experience of compassion transforms the virtuous person as well as the situation to which the person responds. The virtue of compassion harnesses the energy of the evocative emotions that arise when we encounter those who wrestle with dehumanizing suffering: grief, incredulity, sorrow, dismay, rage, gratitude, shame, sympathy, outrage, solidarity, depression, inspiration. It then channels that passion into an active commitment to end the other's suffering through everything from imagination to hands-on engagement. In the process, compassion flushes out practical demands of frequently abstract and ahistorical principles such as human dignity, justice, or human rights.

For example, perhaps more than any other experience, encounters with radical or dehumanizing suffering bring into sharp focus the distinction between what is and what ought to be. Systematic theologian Edward Schillebeeckx calls these jarring encounters "contrast experiences" that contribute to our understanding of human nature and morality if only by pointing to situations and experiences we recognize as contradicting human nature or antithetical to moral development. Contrast experiences, in his estimation, have the potential to create provocative reactions, particularly in cases of unjust suffering: "No, it can't go on like this; we won't stand for it any longer!"[40]

Compassion unleashes the interruptive and liberating power of contrast experiences and hones our ability to feel, to imagine, and to enact viable alternatives to what is. Aquinas illustrates this point.

James Keenan describes Aquinas's *Summa Theologica* as a three-part dialogical treatise that begins with the transcendent nature of God, turns to more earthly examinations of human responses to God, and then reorients moral agents back toward God through a discourse on Christ and the sacraments.[41] This movement, particularly in terms of Aquinas's examination of our response to God through virtuous living, underscores the emphasis that he placed on the dynamic process of moral development. His ideas radically departed from the more static confessional approach that dominated much of Christian history until that point. Aquinas reminds us that moral living is an evolving and dynamic process of responding to God's love. In addition, Aquinas's thorough treatment of the theological and cardinal virtues underscores the importance of relationality—with God, with self, and with others—as the necessary ingredient for human development. In fact, moral growth and personal transformation take place in the process of responding to these relationships.

Situations of suffering have the potential to create unique relationality in each of these three types of relationships. Aquinas notes the depth of the internal disposition connected with mercy, since mercy is the virtue that stems from experiences of "looking upon another's distress as one's own."[42] Perceiving another's affliction as one's own creates the possibility for relationality, if only briefly, between the non-suffering perceiver and the sufferer he or she perceives. This connection plants the seed of a particular disposition, which, when intentionally cultivated, gives rise to an increased capacity for critical analysis and external actions commensurate with that depth of feeling. In other words, acutely feeling another's suffering can encourage an equally acute reflection on the person's reality and a more effective response to it.

For example, if we truly commit ourselves to reflecting on the suffering of homeless persons as our own, we are more likely to feel the cold differently in the winter and the heat differently in the summer. We are more likely to feel more accurately the powerlessness that comes with being invisible on the streets or in the shelter system, of having no control over daily needs such as whether and what one will eat, where to find a toilet, or being able to change one's socks. We are more likely to feel the dread of more substantial issues such as whether pesrons will lose their children, if they will be sexually assaulted, or if they will contract tuberculosis. In other words, if we commit ourselves to suffering with persons in this visceral and imaginative way, we begin to approach justice or human rights in more visceral and imaginative ways—less as abstract concepts and more as physical and emotional longings.

When justice becomes something we long to experience rather than something we struggle to understand cognitively, we begin to appreciate the difference between being fed and being nourished, or the difference between being housed and being at home, or the difference between labor and meaningful work, or the difference between being medically treated and being medically cared for, or the difference between being the recipient of charity and being a collaborator in justice.

Compassion helps us to experience what justice *feels* like. These physical longings for justice or desires for tactile experiences of it might sustain increasingly difficult and demanding practices that seek after justice, or human rights, or human dignity. For instance, our response to homeless persons might dynamically evolve from donating toiletries to shelters to distributing them ourselves at the shelter, to counting persons at the shelter among our friends, to standing with our friends to advocate for affordable housing in our local community. The virtue of compassion therefore integrates these feelings and critical capacities for understanding with equally difficult and even uncomfortable actions.

A compassionate person has an increased capacity to feel, to understand, and to respond to others' affliction. Part of that increased capacity depends on a willingness to be disrupted by the contrast experiences of suffering and not merely smoothing over their jagged edges with sentimental words and actions. Rather, in order to integrate our passion and action, compassion's transformative component rests in our ability to ask of ourselves the evocative questions that suffering persons ask themselves: Why am I suffering in this way? What is to become of me? Who and where is God in the midst of this pain? Why are not more people not affected by my situation? Why can't more people recognize their connection to my affliction? What can *I* do to overcome this affliction? What should *others* do to overcome this affliction?

Compassion as Virtue of Communal Narratives

It is now clear that, given their historical consciousness and evocative nature, virtues are not ideals pursued through deductive reasoning or habits that seek after abstract principles. In addition, virtues should not be understood as individualized, privatized, or atomized expressions of moral development, since these habituated dispositions grow out of communal values and beliefs. As such they are best practiced in the context of a community of persons who seek to perfect them. In other words, virtues are embedded in the shared beliefs and values, dispositions and practices, stories and rituals of communities. It is precisely this characteristic of virtue ethics that resists the privatized, individualized, and unreciprocated expressions of compassion that prevail in our North American culture. And it is precisely this characteristic of compassion that can help us to cultivate values, beliefs, and practices that resist our tendencies toward individualism, consumerism, and bourgeois Christianity by underscoring the participatory, relational, and narrative aspects of our religious and civic traditions.

Alasdair MacIntyre, who sparked the renaissance of virtue theory in the twentieth century, notes that "there is no way to possess the virtues except as part of a tradition in which we inherit them and our understanding of them from a series of predecessors."[43] In many ways MacIntyre's point justifies the very purpose of this chapter: to appreciate the rich content of the tradition of compassion we inherit from our predecessors so that we might adapt it and perfect it in our current circumstances. As such, virtues are "individual and corporate" actions toward some ideal of excellence that rely on the traditions and narratives of our ancestors in order for us to achieve them.[44] For example, Americans have long valued religious freedom and believed it to be an inherent component of human dignity. The virtue of tolerance as it is practiced in our culture, therefore, is not only different from tolerance as it is practiced in other cultures, but it is different from generation to generation of Americans. Each generation since the nation's founding has attempted to be more perfectly tolerant in light of its respective circumstances by habituating dispositions handed on to it. Therefore, virtues reflect the *content* of tradition, or the values and beliefs of groups of people, as well as the *process* of tradition, or the way those values and beliefs are bequeathed and practiced over time. Those who practice them automatically participate in something larger than themselves. Therefore, compassion cannot be a private affair.

In moving MacIntyre's point forward, Christian ethicist Stanley Hauerwas argues that we can best understand the corporate experience of virtue if we focus on the role of narrative or storytelling in shaping collective beliefs and values and the practices that arise out of them. He notes that "the social and political validity of a community results from its being formed by a truthful story, a story that gives us the means to live without fear of one another."[45] Narratives create the moral principles we use to shape our common life. Hauerwas notes that the narrative character of the virtues is most evident in the way that the narrative of Christ continues to shape the identity and practice of the Christian community. This book examines the ongoing significance of the story of the good Samaritan for Christian communities attempting to love our neighbor in an age of globalization.

In addition, Hauerwas insists that only a "thick" narrative can help society resist the temptation for self-deception or the dangerous outlook that "forces us to see our neighbor as a stranger."[46] When neighbors become strangers, we can more easily separate ourselves from them, more easily deny our connections to them, more easily shirk our responsibilities to them.

Thinking about compassion in narrative terms underscores the viability of this virtue in our contemporary global context where the stories of a limited few increasingly dictate the stories, and therefore the virtues, of the whole. Because it pays attention to the stories that are frequently not absorbed into our communal narrative, compassion helps to thicken that collective narrative where the suffering neighbor is concerned. Through attention to the suffering of others, compassion brings often ignored or forgotten stories to our public consciousness, stories from the underside of history whose wisdom challenges the often incomplete master narratives that shape public virtues.

Consider the narrative aspects of the virtue of compassion in the context of our national response to Hurricane Katrina. The virtue of compassion can call our attention to stories about concentrated poverty in New Orleans that gradually destroyed neighbors and neighborhoods long before Hurricane Katrina made landfall. These stories challenge the myth of America as the land of opportunity and equality as well as the mythical values of individualized self-sufficiency.

The virtue of compassion might enable us to hear stories about being forced to choose between paying the rent and paying for a new transmission, stories that challenge prevailing narratives about the causes of homelessness shape our responses to those who wrestle with housing insecurity.

Moreover, if Hauerwas is correct in suggesting that virtues arise out of and are perfected by participation in narratives, and if Aristotle is right in suggesting that perfecting the virtues is a conduit for human flourishing, then we must explore the ethical value of sharing and listening to stories of suffering. Storytelling can be an act of resistance for those whose experiences of suffering are characterized by invisibility, assaults on personal identity, or paternalistic treatment at the hands of others. In sharing their narratives, suffering persons become visible moral agents who reclaim their identities and demand account-ability. This underscores the transformative power of the virtue of compassion. In addition, when we listen to stories of suffering, we enter into a relationship with the storyteller. These relationships have the collective power and resources to reshape the erroneous values and beliefs that wrongly inform the judgments we rely on in order to respond to suffering others. In more positive terms, com-passion has the capacity to renew and restore shared narratives and traditions, as well as those who participate in them.

In many ways this desire to renew stories and traditions spurred MacIntyre to return to virtue ethics in order to move social ethics beyond the post-modern impasse created by emotivism, moral relativism, and empty duty. In a similar way a desire to renew the subversive nature of the narrative of the parable of the good Samaritan motivates this reconstruction of compassion. That particular story created a relationality between Christ and the individual listeners who gath-ered together to hear it, and between them and the two characters on the road to Jericho. Considering compassion as a narrative virtue reminds us of the chal-lenge to hear the story in new ways, in new contexts, and with the intent to create new relationships.

COMPASSION AS A VIRTUE FOR SOCIAL ORDER

In his assessment of the viability of virtue ethics for contemporary Christian ethics, Joseph Kotva expresses two concerns with direct connections to our re-construction of compassion. He wonders if the virtue approach encourages a self-centered moral "narcissism," which perpetuates American isolated individu-alism. He also questions if virtue ethics can actually support communal or col-lective action.[47] The ideas of Enlightenment philosophers on the topic of com-passion correspond to Kotva's legitimate concerns. These thinkers highlight compassion's socially transformative potential, another much needed facet of loving our neighbor in a global age.

While several philosophers of the Enlightenment carried forward the Aristo-telian tradition of emotive reasoning, their orientation toward ethical questions differs significantly from their predecessors. The Greeks and Christian philoso-phers looked forward to the ultimate goal or *telos* of human activity in order to evaluate more accurately individual and collective moral behavior in light of "the good life." The Enlightenment philosophers, on the other hand, gazed back-ward through accumulated layers of cultural developments, political arrange-ments, and religious sensibilities to humanity's original, pre-social, and natural state in order to offer a universal ethical prognosis for the present.[48] Basing one's moral decision on ultimate ends, in their estimation, dangerously placed human reason at the disposal of transcendent categories with little empirical evidence and claims that seemingly contradicted rational analysis. Therefore, adapting Plato's famous allegory, Griswold notes that the Enlightenment phi-losophers believed that "fires lit in a cavern that is properly organized will suffice pretty well" and that we are "better off to liberate ourselves from the myth that there is light outside of the cave."[49]

To that end, moral and political philosophers such as Smith, Rousseau, and Schopenhauer suggest that compassion—or its secular counterpart, sympathy—provides an important innate tool that can focus moral attention on the temporal reality and create positive social conditions for the greater good. These emphases were only bolstered by their anthropological analysis of humans in our purest natural state, where capabilities for emotive connections to others were central to the human experience. Unlike their Stoic predecessors, therefore, the Enlightenment philosophers viewed vulnerability through compassion as critical for shaping proper human relationships and more just social structures. They offer a variety of approaches for cultivating compassion—or its components such as sympathy—as a social virtue capable of ordering collective life.

Adam Smith

Although most often recognized for his political and economic theory, spelled out in *The Wealth of Nations* (1776), Adam Smith (1723–90) also dabbled in the imagination, the arts, and the virtues, a reflection of his social and intellectual location in the midst of the Scottish Enlightenment. Smith thought it would be possible to improve the lives of the increasingly poor masses of his day by identifying inherent human capabilities for building a just social order. Sympathy and self-interest are two such capabilities. He develops the first in the context of his virtue theory, *Theory of Moral Sentiments* (1759), and the second in *The Wealth of Nations*. Both contribute to the evolution of compassion, despite their seemingly contradictory motivations—the interests of others in moral virtue and the interests of the self in economics. "How selfish soever a man may be supposed," he says in the opening sentence of *The Theory of Moral Sentiments*, "there are evidently some principles in his nature, which interest him in the fortune of others, and render their happiness necessary to him, though he derives nothing from it, except the pleasure of seeing it."[50] Smith brings to compassion practical imagination, attention to the circumstances of suffering, and reflexive self-awareness on the part of compassionate persons.

As a thinker of the Enlightenment, Smith certainly endorses reason as the ultimate human capacity and source of liberty, since reason gives us the emotional distance and freedom from others and even from ourselves to become impartial and disinterested "spectators." From this more prudent position, we judge more accurately the circumstances of our surroundings and fellow moral agents. The impartial spectator is a "thoughtful, critical observer, directed by virtuous considerations, whether of the intellectual sort or some other, and seeking to understand."[51] Despite this emphasis on detached observation, it is the inclination of the spectator to understand both self and others that integrates the imagination into Smith's virtue and economic theory. We will see in the fourth chapter that the ability to imagine is essential for making judgments about another's affliction.

Smith expects the moral spectator to observe situations and then imagine other agents' passions in the context of those situations—whether joy and gratitude or anger and misery. He calls this ability "fellow-feeling" sympathy. We can have sympathy for all the passions that our fellow agents experience; he reserves compassion or pity for those passions that arise from experiences of suffering or pain. In such instances, Smith claims, we rely on our imaginations to "place ourselves in his situation" and "conceive ourselves enduring all of the same torments . . . and become in some measure the same person with him."[52] Once we have "adopted and made them our own," Smith says, sympathy begins "at last to affect us, and we then tremble and shudder at the thought of what he feels."[53] Smith understands the imagination in practical terms as a faculty through which we can "create a distinctively human sphere in the natural world" where we work out relationships among persons. Knud Haakonssen considers Smith's sympathy a kind of "practical imagination," one that "looks for order, agreement and coherence in the word."[54] In other words, imagination is an essential faculty for building a more just society.

In addition, despite the role of self-interest in his economic theory, Smith insists that sympathy is truly oriented away from the impartial spectator and toward others for their sakes. Alexander Broade notes that from Smith's perspective we don't feel for others so that their passions become our own, but rather so that we might better understand who *they* are and what *they* experience.[55] Smith says, "The spectator must, first of all, endeavor as much as he can to put himself in the situation of the other, and to bring home to himself every little circumstance of distress which can possibly occur to the sufferer."[56]

Moreover, unlike his predecessors in moral theory such as Hume and Hutchinson, Smith argues that sympathy arises from the spectator's observation of the situation, circumstances, or conditions that cause another agent's passions and not simply from his or her observations of the person's passions alone. "Sympathy does not arise so much from the view of the passion, as from that of the situation which excites it. We sometimes feel for another, a passion of which he himself seems to be altogether incapable."[57] In other words, sympathy is historically conscious or aware of the historical conditions that incite others' passions. For instance, Smith's impartial spectator would think sympathetically with the people of New Orleans based on his or her observations and imaginary ruminations on the circumstances of that social disaster and not simply on the reactions of native citizens to these conditions. This historical consciousness expands social consciousness, calling our attention to the often overlooked causes of another's suffering.

In addition, "fellow-feeling" enables impartial spectators to move beyond the boundaries of their own needs and perspective in order to consider situations from others' points of view. This creates the possibility of understanding their own circumstances from others' perspectives, a kind of reflexive self-awareness. "As they are constantly considering what they themselves would feel if they were the sufferers," says Smith of people who have fellow-feeling for others, "so he is led to imagine in what manner he would be affected if he was only one of the spectators of his own situation."[58] This kind of endeavor takes hard work, since it is not necessarily inherent in our social nature. However, Smith is confident that it brings a great deal of pleasure both to moral spectators and to those with whom they have fellow-feeling. Quite simply, it is good to be able to share in another's passions, to know that others are sharing in ours, to revel in the insights that this increased awareness brings, and to adjust one's behavior in light of this wisdom. Knud Haakonssen notes that "one only learns to see one-self as a person and as a member of a moral universe of agents through sympathy with others' view of one's identity and situation in the world."[59]

Perhaps most important for our discussion of the socially transformative power of virtues such as compassion, Broade points out that Smith had confidence in our imaginative capabilities to bridge the distance between the spectator and the agent in particular circumstances. "Nothing pleases us more than to observe in other men a fellow-feeling with all the emotions of our own breast," Smith observes.[60] Fellow-feeling motivates social change through compromise and accommodation, particularly in transactions in the marketplace. In working to understand the same circumstances or conditions from different perspectives, we become more willing to compromise on the positions we ourselves hold. This willingness to accommodate others using sympathetic feeling facilitates the virtue of justice—particularly comparative justice—since it mediates that tension within moral agents between self-interest and other-regard, as well as the relationships among people who do not know one another in the marketplace. The metaphorical "invisible hand of the market," which relies on self-interest and competition to guide humanity naturally toward progress, does not work without sympathetic feelings that make judgments of prudence possible.

Jean-Jacques Rousseau

Jean-Jacques Rousseau (1712–78) questioned many of his peers' unfettered optimism in the potential for human progress and development, an optimism rooted in a humanism that celebrated the moral potential of the rational self. His questioning stems partially from his insistence that the human condition throughout history can best be understood as one of suffering. Rousseau was acutely aware of the signs of his times. Many are precursors to our own—a dramatic gap between rich and poor, increasing political disenfranchisement, emphasis on self-preservation as the most efficacious social glue, and human worth measured in units of economic productivity. He wondered whether human beings were truly moral by nature and if we are unquestioningly destined for civil society. In fact, in his treatise on education Rousseau notes that "suffering is the first thing [Émile] ought to learn, and that which he will have the greatest need to know" if he wants to shape his intellect and his heart.[61]

Mark Cladis suggests that Rousseau's orientation placed him at the intersection of the competing world views of "Enlightenment optimism," with its hopeful prospects for voluntary social organization, and "Augustinian pessimism," with its realistic acknowledgment of the permanent condition of human finitude and sinfulness. His basic understanding of the primary sources of human motivation—self-preservation and pity—reflects the impact of these two trajectories in his thought. Certainly, in ways that echo the social contract theories of Smith or Hobbes, human beings are driven by egotistical self-interest. But Rousseau insisted that we simultaneously experience a "natural repugnance to see any sensitive being perish or suffer, especially human beings."[62] Rather than pit these seemingly conflicting tendencies against one another, Rousseau articulated a "religion of the heart." This religion arouses our imagination by "transporting" individuals beyond their immediate needs and natural *amour propre,* or self-love, through a meaningful identification with the suffering of others in the experience of *pitié,* or sympathy. Rousseau contends that sympathy—a love that is directed toward another—counters the social excess and inequality that seem to stem from a preoccupation with self-interested self-preservation.[63]

Where encounters with others' pleasures make us envious and ungrateful and generally perpetuate social inequalities, encounters with others' pain frees us from self-concern and transports us "outside of ourselves" to identify with the suffering person and "leave, as it were, our own being to take on" their being.[64] It is through this emotional identification with others that Rousseau believed abstract or strictly rational theories of justice and the good might be transformed into "real affections of the soul enlightened by reason" and as such a natural extension of "our primitive affections."[65] Thus, it is an emotion absolutely necessary for individual and social development.

For example, in his *Discourse on the Origins of Inequality*, he traces the development of virtue from humanity's blissful immoral state as "Solitaires" in the Garden to the manifestations of our fallen nature in various stages of social and industrial development. He notes that a willingness to become vulnerable to another's suffering serves as a catalyst for moral development. Where Smith suggests that self-interest is the driving force of moral and social development, Rousseau emphasizes sympathy as a capacity that enables persons to reevaluate and resist the corruption of civil society. It does this by placing a healthy emphasis on self-love. That capacity could be cultivated by exposing a person to situations and objects "on which may be exerted the expansive force of his heart, which will increase it and extend it over other beings, which will ever call his attention away from himself; and to avoid with care those objects which contract and concentrate the human heart."[66]

Arthur Schopenhauer

Arthur Schopenhauer (1788–1869), often recognized for his rather bleak and Hobbsian perspective on human existence, argued against the emphasis on reason or rational thought as the foundation of the moral life. Rather, he suggested that *Mitleid,* or compassion, serves as a more appropriate foundation for moral action. "Boundless compassion for all living things is the firmest and surest guarantee of pure moral conduct," he argued. "Whoever is inspired with it will assuredly injure no one, will wrong no one, will encroach on no one's rights; on the contrary . . . he will help everyone as much as he can, and all his actions will bear the stamp of justice."[67]

Schopenhauer bases his argument on three observations with direct connections to the human condition in our contemporary reality. First, with a passion that eventually inspired Friedrich Nietzsche, he identifies "the Will" or the voracious human appetite for survival as the driving force of all human experience and concern; as such, the Will is the source of "pursuit, hunting, anxiety and suffering." In fact, it is the insatiability of the Will that makes suffering an inescapable reality for all living things—we either struggle to obtain the resources necessary to satiate ourselves or struggle to defend our resources against the advances of others. In a way that speaks directly to the American experience, Schopenhauer notes that even persons "who are healthy and wealthy, and the beneficiaries of what otherwise look to be all the blessings life has to offer" are actually "suffering the cycle of desire, frustration, greater desire, satiety and boredom."[68]

In addition, the Will and the suffering it creates form a common denominator among all persons. The Will is "a thing-in-itself" that simultaneously exists in all persons while transcending the limits of physicality. The only way for humans to rise above the demands of the Will and the anxiety and suffering it causes is to concern ourselves with the suffering of others by acknowledging the same Will at work in them, the same Will that lies at the root of their struggles, the same Will that often places us in adversarial relationships in an increasingly competitive world. This acknowledgment of the suffering of another, a type of knowledge that Schopenhauer reserved for saintly asceticism or perceptive aesthetics, restrains the ego's servitude to the Will, thus undermining its dominance. In other words, Schopenhauer understands compassion as a means by which we can acknowledge commonality with others who struggle like us under the dictatorship of the Will and a tool by which we can limit the power of the Will in our individual lives.

Moreover, unlike his contemporaries, Schopenhauer points to the web of suffering and unjust relationships that exist among persons as a result of egotistical drive of the Will. He therefore challenges whether self-interest is morally neutral. He notes, for example, that freedom for self-interest often denies the freedoms of others and that the accumulation of wealth for some requires the depletion of others' resources. Given this inescapable web of relationships, he suggests that it is not enough merely to offer negative moral rules, as epitomized in Kant's categorical imperative. Rather, the Will needs to be restrained by the obligation to recognize that same anxiety-generating Will in others and mitigate its negative effects whenever possible. Therefore, relying on compassion as his central moral principle, Schopenhauer admonishes: "Injure no one; on the contrary, help everyone as much as you can."[69] It is only through suffering with another, or the sense that "when I look at people in pain I am really looking at myself" that we are motivated to do moral acts. Schopenhauer's understanding of compassion reminds us that it is not enough to simply avoid wrong doing. Moral activity requires actions on behalf of others.

Takeaways from the Philosophical Tradition

The political philosophers of the Enlightenment, and even those of the post-modern period, offer important insights for the continued evolution of compassion. While they rightly assent to the centrality of self-interestedness in social relationships and structures—a seemingly timeless feature of the human condition—they do not necessarily believe that compassion is antithetical to self-concern. Acknowledging one's vulnerability in the plight of another certainly entails self-interest, but with the right balance between self-interest and "other-interest" these philosophers ardently believed that compassion could shape social structures and relationships. Smith reminds us that compassion attunes the perceptions of moral agents to the reality of suffering in their midst and as such can empower individuals to redirect social forces of free markets. Rousseau relies on it to cultivate affections needed to complement reason. Schopenhauer uses it to acknowledge the common denominators that bind humanity in shared experiences of suffering.

In addition, these thinkers have great confidence in compassion's ability as a social emotion, as a means of connecting persons who otherwise would not know one another and therefore care little for one another. Certainly compassion exists as an interaction among individuals, and yet the Enlightenment philosophers do not limit compassion to the private sphere. They apply it to collective initiatives such as the economy, in Smith's case; civic institutions as such evidenced by Rousseau's passionate plea for an education of the heart; or Schopenhauer's recommendation for public discourse regarding moral development.

PHILOSOPHICAL FOUNDATIONS FOR NEW COMPASSION

Resources in the philosophical tradition can help us move the tradition of compassion forward in order to meet the demands of our global age. If we integrate these resources, a new permutation of compassion and its praxis begins to emerge.

First, the philosophical tradition reveals that in order to love our suffering neighbor in an age of globalization we must perfect our *capacity to perceive* others in their affliction. Plato says as much in his endorsement of the primacy of wisdom that perfects our sight, as does Aristotle in the emphasis he places on the emotions in illuminating our inherent vulnerability and relationality. Recall, also, Kant's recommendation that we expose ourselves to situations of injustice in order to cultivate a desire in the will to uphold the universal moral law to treat all persons as ends. And the entire orientation of virtue ethics, epitomized by Niebuhr's "What's going on?" reinforces the importance of perceiving our social reality accurately before we decide how to respond.

Second, compassion involves a *willingness to interpret* contexts of injustice from the perspective of those who suffer. The three aspects of the virtue of compassion underscore this point. In order to figure out what's going on in a given situation, we need to turn to those closest to it. In addition, as an emotion that informs the way we understand others' suffering, compassion's depth of feeling can create "contrast experiences" that might interrupt prevailing ways of understanding others' pain. And finally, compassion's narrative component exposes us to different stories and storytellers who give us a new perspective and new imperatives to adapt our responses to injustice.

Finally, compassion requires an *active commitment* to create new relationships that can transform the neighbor, ourselves, and the social reality. Recall that Aristotle and Aquinas both identify an ability to enter into relationships with suffering persons as essential for perfecting either justice or charity, the primary virtues in their respective theories. Smith, Rousseau, and Schopenhauer endorse the capacity to relate to another's suffering as an invaluable civic virtue that strengthens the public bonds among individuals. These themes recur in the theological tradition, albeit with different emphases and applications. We turn to that now.

3

What Are They Saying about Compassion in Theological Ethics?

But wanting to justify himself, he asked Jesus, "And who is my neighbor?" Jesus replied, "A man was going down from Jerusalem to Jericho, and fell into the hands of robbers, who stripped him, beat him, and went away, leaving him half dead. Now by chance a priest was going down that road; and when he saw him, he passed by on the other side. So likewise a Levite, when he came to the place and saw him, passed by on the other side.

But a Samaritan while traveling came near him; and when he saw him, he was moved with pity. He went to him and bandaged his wounds, having poured oil and wine on them. Then he put him on his own animal, brought him to an inn, and took care of him. The next day he took out two denarii, gave them to the innkeeper, and said, 'Take care of him, and when I come back, I will repay you whatever more you spend.'"

"Which of these three, do you think, was a neighbor to the man who fell into the hands of the robbers?" He said, "The one who showed mercy." Jesus said to him, "Go and do likewise." (Lk 10:29–38)

In this parable Jesus sketches the blueprint not only for Christian moral living, but also for upstanding citizenship in the human community. The story and its protagonist have "name brand" notoriety.

For example, an Internet search reveals thousands of Good Samaritan hospitals, hospices, food pantries, philanthropic foundations, religious missions, and civic associations around the world. There are contemporary interpretations of the parable in different cultures, as well as Good Samaritan coloring books and puppet shows. News stories of modern-day Good Samaritans in every imaginable scenario abound, as do the criteria for Good Samaritan awards in schools, professional organizations, and first-responder units. Students seeking every type of degree—from GEDs to MDs—can apply for Good Samaritan scholarships to support their education in everything from public health to music, as well as Good Samaritan financial aid packages to assist them in overcoming a variety of socioeconomic disadvantages. Recreational vehicle drivers can slap a smiley face bumper sticker on their rigs and join the Good Sam Club to "have fun, stop to help one another, and meet responsibilities to the environment, highways, and parks." A Good Samaritan Club in Canada saves its members money on prescription drugs. If you plan to sponsor a major event where alcohol will be served you can hire the International Good Samaritans; their trained designated drivers will get your guests and their cars home safely. There are even Good Samaritan statutes that require citizens to do as much good as possible for anyone in need, and others that protect Good Samaritans from litigation should their intervention in some way cause unintended harm.

This rich sampling of examples of Good Samaritanism underscores a point from the first chapter—that compassion is an incredibly prevalent and frustratingly ambiguous way of engaging in our social reality. William Spohn, moreover, suggests that this should be the case, particularly for Christian disciples, if we consider Jesus' imperative at the conclusion of the parable: "Go and do likewise." Jesus does not want his disciples to stick close to one another and mimic or imitate the compassion of the Samaritan or of Christ himself. This kind of group-think does not require acute perception or reflection. It perpetuates routine action that lacks intention and moral agency. Rather, by commanding the disciples to *depart from him* and do likewise, Jesus tells us to strike out on our own journeys down to Jericho and replicate his compassion to fit the circumstances that define our stretch of that treacherous road.

However, not all self-proclaimed expressions of Samaritanism are equally viable means of suffering with others. For example, the disabled veterans of the Good Samaritan Club in Lansing, Michigan, who "perfect the art of giving from the heart" by anonymously securing "items needed by low-income families" perform a different kind of compassion than the Good Samaritan Toast Masters club that has "helped millions of men and women become more confident in front of an audience." As we saw in the first chapter, in our global age, where values of individualism, consumerism, and materialism, as well as the power dynamics of white privilege shape our perceptions of and responses to those who suffer, it is important that we ask ourselves the question that Jesus asked of the scholar of the law who prompted the parable's telling in the first place: Which of these is the neighbor to victims of injustice?

A brief overview of the theological tradition yields a panoply of examples of individuals and communities whose struggle to live according to this central mandate of Christianity can help us in answering this question. They offer resources for a reflective and innovative approach to compassion that challenges American bourgeois Christianity as well as the values and beliefs that foster an imitative, routinized, and largely empty means of suffering with others. In the scholarly writing and personal witness of many in the Christian tradition we find examples of loving our neighbor that can bolster the definition of compassion that we started to construct in the last chapter: a compassion that requires special attention to persons laid low by injustice; a compassion that involves a life-altering change in the way we understand ourselves, God, and the world around us; and a compassion that demands an active and relational resistance to the causes of injustice.

Three characteristics of compassion emerge in our perusal of the tradition: (1) compassion is a dangerous and political expression of neighbor love, (2) it is concerned with the common good of all persons, and (3) it is a virtue that seeks after human material and spiritual development. We can find the roots of these expressions of neighborly love in biblical texts, in the theological ruminations of the tradition's significant thinkers, and in the social doctrine of the Catholic Church.

SACRED NARRATIVES OF DIVINE COMPASSION

Scripture scholar Dianne Bergant argues that a close reading of both the Hebrew Bible and the New Testament reveals a compassionate God behind "each and every divine activity, whether creation, liberation or judgment."[1] For example, Yahweh proclaims to Moses through the burning bush: "I have observed the misery of my people who are in Egypt; I have heard their cry on account of their taskmasters. Indeed, I know their sufferings, and I have come down to deliver them from the Egyptians, and to bring them up out of that land" (Ex 3:7–8). This emotion prompts Yahweh's dramatic acts on behalf of the Israelites that liberate them from bondage in Egypt. Or consider Matthew's description of Jesus' encounters with the people throughout his ministry: "When he saw the crowds, he had compassion for them, because they were harassed and helpless, like sheep without a shepherd. . . . He had compassion for them and cured their sick" (Mt 9:36; 14:14). In fact, Jesus' compassion for a crowd that gathered when he came ashore from the Lake of Galilee spurs the feeding of the five thousand—a miracle that illuminates the significance of the Eucharist in calling forth the gifts of the community in order to feed compassionately our physical and spiritual hungers.

A brief analysis of compassion in sacred texts gives us a deeper sense of the kind of suffering that contradicts God's initial intentions for creation as well as God's moving responses to this suffering.

Compassion in the Hebrew Bible

In her examination of the Hebrew Bible, Bergant suggests that compassion is derived from the Hebrew root *rhm*, which refers either to the special love of parents for children or to the life-giving and creative concept of the womb. This metaphor is used to describe Yahweh in all but five of its fifty appearances in the Hebrew Bible. In these passages we discover that compassion entails an attentiveness to and presence with those who suffer injustice. Bergant categorizes this attentiveness in four distinct contexts: mercy after wrath, repentance of sin, covenant renewal, and national restoration. The latter two are pivotal for the continued evolution of compassion in a global age.

God expresses both self and presence among the people through compassion, indicated in the often-repeated dyad that praises Yahweh as "gracious and compassionate." Hosea captures God's love for the people: "How can I give you up, Ephraim? How can I hand you over, O Israel? . . . My heart recoils within in me; my compassion grows warm and tender. I will not execute my fierce anger; I will not again destroy Ephraim, For I am God and no mortal, the Holy One in your midst, and I will not come in wrath" (Hos 11:8). Moreover, passages that use the root *rhm* reveal that God's presence is made known to the people of the covenant—both individually and collectively—particularly in times of dehumanizing suffering or oppression. In return for Yahweh's compassionate presence at these difficult times, the people express their willingness to remain present to Yahweh through compassionate care of the marginalized within their community, a commitment that ultimately mirrors Yahweh's active presence among them. For example, this is a central refrain of the social laws of covenant between Yahweh and the people in which Yahweh reminds them to "hear the cries of the alien," to "lend money to poor neighbors," and to return a neighbor's cloak taken in a pledge "before sundown," just as Yahweh has done for them. "If you do abuse them [the alien, neighbor, or coatless neighbor], when they cry out to me, I will surely heed their cry. . . . I will listen for I am compassionate" (Ex 22:20–26). In short, to be in relationship with God requires that one love others as God loves others, that is, with compassion.

Bergant also notes that compassion is more than an individual response to the invitation of the covenant. It also expresses the collective hopes for the restoration of Israel. For example, Moses reminds the people that if "you return to the LORD your God, and you and your children obey him with all your heart and with all your soul," then "the LORD your God will restore your fortunes and have compassion on you, gathering you again from all the peoples among whom the LORD your God has scattered you. . . . Even if you are exiled to the ends of the world, from there the LORD your God will gather you, and from there he will bring you back" (Dt 30:2–5). The emotive qualities of this love are also evidenced by the people's trust that God will protect them from their enemies by challenging the fidelity of lesser gods—"Indeed the LORD will vindicate his people, have compassion on his servants. . . . He will say . . . 'See now that I, even I, am he; there is no god besides me'" (Dt 32:36–39). God's love can also be found in the people's hope for God's compassion to overcome their captors so that they might be moved to release the Israelites from bondage. For example, King Solomon prays to Yahweh: "Forgive your people who have sinned against you . . . and grant them compassion in the sight of their captors, so that they may have compassion on them" (1 Kgs 3:50). And the people are frequently reminded, "For as you return to the LORD, your kindred and your children will find compassion with their captors, and return to this land. For the LORD your God is gracious and merciful, and will not turn away his face from you, if you return to him" (2 Chr 30:9).

Finally, the great prophets of Israel—Jeremiah, Isaiah, Hosea—speak of Yahweh's continual compassion for those who repent after failing to honor the two basic prohibitions of the covenant—idolatry and disregard for those on the margins. The people experience the depth of God's love in acts of mercy and forgiveness, liberating experiences that depend on the people's willingness to return to their relationship with Yahweh. Consider the following examples:

> Sing for joy, O heavens, and exult, O earth;
>   break forth, O mountains, into singing!
> For the LORD has comforted his people,
>   and will have compassion on his suffering ones.
>   (Is 49:13)

Can a woman forget her nursing child,
or show no compassion for the child of her womb?
Even these may forget,
yet I will not forget you. (Is 49:15)

For a brief moment I abandoned you, but with great compassion I will gather you. In overflowing wrath for a moment I hid my face from you, but with everlasting love I will have compassion on you, says the LORD, your redeemer. . . . For the mountains may depart and the hills be removed, but my steadfast love will not depart from you, and my covenant of peace will not be removed, says the LORD, who has compassion on you. (Is 54:7–8, 10)

The purpose of compassion, therefore, is restorative justice for the entire community, or a renewal of the community's capability to flourish through a renewed capacity for relationality. "And after I have plucked them up, I will again have compassion on them, and I will bring them again to their heritage and to their land, every one of them" (Jer 12:15). Yahweh knows the people's material and spiritual needs and either provides for these needs or urges the Israelites to provide for themselves through just relationships with one another. Therefore the compassion of God is "more than comforting; it is creative," and, like the womb, "brings to rebirth life that was threatened or perhaps even lost."[2] These features point to the relationship between compassion and social change, to compassion's subversive power for transformation through relationship with God and others, or compassion's creative potential to give birth to something completely new. It complements the basic definition of *justice* in biblical texts, which John Donahue explains as "fidelity to the demands of a relationship," particularly relationships with those on the outer fringes of our circles of concern.[3] And this relational characteristic underscores biblical compassion's connection to the virtue approach to the moral life through which one strives to do as God has done throughout human history.

Compassion in the New Testament

The New Testament also conveys the pervasiveness of God's compassion. The Gospels are filled with accounts of Jesus' emotional encounters with the poor and afflicted in the occupied territory where he lived, worked, and loved: lepers and epileptics, a hemorrhaging woman and a man with a withered hand, the blind and deaf, those possessed by demons and crippled by paralysis, and those threatened by patriarchy. Several common themes unite the different stories of Jesus' miraculous healings. For instance, many of these ailments, and more precisely the social attitudes about them, precluded these persons from participating in the wider community. Jesus physically ministers to them—he touches them, speaks to them, listens to them, and incorporates their wisdom into his own. In addition, his healing not only restores these ostracized persons to fuller communion with others, but it also confronts the values, beliefs, and practices that ostracized them in the first place. Jesus' healing restores individuals and whole communities.

The composers of the Synoptic Gospels used at least three different Greek words to capture Christ's various emotional reactions to his suffering neighbors. Bergant notes that translators use the Greek word *oiktiro,* or "sympathy," for Christ's description of God, as well as to describe the ways in which people are to treat one another.[4] Consider, for example, Luke 6:36 and Matthew 5:48. "Be compassionate *(oiktirmones)* as your Father is compassionate." A second word, *eleos,* or "compassion," describes the general emotion aroused by the unjust suffering of others and reflects God's steadfast love in the covenant. This is reiterated in Paul's letter to the Romans: "For he says to Moses, I will show mercy [*eleeso*] to whom I show mercy; and I will have compassion [*oiktireso*] on whom I have compassion" (Rom 9:15).

A third word, *splanchon,* is reserved to describe Christ's personal experiences of compassion. Always used in the plural and in the verb form, *splanchon* is a Greek term for the innards of a religious sacrifice. *Splanchon* points to Jesus as the sacrificial offering that renews the covenantal relationship between Yahweh and the people. This sacrificial image supports what Wayne Whitson Floyd identifies as the "redemptive commitment" that Christ makes with his compassion. Christ totally emptied himself, or gave himself over completely to the suffering of others, in order to eradicate suffering.[5]

Bergant also notes that *splanchon* does not have a long history in the Jewish lexicon and would have denoted "profound feelings or emotions" connected to the lower part of the torso.[6] In biblical texts *splanchon* always has Jesus as its subject, and he uses it to describe the emotional attachment of the father to the prodigal son (Lk 15:20), of the Samaritan to the wounded man on the side of the road (Lk 10:33), and of the just employer to his wards (Mt 18:27). Metaphorical use of this word, therefore, reinforces the intensity of his emotional response to suffering and illustrates the deep relationality that binds Christians together. These parables call for Christians to embody Christ's commitment to give himself completely to those in need and remind us to upend unjust social, religious, and cultural structures that create suffering. The use of *compassion* in these texts indicates that Christians are to witness God's compassion "to those from whom we feel most alienated, those with whom we have been in conflict, those who might take advantage of us, or from whom we expect no return favor."[7] The parables of compassion attempt to teach us about God's active disposition against human suffering and to offer examples of counter-cultural human relationships that participate in the "kin-dom" of God. All of these features give compassion a messianic quality.

The Good Samaritan

Luke's Gospel contains the most parables. John Donahue notes that Lukan parables differ from their synoptic counterparts in their emphasis on "the mystery of human interaction" rather than "the mystery of nature or the threat of judgment."[8] Luke probes the depth of human experience—of suffering, of forgiveness, of regret, of community, and of compassion—in order to illuminate what Donahue identifies as the "ethics of Christian discipleship." Donahue suggests that this includes a willingness to take up one's cross, to show concern for non-Jews, to show mercy to sinners, to care for those on the margins, to live a life of prayer, and to treat wealth and possessions with careful suspicion.[9]

Jesus offers the parable of the good Samaritan in response to a lawyer who tests Jesus' knowledge of the Mosaic law—to love God and to love neighbor. He does so by asking Jesus, "And who is my neighbor?" Jesus does not directly answer his question, but rather asks the more difficult and unasked question— *how* we ought to love our neighbor. This points out the error in the lawyer's line of thinking. The priest and the Levite fail to act because of the ritual purity laws; these laws kept them from responding to the man in need. They simply cross to the other side of the road. Donahue notes that they are caught in a moral dilemma—to observe either "the torah on uncleanness or the torah on love of neighbor."[10] But the Samaritan, whose ancestors ironically were ostracized for their interpretation of the Mosaic law, successfully forgets the ethnic and religious animosity between his people and the Jews. Therefore, the parable demands that we abandon "all status, privilege, and exclusiveness, that is, . . . those things which for Luke stopped the Jewish people from responding to the outreach of Jesus."[11]

Pheme Perkins suggests that in offering this answer Jesus clarifies not only who constitutes the neighbor, but also what it means to love that neighbor.[12] Love of neighbor was certainly a familiar theme within the Palestinian and Hellenistic Jewish communities where Jesus taught. In fact, Mosaic law specifically included love of the neighbor in order to delineate clearly the boundaries of the Israelite community as well as to ease tensions that existed between it and other groups in the Ancient Near East as a result of the Israelites' refusal to assimilate the practices of other cultures. However, in Perkins's estimation, the parable expands our understanding of the love commandment as it appears in the Synoptic Gospels. It is strongly connected to love of God. There are no boundaries on who should receive this love, and it becomes the cornerstone of Jesus' call for a liberated humanity.

However, Perkins also points to three less frequently contemplated elements of the parable that give it its "critical edge." First, Jesus directs the parable to the wealthy, symbolized by the character of the Samaritan. The rich do not have to depend on reciprocated love or the charity of others in order to survive. As such, they ought to be motivated out of concern for the other for the other's sake alone, and not with an eye for potential benefits to themselves. And yet, like the Samaritan, they risk much in becoming vulnerable in another's suffering. Their personal security, social assets, fear, and even righteousness make it easy to cross to the other side of the road. Jesus reminds them that their redemption lies in the ways they are moved by those on the margins. Compassionate love is not sentimental, not ideological, and above all, it is not easy. It might be best understood in terms of the accountability we have to others in light of our shared humanity and a willingness to cross over many self-imposed and culturally imposed boundaries.

Second, Jesus suggests that we "miss the point" if we busy ourselves with a moral or economic calculus in order to determine what we owe our neighbors. "The man is treated as if he were a 'best friend.' Nothing is calculated, nothing is too much."[13] There is no mathematical equation for compassion. Rather, it requires the intangibles of human relationship and, more specifically, the goods of friendship: deep listening, companionship, shared material and emotional resources, affirmation, accompaniment. Edward Vacek's definition of what it means to be a friend points to the depth of relationship that compassion creates: "Friends ask that who they are make a difference to who we are, and they ask to be a part of who we are and what we do."[14] The Samaritan accompanies the injured Jew to a safe place on the Jericho road because that person mattered deeply to him and he wanted to matter deeply to him in return.

Finally, given the historical relationship between the Jews and Samaritans, which included a variety of acts of politically and religiously motivated terrorism as well as routine discrimination, the Samaritan's compassion challenges the prevailing social logic of the day with all of its false assumptions, erroneous beliefs, and misguided values. Compassionate love is counter-cultural. It creates upheavals in the ways we understand ourselves, others, and the world. For example, compassion suggests that our rivals—personal, professional, cultural, national, economic—are in fact our companions. It reminds us that love of God without equal love for the neighbor is sinful. It suggests that unjust suffering does not happen only to people to whom we have no attachment or even to the people we might expect to suffer; rather, it affects members of our immediate communities whom we pass by everyday. It reminds us that the destination is not as important as the path we traverse to reach it, and that becoming vulnerable in the suffering of others makes us invulnerable to the desensitizing pressures of society. It proclaims that extravagant self-gift is not foolish but rather a wise investment, and that ministering to others is nothing if not primarily a commitment to accompany others no matter the cost.

Compassion overrides social, cultural, racial, economic, and religious boundaries. It accepts personal accountability for the stranger-turned-neighbor and stops at nothing to ensure that person's physical and emotional well-being. It brings disparate people together in a personal, embodied, and emotional relationship.

Concluding Remarks

Several biblical texts support an evolution of compassion in our global context. For example, compassion is primarily a voluntary response to another's suffering that participates in God's own voluntary response to the suffering in human history. In short, a compassionate response is not an isolated or random act of kindness but rather an intentional relationship—with others and with God—sustained over a lifetime. It is a commitment to see the world as God does, and to respond to it as God does. For example, Diana Fritz Cates notes that "being compassionate and just within our modern global context requires recognizing that every human being is a 'neighbor' who has some claim on us to be received and responded to with attention, affection, beneficence, respect, and fairness."[15]

Furthermore, compassion does not merely attend to the symptoms of another's affliction, but it also restores them to full membership in the community. This is most evident in Yahweh's compassionate action on behalf of the nation of Israel. God, moved by the people's cries, liberated them from slavery in Egypt, promised fidelity to them in the relationship of the covenant, forged bonds of justice among them, and created them anew as a nation set apart. God's compassionate activity focuses on restoration. It is precisely this that underscores compassion's political nature, or its concern with questions regarding human flourishing. Creating a just social order in which all are able to flourish serves as the common denominator of God's response to social oppression.

We can also find this in Christ's compassion for the individuals who cry out to him from the social, cultural, religious, and economic margins of first-century Palestine. He is moved to heal them of the socially created conditions that keep them separated from God and others—ritual impurities, demons, blindness, leprosy, ethnic and gender discrimination, and religious abomination. In this way Christ's compassion not only heals afflicted individuals but also challenges the beliefs and values that relegated these persons to the margins in the first place. He redresses the social causes of their afflictions as well as the symptoms of their suffering.

Finally, compassion demands much of those who practice it. Certainly, it demands that we give freely of ourselves to others in need. However, its redemptive and messianic qualities also interrogate the prevailing logic of our contemporary reality that sustains structures of injustice: that people deserve their blessings or misfortunes, that productivity guarantees fulfillment, that flourishing is best understood in material terms, that only misguided individuals perpetuate racism, that free-market capitalism will "raise all boats," that charity is enough to buoy those struggling to keep their heads above water. Compassion also interrogates the values that arise from that prevailing logic and that perpetuate unjust practices: isolating individualism, justifiable privilege, impenetrable security, demoralizing cynicism, and comforting Christianity. And finally, and perhaps most dauntingly, compassion also interrogates us for our participation in this logic and for our endorsement of these values and practices.

But compassion in biblical texts is not only critical. It is also wildly constructive. Both the covenant between Yahweh and the people of Israel and images of the "kin-dom" of God promised by Christ offer a liberating alternative to the prevailing conditions on the road to Jericho: radical equality between men and women, preference for the least, forgiveness of sinners, counter-cultural friendship with the stranger and the enemy, counter-intuitive vulnerability through the gift of self. Rabbi Tsvi Blanchard calls these alternatives a "redemptive vision" because they inspire us to transform our social reality by participating in God's liberating action in history.[16] Jim Wallis suggests that the Hebrew prophets remind people in positions of leadership and affluence about the redemptive possibilities of this vision for all people: "without a vision the people will perish."[17] Compassion, therefore, entails seeing, interpreting, and acting in the world anew.

COMPASSION AND POLITICALLY DANGEROUS DISCIPLESHIP

With these biblical foundations in mind, we can begin to identify the ways in which compassion bolsters the political nature of Christian discipleship engaged in the world. This is particularly true when we associate the term *political* with the collective activities connected to the shared project of human flourishing rather than with the activities related to elections and mechanisms of government. For example, Gaspar Martinez suggests that in the context of faith, we might think about the political aspect of persons and communities as the "ability to see more, and to see with the eyes of faith, the invisible, unnoticed, inopportune suffering in every society and in the destitute countries of the world."[18] According to this line of thinking, compassion is inherently political. Authentically political people are necessarily compassionate.

Martinez's definition also complements notions of discipleship in the Christian tradition. For example, Norbert Lohfink notes that biblical discipleship requires two elements: an interior conversion marked by a willingness to love and be loved, and an external commitment to actively embody that love within systems of oppression.[19] In addition, discipleship demands a commitment to following the way of a *political* Christ, who, James Keenan explains, was traditionally interpreted as the central character of the parable of the good Samaritan: "the traveler on the road," or "the one who showed mercy" or the one who did not "look for a neighbor to love but rather [was] a neighbor who loves."[20] This discipleship of neighbor love mandates a reversal of power structures within families and religious communities, as well as an equitable distribution of resources and fuller participation in communal life. Compassion is necessarily a political act because it creates relationships that challenge the status quo.

The political nature of Christian compassion, epitomized by the discipleship of the Good Samaritan, has evolved through the centuries as different communities in varying socioeconomic contexts have attempted to minister to the victims of injustice along the road to Jericho. Throughout the centuries theologians have explored the requirements of discipleship in their own social contexts and have offered insights about how we might "go and do likewise" in our global age.

Augustine and Humble Tribulations of the Heart

Augustine of Hippo (354–430), thoroughly educated in the ways of Roman citizenry and restlessly drawn to the way of Christ, did not necessarily make the synthesis of citizenship and discipleship a pastoral priority at a time when it would have been permissible and even advisable for Christians to consider more intentional integration of the two. This is certainly a result of the inherent dualism in Augustine's Platonic philosophy. He segregated and prioritized a variety of dichotomies: the spirit over the body, the transcendent realm over the temporal realm, the City of God over the City of Man. This tentative political stance also reflects Augustine's historical location. He was born forty years after Christianity became the religion of the Roman Empire and he wrote on the brink of its collapse, an event for which Christians in his day were made scapegoats. In order to quell suspicion and maintain social stability, he reminds his flock that Christ's kingdom is other-worldly, that pilgrims of the City of God are not commissioned to bring about God's kingdom in the City of Man, and that earthly justice simply involves doing good and avoiding harm whenever possible. These are not the anthems of radical social change.

Moreover, Augustine does not develop a specific theory or treatise on compassion or what he calls "suffering in the heart of the man who feels for the sorrow of another."[21] In fact, in his autobiography, *Confessions*, he chastises himself for the kind of shallow compassion he experienced at the theaters, and he does so for reasons that Plato, with his own distaste for the emotions connected to human suffering, would certainly appreciate. "But how real is the compassion evoked by fictional dramas?" Augustine critically inquires. "The listener is not moved to offer help, but merely invited to feel sorrow; and the more intensely he feels it the more highly he rates the actor in the play."[22] This kind of superficial emotion at another's misfortune only gave rise to other misguided lusts and desires that consumed Augustine in his pre-conversion years with a "foul disease" of longing for everything but God. He firmly concluded, therefore, that "a person who sorrows for someone who is miserable earns approval for the charity he shows, but if he is genuinely merciful he would far rather there were nothing to sorrow about."[23]

Nevertheless, these comments, as well as Augustine's ruminations on love of neighbor, point to the dangerous and political nature of Christian responses to those who suffer: love of neighbor creates a vulnerability that binds persons together rather than buttressing the separation between them; it is not a passive expression of grief but rather an affection that spurs rightly ordered action with tremendous potential to change persons; and it includes an experience of humility or the "tribulation of the heart" that resists self-deception. Each of these aspects can assist us in breaking through the prevailing logic of our twenty-first-century sensibilities.

For example, Augustine unifies the inherent dichotomies in his Platonic world view and moral framework with the assertion that all persons ought to direct their loves toward the immutable and transcendent *Summum Bonum* on which we are all radically dependent. In other words, we ought to orient all of our desires, passions, and capabilities toward love of God and to use all material goods to a similar end. When properly ordered in relation to this greatest good, our many passions, desires, and capabilities work in concert to create interior contentment, the type of contentment that Augustine sought most of his life. Recall his famous observation in his autobiography: "Our hearts are restless until they rest in you."

Moreover, Augustine notes that the command to orient all loves toward our love of God requires that we also love our neighbor. If we are truly to love God, then we must recall Matthew's parable of the last judgment and recognize God in the neighbor, particularly the suffering neighbor. In fact, in *On Christian Doctrine* Augustine argues that the "counsel of compassion" nurtures a particular kind of wisdom that enables compassionate persons to see God more clearly and love God more fully; through compassion "he cleanses his soul, which is violently agitated, and disturbs him with base desires, from the filth it has contracted. And at this stage he exercises himself diligently in the love of his neighbor; and when he has reached the point of loving his enemy, full of hopes and unbroken in strength, he mounts to the sixth step, in which he *purifies the eye itself which can see God.*"[24]

This unity of love of God with love of neighbor creates social order and stability within communities because our union with this greatest good involves a constant struggle to love the right things in the right way, a struggle that leaves us increasingly vulnerable and dependent on God's grace. Augustine's anthropology accentuates the experiences of vulnerability inherent in both human physical and moral nature. As such, it bridges the fourth-century gap between the givers and receivers of compassion, a gap that persists today. In other words, Augustine lifts up the common denominator of human experiences of vulnerability and suggests that intentional sharing of these vulnerabilities can create a sense of unity among otherwise disparate persons. "Brethren, I know not how it is, but when the hand of him who has is laid in the hand of him who has not, the soul of him who gives to the poor feels as it were the touch of common humanity and infirmity."[25]

In addition, Augustine insists that love is an experience of affective longing for goods of various grades of perfection and a rational capacity to orient our passions toward the highest good of all, God. If the will is rightly ordered toward active love of God, then, Augustine believes, our love for the neighbor will be rooted in the benevolence of a "giver" and as such embody a deep-seated desire to avoid harm and do good whenever possible. This links acts of compassion with Augustine's basic expectation of justice: to order all material possessions and personal capabilities toward union with God and giving each his or her due in the process.

In addition, rightly rooted love of neighbor also expresses what Augustine calls the "humility of a server" or the desire to resist self-righteousness. Humility prevents us from thinking more highly of ourselves than we should or from self-obsession that leads us to miss what is going on along the byways of our journey down to Jericho. Augustine identifies this basic form of self-deception as the common cause of human sin, or that which keeps us from seeking God as the greatest human good. It also obscures the way we perceive and understand ourselves and what we owe others. Equipped with the humility of a server, we avoid the risk of mistaking ourselves for God or erroneously believing that we are somehow more virtuous than those we seek to serve. Daniel Williams suggests that this vigilance requires a difficult "self-denial, restraint, humility, respect and trust" and reminds us that "we can only have the good by not *grasping* anything or anyone through domination, manipulation, or unlimited acquisition" but rather through ongoing commitment to better understand ourselves in rightly ordered relationships to God and others.[26]

Finally, Augustine suggests that this sympathy and humility then creates what he calls a "tribulation of our pilgrimage," namely, an uncomfortable awareness of our own sinfulness and need for repentance. For example, he reprimands those who hope to bypass the discomfort of compassion and notes that without it, people remain apathetic. "Fools, again, who avoid the exercise of compassion as a vice, because they are not sufficiently moved by a sense of duty without feeling also distressful emotion, are frozen into hard insensibility, which is very different from the calm of a rational serenity."[27] The distressful emotion connected to compassion reflects the humility that Augustine calls for, since it reminds us of our broken and sinful natures. "But, dearly beloved, among all tribulations of the human soul is no greater tribulation than the consciousness of sin. For if there be no wound herein, and that be sound within man which is called conscience, wherever else he may suffer tribulation, thither will he flee, and there find God."[28]

Augustinian tribulations of the heart reflect the type of desire for God's compassionate love that the Hebrew prophets sought to evoke from the people of Israel when they failed to uphold the covenantal requirement to care for the neighbor. These emotional disturbances prompt an examination of conscience that might raise awareness of our connections to the causes of others' suffering, if only through a failure to bother to be concerned about them.

Augustine's approaches to compassion reinforce often overlooked political aspects of loving our suffering neighbor in a global age. For example, he resists the dehumanizing paternalism that often accompanies our responses to those who suffer, an unequal power dynamic that creates a palpable distance between server and served. Instead, he suggests that a deep sense of mutuality rooted in shared vulnerabilities ought to motivate compassion, and that one of our objectives ought to be an increased awareness of our intractable relationality in the pursuit of the greatest good. Moreover, Augustine's insistence on humility demands a willingness to admit to our limits and inevitable shortcomings—whether in understanding a situation of injustice, in devising an appropriate response, or even in following through with our intention to love the neighbor. This capability to recognize our limits places moral agents on a more equal footing, not only with others with whom we serve in our increasingly pluralistic society, but more important, with the recipients of our compassion.

Bringing a sense of self-doubt or a lack of pretension to global discussions of human development breaks through the prevailing logic of privileged persons that doubts whether radical social change is necessary or even possible. It allows space for the moral imagination to conjure radically different alternatives to the way things are. Moreover, when we envision ourselves as servers, or those who wish to divest ourselves of the power that comes with our privilege, we might more accurately see ourselves as others do and therefore understand more clearly our connections to others' suffering. Finally, Augustinian tribulations of the heart and the moral awareness they evoke are invaluable in a global context in which we avoid the stress and anxiety of moral responsibility to others or can easily distance ourselves from our implications in their condition. For example, this heightened moral awareness might call our attention to the relationship between gentrification and lack of affordable housing, voluntary white segregation and black hyper-segregation, the desire for cheap goods and labor conditions, and homeland security measures and the struggles of undocumented workers.

The Cappadocian Bishops and Compassionate Philanthropy

Three Christian bishops of Cappadocia in the fourth century—Basil, Gregory of Nyssa, and Gregory Nanzianzus—challenged prevailing Greco-Roman sensibilities that accepted poverty as inherent to society, denied the poor any social standing, and institutionalized giving to the destitute as a civic duty that served the state. These cultural sensibilities negatively influenced Christian responses to famine that economically devastated the region toward the end of the fourth century. They also negatively shaped attitudes about leprosy and other diseases that devastated large groups within the population. In order to correct the apathy that prevailed among their relatively wealthy congregations, in their "poverty sermons" the bishops expanded on familiar Greco-Roman practices that encouraged their congregants "to notice the poor" and to respond to them with acts of compassion.[29]

In these sermons the bishops pointed out that starvation results from physical *and* social malnourishment. Both are unnatural and a result of the fear of the wealthy in a time of scarcity and disease. Basil says with firm conviction: "Our uncontrolled and culpable behavior is manifestly obvious: seizing on behalf of others we do not share. . . . We are nourished when hungry, yet we rush by the one in need. . . . We have become skinflints and asocial in relation to the poor. For this cause, the farmlands are dry: because love has fled."[30] In order to redress the problem of famine and disease, the bishops chose to redress these divisive fears.

For example, they use the foundational idea of *leitourgia*, or the Greek practice of civic worship of the gods through private acts of service, to suggest that we ought to care for the poor for their own sakes as a group with special standing in the eyes of Christ rather than simply in order to please the gods or to secure good civil standing. In fact, in these sermons they articulate some of the earliest ethical implications of the doctrine of the incarnation: a God who becomes human and most closely identifies with the poor, as evidenced by their frequent references to the parable of the last judgment in Matthew 25, gives the poor a special social status and places special moral weight on our responses to them. For example, Gregory of Nanzianzus entreats the members of his congregation to overcome their fears of leprosy and to rectify the social symptoms of the disease by finding Christ among the suffering: "While there is yet time, visit Christ in his sickness, let us give to Christ to eat, let us clothe Christ in his nakedness, let us do honor to Christ . . . but let us give him this honor in his needy ones."[31]

In addition, while the bishops endorsed the practices of gift exchange that were integral for maintaining social order in the economically stratified Roman society, they also encouraged a "fictive kinship" between donors and recipients that was rooted in an acknowledgment of shared humanity. "And will we disparage our own kin and race as baser than the animals?" Gregory of Nyssa asked his flock. "Let these things not be. . . . Resolve that this inhumanity will not triumph. . . . Remember who they are to whom we meditate: on human beings, in no way distinct from common nature."[32] This emphasis on shared humanity shifts the focus from the material goods distributed to those in need, to the relationship that such an exchange might create and the immaterial goods that might arise out of such relationships. The bishops see these immaterial goods of friendship as invaluable for rectifying the social disorder of famine and disease, especially since they identify broken relationships in the body of Christ as the cause of these problems in the first place. For example, in an exhortation against what we today call "planned giving," Basil criticizes those who wait until they die to assist those in need partly because such practices do not cultivate relationships among the living: "You wait until you are no longer men to become their friend? . . . Great thanks for your generosity!"[33]

Three themes regarding the political nature of compassion emerge from these sermons. First, compassion recognizes the dignity of those who suffer and acknowledges them as part of the fabric of society. The Cappadocian bishops recognize that the poor possess a particular agency, perhaps captured best in Gregory of Nanzianzus's insistence that the diseased spread a "reverse contagion" or a contagious desire to minister to the Christ we encounter in others. This contagion of mercy or compassion can overcome the unnatural separation and disparity among persons that fuels famine and disease. Just as Lazarus revealed to Dives his sinful shortcomings, in Gregory of Nyssa's estimation, the poor remind us "that if we wish to heal the wounds by which our sins have afflicted us, heal today the ulcers that break down the flesh."[34] The poor promised an important opportunity for conversion: "The poor are the stewards of our hope, doorkeepers of the kingdom, who open the door to the righteous and close it gain to the unloving and misanthropists," says Gregory of Nyssa. He goes on to note that "mercy and good deeds are works God loves; they divinize those who practice them and impress them into the likeness of goodness."[35] In short, the compassionate vision of the Cappadocian fathers, articulated most recently by the U.S. bishops in *Economic Justice for All,* "enables the Church to see things from the side of the poor and powerless and to assess lifestyles, policies, and social institutions in terms of their impact upon the poor" (n. 52).

In addition, by turning the gaze of their congregants toward the poor in their immediate communities, the Cappadocian bishops also encouraged their congregants to gaze critically on themselves. They raise the awareness that "the insatiable needy desires of the rich in turn worsen the needs of the poor."[36] Basil notes: "The bread you hold on to belongs to the hungry; the cloak you keep locked in your storeroom belongs to the naked. . . . You do an injury to as many people as you might have helped with all these things."[37] Wealth is not necessarily the root of the problem; rather, the challenge lies with ways in which attitudes about wealth shape our relationships with others. Basil says further: "When wells are in disuse they grow foul. And so do riches grow useless if left idle and unused in any place; but moved about and passing from one person to another they serve the common advantage and bear fruit." Compassion, therefore, helps us to see the connection between our over-nourishment and the malnourishment of others, or in contemporary contexts, it helps us to connect the dots between our over-development and the under-development of others. Compassion encourages a generosity of goods and of self that cultivates a commitment to simple living among those privileged enough to be voluntarily poor: "Are you poor?" Basil asks. "There is someone much poorer than you. . . . Do not shrink from giving of the little you have; do not treat your own calamity as if it is worse than the common suffering."[38]

Finally, compassionate care for the suffering poor is a requirement both of discipleship and citizenship, given that the bishops insist that the unnatural suffering of famine and disease arise from unnatural relationships among persons. These unnatural relationships contradict the vision of the "kin-dom" of God. Therefore, they encouraged the Christian community to rectify the natural ailments of the earth and the physical ailments of individuals by binding the fractures in their social relationships that caused scarcity of resources or fear of disease. Relational "fences" could be mended by generously giving of self and material goods, by bolstering the bonds of common humanity, and by ministering to the suffering Christ encountered in the midst of the community. These were counter-cultural practices in an economically stratified Greco-Roman culture. Holman notes, "For Basil, community life, love of kin, interdependence, and a complex network of social obligations were not artificial social constructs; rather civic identity itself and community interdependence were a natural good."[39]

Thomas Aquinas, Ignorance, and the Common Good

Dominican philosopher and theologian Thomas Aquinas underscores the political nature of compassion through its relationship to the common good, a concept that epitomizes his medieval synthesis of Aristotelian anthropology and the Christian doctrines of creation and incarnation. His definition rests on three claims that shape compassionate responses to suffering persons: God created human beings as social creatures, the goods of creation are to be used by all for the good of all, and the common good of all is the ideal end for all individual agents. Aquinas echoes Aristotle in his claim that seeking the good of civil society or the commonweal is more akin to happiness, or union with God, than procuring individual goods alone. In *Summa contra Gentiles* he notes that "a particular good is ordered to the common good as to an end; indeed, the being of a part depends on the being of the whole. So, also, the good of a nation is more godlike than the good of one man" and "the highest good which is God is the common good, since the good of all things taken together depends on Him."[40] He also notes that "the more perfect something is in its power, and the higher it is in the scale of goodness, the more does it have an appetite for a broader common good, and the more does it seek and become involved in the doing of good for beings far removed from itself."[41]

Recall our discussions of Thomistic compassion (or the *misericordia* that motivates the virtue of mercy) in the previous chapter. Aquinas designates mercy as among the highest of the virtues because "it likens us to God as regards to similarity of works" and because it complements the supreme virtue of charity, which unites us to God in "bonds of love." Mercy primarily entails the ability to perceive another's suffering and to assess whether or not they possess the resources to overcome their condition: "But of all the virtues which relate to our neighbor, mercy is the greatest, even as its act surpasses all others, since it belongs to one who is higher and better to supply the defect of another, in so far as the latter is deficient."[42] In other words, mercy compels non-suffering observers to draw from their own resources to assist the neighbor, especially if the neighbor is of no relation to them, by concern for the greatest good, which is the common good of all. Thomistic compassion is political because it integrates care for individuals who have little or no attachment to us with concern for the well-being of society, of which we are all a vital part.

David Hollenbach identifies a relational quality to Aristotelian and Thomistic notions of the common good. He notes that Aristotle understood "the *polis* as an assembly of citizens engaged in debate about how they should live together" who were bonded together by more than economic exchange or the "architecture of the forum" where they gathered, and that Aquinas claimed that "the common good included the bonds of affection and even love that linked people together in communities."[43] Hollenbach relies on these insights to suggest that we might best understand the common good as "not simply a means of attending the private good of individuals" but rather as "the good realized in the mutual relationships in and through which human beings achieve their well-being."[44]

Thomistic notions of *misericordia* can help us to respond to the many contemporary obstacles to thinking about the goods we hold in common, as well as ways we ought to go about securing them for all. Relational goods such as friendship, neighborliness, or concern ought to be among the surplus goods that compassionate persons use to care for those in need. In other words, compassion focuses on the kinds of goods necessary not just for survival but for flourishing in community. Compassion is an important moral tool for living well together because it reminds us of our social natures and of the inherent goodness, even godliness, of our capability to relate to one another in the context of community.

In addition, Aquinas's ideas about our lack of perception—or ignorance— also underscore the political significance of compassion. Perception is significant in Aquinas's approach to mercy; we need to perceive those who suffer, perceive their ability to secure goods for their own flourishing, and perceive how we might "succor" them with our own goods. Therefore, he makes a provocative connection between ignorance and sin that ultimately holds moral agents responsible for knowing what is going on in our social reality. He could not have fathomed the implications of these ideas for Christians in our contemporary age of instant global communication. Certainly, we can argue that it is impossible to perceive all instances of human suffering and as such plead for exoneration for our failure to respond to these unknown people in unknown situations. However, Aquinas points out that while ignorance is a cause of involuntariness of the will because it "deprives one of knowledge," not all ignorance is equally involuntary. Voluntary ignorance is a source of moral culpability. Ignorance of this kind happens, he says, "either directly, as when a man wishes of set purpose to be ignorant of certain things that he may sin more freely; or indirectly, as when a man, through stress of work or other occupations, neglects to acquire the information which would restrain him from sin."[45]

For example, moral agents who will themselves not to know something, or selectively choose not to inform themselves about a certain situation so that they might excuse themselves from responsibility on the grounds of ignorance, act with "affected" or direct voluntary ignorance. Moral agents who look away or avoid any interaction with homeless persons that might better inform them of those individuals' situation, for instance, are culpable of this kind of ignorance. "Consequent" or indirect voluntary ignorance is also inexcusable because it involves a failure to acknowledge, perceive, or understand something we can and ought to know. For instance, moral agents who refuse to inform themselves about the homelessness crisis in their community or who refuse to learn about the way in which their lifestyle affects the homeless are guilty of indirect voluntary ignorance. In both instances, Aquinas refuses to excuse such moral agents from their failure to bother to know or for the actions that arise from their limited perceptions.

Aquinas considers voluntary ignorance, through either a direct willingness not to know or an indirect failure to bother to know, a sin. And like virtues, sinful dispositions and action can be habituated. In other words, he indicates that it is not sufficient for moral agents to avoid doing wrong things. Rather, they should continually strive actively to know more and more—about universal conditions and particular realities—that not only affect them but, more important, that affect the people they fail to acknowledge. Failure to do so is not excusable; in fact, it is sinful.

Twentieth-century Theology

The Second Vatican Council (1963–68) buttressed the centrality of compassion in Christian discipleship. Consider the central mandate of the council's constitutional document *The Church and the Modern World*: "The joys and the hopes, the griefs and anxieties of the men of this age, especially those who are poor or in anyway afflicted, these too are the joys and hopes, the griefs and anxieties of the followers of Christ" (no. 1). This proclamation not only bolstered those in the church who were engaged on the front-lines of injustice around the world, but it also endorsed human experience—especially the joys and hopes, griefs, and anxieties of "those who are poor or in anyway afflicted"—as a new "site" of theological reflection. In fact, Gregory Baum posits that we can trace a resurgence of compassion in the Christian tradition to the council's endorsement of authentic openness to ecumenism and interreligious dialogue, as well as the much contested contributions of liberation theologies—which make social suffering a primary theological category—in the areas of Christology, eschatology, and soteriology.[46]

Feminist Theology and Socially Critical Compassion

Contemporary feminist scholars bring to the tradition nuanced understandings of human suffering, an emphasis on human interdependence, an appreciation for the demands of Christian discipleship, and alternative approaches to the incarnational imperatives of Christian ethics. These ideas assist in the evolution of the politically dangerous characteristics of compassion in the Christian tradition.

For example, Wendy Farley claims that compassion is nothing if not political, and she names institutional and structural sin, rather than the individual choices, as the cause of the radical suffering that dehumanizes so many people in our world: "Because so much suffering and destruction are the effects of political and social policies, compassion engages in political activity."[47] Therefore, she understands compassion as a "virtue of resistance" or "a power that gives people their own power" to challenge rather than to accept these institutional and systemic injustices, and to reclaim rather than to surrender their identities and destinies. She notes that compassion is both a "disposition to love in a world full of suffering," as well as "a mode of world-engagement." Compassion "resists the power to hurt, maim and dehumanize" by encouraging encounters with others, who through their pain, liberate us from our egocentrism and reveal to us a more accurate perception of the workings of the world.[48]

Farley contends that compassion channels the emotions that arise from these encounters, emotions that are necessary for an active and persistent political resistance. It "provides justice with a *hatred* of suffering and a *love* of creatures, without which justice can become demonic."[49] Therefore, compassion is ultimately a public and political expression of concern about the tragic, or humanly created, injustices of our world. Compassion respects no social or national boundaries. It requires solidarity with those who continue to be crucified by unjust socioeconomic and political structures and institutions. Compassionate persons engage in ongoing self-examination to determine if they are following Jesus' command to do likewise.

Feminist ethicist Margaret Farley claims that encounters with suffering others create opportunities to discover our ignorance of others' suffering and to respond with a "self-critical openness" to the other.[50] This vulnerable orientation reveals more clearly what suffering with others truly requires of non-suffering persons. Farley suggests that compassion values the particular stories of individuals, celebrates rather than suppresses difference, and appreciates the embeddedness of persons in cultures and relationships. In the context of her work with women surviving HIV/AIDS in Africa, she argues that compassion demands difficult reflection on religious attitudes, practices, and teachings that contribute to the spread of the disease.

Asian feminist Chung Hyun Kyung discovers that in order to resist *han*, or dehumanizing suffering, Korean women point not only to the common denominator of suffering that women share, but also, and more hopefully, to their common desire to end that suffering through attention to the material and immaterial conditions necessary for flourishing.[51]

M. Shawn Copeland suggests that in order to understand Christ better, we ought to examine closely his call to discipleship, particularly to a discipleship that is connected to the painful, intimidating, and political scandal of the cross. She suggests that to be a disciple is to live "at the disposal of the cross—exposed, vulnerable and open to the wisdom and power and love of God." This certainly challenges the attributes of Christian discipleship in contemporary

America, with its emphasis on personal security, invulnerability, suspicion of difference, and a therapeutic approach to faith rather than a demandingly counter-cultural relationship with a Jesus who is concerned with unjust suffering. To live in the world as Copeland's interpretation of discipleship suggests requires a "praxis of compassionate solidarity" that contains an important "critical self-examen" for those with the luxury merely to observe rather than to experience the deadening affects of social suffering. Copeland suggests that this self-critical awareness makes discipleship dangerous. "Discipleship costs," she says. As we saw clearly in the Lukan parable of the good Samaritan, "the praxis of compassionate solidarity that [Christ] inaugurated on behalf of the reign of God disrupted social customs, religious practices and conventions of authority and power."[52]

Lisa Sowle Cahill suggests that "christologies focused on the historical Jesus, so crucial for liberation and feminist theologies," facilitate "prayer to and worship of a merciful, forgiving, compassionate and generous God," thereby enabling action within disciples that "serves, includes, and empowers those who have suffered domination and violence."[53] In short, compassionate discipleship involves a love of neighbor that honestly assesses what might be required of the disciple to return the neighbor to a state of flourishing, even to the extent that it requires self-criticism and adjustment of that disciple's own state of flourishing.

Liberation Theology and Conversion of the Comfortable
The Latin American liberation theologians of the twentieth century suggested that the poor are prophetic catalysts for social change since their social situations, memories of the past, and dreams of the future have "irrupted" into the wider social consciousness. As such, the poor bring with them new moral awareness and responsibilities. For example, this irruption forces the comfortable of the world to acknowledge that "poverty means death" for a majority of our fellow citizens on the planet, and as such poverty is best understood as a form of "institutionalized violence" that unjustly crucifies people at alarming rates.[54] Since this institutionalized violence is humanly created and sustained, liberationists demand that we name it social sin and that we actively seek repentance through commitments to untangle webs of dehumanization and oppression. The unjust suffering of the poor uncomfortably forces the privileged to confront the causal relationship between our privilege and others' unjust death. The irruption of the poor into our social consciousness serves as the antidote to the numbing effects of structural violence through the human capacity for relationality and desire for a God we encounter in relationships with others. Gustavo Gutiérrez speaks of the sacramentality of the neighbor when he notes that "it is in the temple that we find God, but in a temple of living stones, of closely related persons, who together make history and fashion themselves. . . . We find the Lord in our encounters with others, especially the poor, marginated and exploited ones."[55]

In addition to this moral framework that perceives, interprets, and resists social sin, liberation theologians advance the tradition of compassion by connecting it to transformative experiences of conversion and political practices of social resistance. Jesuit systematic theologian Jon Sobrino autobiographically captures the transformative aspects of compassionate conversion to the reality of the poor. He contends that mercy, or the "basic structure of the response to this world's victims," invites a personal and social conversion to an unfamiliar and uncomfortable reality. Sobrino prefers mercy because it allows the reality of suffering and those who suffer to make a claim on us. He speaks of a personal realization he made after years in El Salvador where he "witnessed appalling poverty, but even though I saw it with my eyes, I did not really see it; thus that poverty had nothing to say to me for my own life."[56]

He discusses the tribulations of "awakening" from a dogmatic slumber and the "sleep of inhumanity" with the realization that justice does not involve Westernizing the oppressed peoples of El Salvador. Rather, it entails the risk of allowing ourselves to be Salvadorized through experiences with them.[57] For instance, often it is much easier, much safer, and much more comfortable to convert others to our ways of thinking, of praying, of being the people of God than it is to permit others to make claims upon us, our theology, our prayer, our church. However, once liberated, Sobrino saw the world from the perspective of the crucified, and he realized new truths about what it means to be human, what it means to love your neighbor, what it means to be church. In the process he also became suspicious of Western notions of anthropology, ecclesiology, and flourishing. He notes that joyful realization attuned him to the affective goodness and effective practicality of the good news. Mercy infuses the moral imagination with possibilities for social justice that only those converted to the reality of the poor can fathom.

In addition, liberation theology also highlights the dangerous nature of compassion when it is embodied in collective commitments to remove the crucified peoples from their crosses. Sobrino recognizes that the crosses of the "have nots" are created by the "haves" through deeply embedded social, economic, political, and military structures that benefit an elite minority but that directly and indirectly involve the participation of the vast majority. Therefore, to tackle institutional violence is to challenge and dethrone entrenched power structures. This is a life-threatening mission. He notes that "when mercy is taken seriously as the first and the last, it becomes conflictive. No one is thrown in prison or persecuted simply for having practiced works of mercy. Not even Jesus would have been persecuted and put to death had his mercy been mere mercy."[58] Just as the Samaritan put himself in danger to assist the victim in the ditch, and in so doing challenged cultural norms and social structures, Sobrino suggests that individual Christians and Christian churches ought to do the same.

When rooted in the framework of liberation theology, compassion becomes a disposition and set of practices that transform compassionate persons through conversion experiences. Suffering with others changes our values, our vocational desires, our ways of making sense of our social reality. In addition, compassion demands a set of risky practices that challenge power structures that perpetuate self-centered egoism or the oppression of others. Since it responds to the institutional violence of social sin, compassion is necessarily a collective and political experience.

COMPASSION AND SOCIAL TRANSFORMATION

The tradition of modern Catholic social thought begins with Leo XIII's 1891 social encyclical that responded to plight of the workers in industrialized Europe and continues with similar statements by popes, bishops, synods, and conferences, and the documents of Vatican Council II. It serves as a template for connecting compassion more closely with Catholic approaches to the just ordering of society and to strategies for authentic human development. Although the ability to suffer with others is not named directly in the documents that make up the body of the tradition, compassion is nevertheless a disposition that motivates and directs individual Christians and the institutional church in responding to the signs of the times in various historical and cultural contexts.

We can draw connections between compassion and three central principles in Catholic social teaching that focus on authentic human development: the common good, solidarity, and subsidiarity. Compassion both complements and challenges these principles, particularly when we consider them in light of the reality of globalization. By complementing these principles, compassion plays an essential role in global human-development strategies that focus on flourishing because it helps us to perceive and to engage in situations of dehumanizing suffering; by challenging them it also guides our first-world imaginations in resisting the causes of those injustices.

Compassion and the Common Good

Concern for the acute sufferings of the working poor interrupted the church's inward-gazing and defensive posture in the eighteenth and nineteenth centuries. According to *Rerum Novarum,* the "misery and wretchedness pressing so unjustly on the majority of the working classes" evoked an outward-facing engagement in the world and awareness of the church's responsibility as an agent in civil society" (no. 3). However, in the first half of the twentieth century, that concern was paternalistic in nature and tended to value social order and stability more than radical social change. *Rerum Novarum* and *Quadragesimo Anno,* two of the earliest social encyclicals, emphasize that a contractual or commutative justice guides the relationship between employers and workers, and that a very rudimentary distributive justice directs the accumulation of private property. "Capital cannot do without labor, nor labor without capital," Leo XIII states in *Rerum Novarum.* Therefore, each needs to be "reminded of its duties to the other, and especially of the obligations of justice" (no. 19).

The rapid and increasingly global processes of socialization in the post–World War II period, however, raised new questions about the end goals of human progress, the means of human development, and the impact of unfettered progress for progress's sake on human beings. The gap between rich and poor within states and among the nations of the world demanded a new vision for social order and more just alternatives for stability. As *Mater et Magistra* states, "The nations of the world are becoming more and more dependent on one another and it will not be possible to preserve a lasting peace so long as glaring economic and social imbalances persist." John XXIII continues, "We are all equally responsible for the undernourished peoples" (nos. 157, 158).

In order to educate "those who are most blessed with this world's goods" about this responsibility, Pope John XXIII returned to Aquinas's concept of the common good in order to bring a communal or social corrective to human flourishing and development strategies that were increasingly steeped in the then-emerging values of individualism, consumerism, materialism, and free-market capitalism. For example, in *Mater et Magistra* he defines the common good as "the sum total of those conditions of social living, whereby men are enabled more fully and more readily to achieve their own perfection" (no. 65). In speaking of the "sum conditions of social living," John XXIII directly points to the often immaterial and spiritual aspects of life in community that are still overlooked aspects of human flourishing, such as work that nourishes creativity, strong family ties, and the capability to maintain a relationship with the transcendent. Moreover, he suggests that the common good of all depends on a willingness to empower people to participate in and contribute to various aspects of social life.

John Paul II underscores this motif with the sense that authentic human development depends on a vibrant common good that refuses to allow the good of an individual to be separated from the health of community. He suggests that life in a vibrant community is a good in and of itself and not merely a means to individual flourishing, writing in *Centesimus Annus* that "development must not be understood solely in economic terms, but in a way that is fully human" (no. 2). "It is therefore necessary to create life-styles in which the quest for truth, beauty, goodness and communion with others for the sake of common growth are the factors which determine consumer choices, savings and investments" (no. 36).

Compassion bolsters the communal effort to create a vibrant common good that recognizes life in community as an inherent human good in and of itself. This is an effort that is increasingly needed, given the toll that globalization exacts from all persons, whether the oppressive conditions of extreme poverty or the more subtle and yet demoralizing conditions of over-development. Both of these circumstances leave us starving for authentic relationships in which we can become more fully human. Compassion, therefore, perfects our ability to perceive those who are excluded from the common good in our contemporary reality with its exclusive lifestyle enclaves, economic nationalism, and fear of vulnerability. For example, the Samaritan rejected the social blinders of religion, ethnicity, and class, and instead accepted the responsibility presented by the humanity he shared with the person in need along the side of the Jericho road.

Compassion also enables us to see the importance of life in community for those of us who voluntarily segregate ourselves from that community—whether through our culturally constructed preferences for independent isolation, our rejection of vulnerability and insecurity, or our fear of those who are in some way or another different from us. For example, armed with the self-critical humility that

Augustine or contemporary feminist ethicists recommend, compassion also helps us to see gaps or holes in our first-world notions of the common good—whether our consumerist preoccupation with the material goods, our obsession with productivity that rejects recreation and undermines the dignity of work, or our preference for autonomous individualism that undercuts the value of life in community. Compassion reminds us that relationality is the greatest of the social goods. It cultivates the first-world person's severely incapacitated capability to sustain relationships at a time when isolated individualism and fear of others is most valued.

Compassion and Solidarity

The principle of solidarity underscores both the inherent social nature of persons as well as the complex social relationships in which we voluntarily and involuntarily participate in our contemporary socioeconomic context. In *Sollicitudo Rei Socialis,* for instance, John Paul II argues that solidarity highlights the causal relationship between super-development and under-development. Solidarity also points to the gap in the "pace of progress" between developed and under-developed nations. Therefore, it generates uncomfortable insights for those of us in the First World who assume that human-development strategies ought to promote our narrow conceptions of human flourishing. Solidarity challenges first-world levels of consumption, expressions of preference, and understanding of freedom as immunities from our responsibilities to others. It highlights that all persons struggle to flourish under the yoke of privilege. The pope notes that "there are some people—the few who possess much—who do not really succeed in 'being' because, through a reversal of the hierarchy of values, they are hindered by the cult of 'having'; and there are others—the many who have little or nothing—who do not succeed in realizing their basic human vocation because they are deprived of essential goods" (no. 28).

John Paul II calls this dichotomy sinful and points to solidarity as the means of resisting this sin. Solidarity fosters a "more human" approach to development for all persons by reasserting that the capacity for "being" in relationship—whether family and friendship, civic or professional—as the key to achieving our true end and experiencing deep contentment.

Unlike other principles of the social doctrine of the church, John Paul II suggests that solidarity is best understood as a "social virtue" necessary for "authentic human development." In other words, it is more closely related to the intuitive, inductive, affective, and imaginative ways of seeing and acting in the world rather than the strictly intellectual, deductive, rational, and logical ways of doing so. It is not "a vague compassion or shallow distress at the misfortunes of so many people" but rather a "persevering commitment to acknowledge that we are *all* really responsible for *all*" (no. 38). In his estimation solidarity does not necessarily entail looking at the world or social policy from a different perspective, nor does it involve affiliation among like-minded persons around particular issues or social concerns. Rather, solidarity is a disposition that responds with habituated *action* to situations of injustice in our global community. It is an active expression of responsibility that acknowledges that socioeconomic disparities are not naturally given or inherent aspects of social life. Nor are they the unavoidable costs of living in our global economy. Rather, as byproducts of the "cult of having," these disparities and dehumanizing conditions are things to be resisted with the immaterial goods of the "cult of being." Primary among these goods are human relationships that, like the compassionate care of the good Samaritan, transcend the barriers that separate persons, recognize the commonality among all persons, and restore wayward members of the human family to their respective journeys down to Jericho.

The pope is correct to reject the efficacy of a "vague" compassion or "shallow distress" at another's misfortunes. These are simply expressions of the "cult of having." However, as we have seen in various examples in this chapter, when inspired with the humility to serve others or when connected to the relational goods of life in community or when vigilant in its perception of social suffering, compassion can give solidarity a much needed critical edge. It does so by making apparent the direct causal relationship between over-development for some and under-development for others. It highlights that preferences for unfettered freedom for some sanction the totalitarianism of poverty for others. It makes us aware that our desire for cheap goods thwarts others in their desire for a living wage. It shows the relationship between voluntary segregation for some and involuntary segregation for others, between immunity to genetic disorders for some and susceptibility to treatable diseases for others, between unlimited energy resources for some and environmental degradation for others.

In addition, compassion works in concert with solidarity to resist our tendency to dilute the transformative potential of the "cult of being" when we limit our sense of solidaristic responsibility to those with whom we share some sort of similarity—whether gender, class, ethnicity, neighborhood, or even experiences of suffering. It highlights the vulnerabilities that all persons share, despite the different ways these vulnerabilities might manifest themselves. A persevering commitment to the good of all might move Americans who have lost loved ones in the war in Iraq to extend the solidarity among them to Iraqi families who are mourning similar losses. Moreover, as we will see in the coming chapters, a compassion that privileges the perspectives of suffering persons can dissect the complex dynamics of white or unearned privilege that make it difficult for first-world Christians to identify the causal relationship between our own over- or super-development and the under-development of others.

Compassion and Subsidiarity

The type of compassion we need in order to suffer authentically with others in our global age reflects many features of the principle of subsidiarity, which provides a method for social change. Pope Pius XI first articulated this, one of the oldest principles of Catholic social thought, in 1931 in his social encyclical *Quadragesimo Anno*. He notes: "Just as it is gravely wrong to take from individuals what they can accomplish by their own initiative and industry and give it to the community, so also it is an injustice and at the same time a grave evil and disturbance of right order to assign to a greater and higher association what lesser and subordinate organizations can do" (no. 79).

Subsidiarity aims to protect the dignity of poor and vulnerable persons from paternalistic treatment at either the hands of the state or good-intentioned social institutions. It insists that those closest to situations of injustice are in the optimal position to evaluate ethically the situation and devise appropriate action to rectify it. People should be given the support they need to respond to the problems facing them in the way they see fit. In other words, in order to respond to those who wrestle with injustice, we should first empower them to make demands on those of us who already have access to power and resources and also allow them the chance to participate in the strategies for change that they themselves outline. In Pius's words: "The State authorities should leave to other bodies the care and expediting of business and activities of lesser moment, which otherwise become for it a source of great distraction" (no. 80). However, these persons should not be abandoned. To the extent such empowerment is not possible, governments and members of civil society have a responsibility to step in and assist.

Compassion thickens the principle of subsidiarity in several ways. As we have seen repeatedly in Aristotle and Aquinas, compassion enables us to perceive more accurately the complexities of particular circumstances of suffering persons or communities. This fosters a bottom-up approach to social change that challenges one-size-fits-all policy solutions and can only be accomplished if we empower the suffering to take charge. In addition, we have seen time and time again in the Christian tradition that compassion prizes relationships among people, and not merely material goods, as the optimal facets of any response to injustice. To that end, it complements subsidiarity, whose central goal is to encourage those faced with obstacles to their flourishing to work together—in a variety of relationships—to address those obstacles. Furthermore, compassion assists subsidiarity in empowering marginalized people by protecting their participation in the common good.

Consider these points in light of alternative responses to Hurricane Katrina, something we will do more extensively in Chapter 6. Coupled with compassion, subsidiarity challenges prevailing notions of disaster response and recovery that often bypass the local community and emphasize instead state and federal initiatives. Imagine, instead, empowering citizens of the now infamous Lower 9th Ward to evaluate, direct, and execute the reconstruction of their neighborhoods. This type of compassion might ensure that these communities actually benefit from the reconstruction efforts, whether in terms of new jobs, renewed bonds in civic associations, or increased participation in local government. In other words, the wisdom and labor of entire communities, long denied access to community planning and meaningful work, could potentially shape the future of New Orleans. Thickened by a desire to love our suffering neighbor, subsidiarity might also encourage those who seek to respond to natural disasters to support neighborhood associations such as the East Biloxi Coordination, Relief, and Redevelopment Association, which aims to bring neighbors back to the community in order to organize and influence government decisions about reconstruction of their neighborhoods. This would be a powerful example of compassionate revitalization that finds a middle ground between liberal demands for structural change at the governmental level and conservative demands for individual responsibility.

Takeaways from the Theological Tradition

Compassion potentially corrects three liabilities of the rich tradition of Catholic social teaching in our increasingly global context. For example, feminist ethicists contend that social teaching is less than attentive to gender-based justice issues such as women's experiences of poverty, war, and even HIV/AIDS. Feminists also contend that, given its natural-law reasoning, the social doctrine of the church employs a top-down approach to social justice that compromises the particularities of the human condition, such as gender, age, physical and mental capabilities, and social and geographic location for the sake of universal claims that serve as a common denominator for all persons, such as the capacity for reason, our social natures, and our obligations to respect all persons.[59] Compassionate perception that is aware of Aquinas's challenge of direct and indirect voluntary ignorance attends to these often overlooked particularities, and its emphasis on relational goods fosters an organic response to social injustices.

Moreover, Catholic social teaching provides principles or directive norms for action but lacks specific methods or concrete practices that attend to the particular realities of suffering communities. For example, principles regarding human rights will necessarily be understood and applied differently in varying social contexts. Some of these applications will be more efficacious than others, but Catholic social teaching does not always assist in making those normative evaluations.[60] Given the emphasis on actively responding to others espoused by leaders of the Christian community in the patristic period and by the liberation theologians in the twentieth century, compassion offers a way to move from scrutinizing the signs of the times toward actually engaging them alongside those who suffer.

Finally, the principles of Catholic social teaching can easily become little more than abstract concepts that we tend to know cognitively or intellectually rather than deep desires or practices we come to know intuitively and experientially. In other words, Catholic social teaching appeals to the mind but does not necessarily stir the heart. A combination of both mind and heart is necessary in order to calculate accurately what might be required to create a more just world and to motivate us to take the risks this kind of justice will require of us. As we will see in the next chapter, compassion is an emotive approach to reasoning that engages both the intellectual and rational as well as the intuitive and affective components of the moral agent. When we are emotionally stirred by another's suffering, we are often moved and empowered to act boldly, creatively, and relationally to respond to that person's plight in ways that mere logical or rational reflection on their condition cannot.

WHICH OF THESE WAS A NEIGHBOR
TO THE PERSON SUFFERING FROM INJUSTICE?

The parable of the good Samaritan offers two questions for Christian disciples to consider. The first, raised by the lawyer—"And who is my neighbor?"—challenges us to consider the *who* of our compassion, or which persons ought to be the recipients of the special love that we offer to those who suffer. This tends to be the focal point of the parable's moral lesson, and its prophetic truth still rings true in our multicultural and economically stratified contemporary context where we can easily miss or ignore those who have been robbed of full humanity. However, we also should not overlook Jesus' question to the lawyer at the conclusion of the story: "Which of these three, do you think, was the neighbor to the man who fell into the hands of robbers?" While the answer appears obvious—the Samaritan, of course—this question probes the less obvious *how* of our compassion, or the ways that we actually go about suffering with others.

This is the question that first-world Christians, with our seemingly endless examples of Good Samaritanism, must ask ourselves. Fortunately, the Christian tradition offers some examples of how we can be neighbors to others in need, particularly in this age of globalization.

For example, from the healing ministry of Christ to the social encyclicals of John Paul II, we can identify an emphasis on *relationality* as the hallmark of compassion. Compassion involves an attuned perception of experiences of social isolation or the inability to maintain healthy relationships with self, God, and others. Compassionate persons attend to the kind of suffering that arises when relationships are unnaturally or unjustly broken or damaged. Yahweh hears the cries of the Israelites struggling under the oppression of slavery and compassionately acts to restore their sense of dignity and community. Feminist ethicists in the twentieth century lift up the subtle ways in which women's experiences of suffering have long been overlooked. Further, authentic compassion seeks to restore persons to the community or to bolster their capacity for relationships with others, whether through the "fictive kinship" recommended by the Cappadocian bishops or the compassionate subsidiarity espoused by Catholic social teaching.

In addition, the Christian tradition suggests that compassion involves a *self-critical awareness* on the part of compassionate persons of our connections to others' suffering. With Augustine's humility of a servant, we are called to examine the various aspects of what John Paul II called our "cult of having" that perpetuates the injustices that shape the existence of so many others. The Cappadocian bishops said as much in the fourth century when they noted that the hunger of famine was exacerbated by a human hoarding of goods and an indifference to the cries of the poor. As such, they demanded a response that takes responsibility for this aspect of others' hunger.

Moreover, compassion is *dangerous* because it often challenges the status quo and the socially entrenched values that support it. It expands the parameters of who is worthy of restoration to the community, as was the case in Christ's healing encounters with social outcasts or Aquinas's refusal to excuse moral agents for failing to take responsibility for informing ourselves about the complexities of the social reality. In addition, compassionate suffering with others demands that we interrogate our erroneous assumptions about the conditions that support human flourishing, often dictated by a "cult of having," in order to make a stronger claim for the immaterial or relational goods that enable individuals to become more fully human in vibrant communities.

In the following chapters, we will construct an approach to compassion that incorporates the expressions of compassion discussed here while simultaneously offering a refined definition and proposal for application. Relying upon the philosophical ideas of Martha Nussbaum's and Johann Baptist Metz's political theology, we will begin to see more clearly that rather than being a privatized response to suffering, compassion is a political response that has the following characteristics:

- Compassion requires an honest assessment of what might be required to restore a suffering person or groups of people to a state of flourishing.
- Compassionate assessment includes a self and institutional awareness of direct or indirect collusion in the causes of suffering.
- Compassion involves an interruptive self-awareness made possible by means of a disruptive conversion to the reality of those who suffer.
- Compassion entails an active commitment to human flourishing rooted in empowerment and resistance to the causes of suffering that brings about a substantial change for the subject and object of compassion.

4

Compassion as "Upheaval" in the Political Philosophy of Martha C. Nussbaum

There's an alarming trend in our world today, our world so dominated by technology and science. This trend says that technology is in and stories are out. All we need to think well are technical models, that stories about human beings and their strivings don't contribute anything. We don't need novelists, or poets, we just need bureaucrats, engineers and formal economists. . . . People who can produce [technical models] are in favor in places where big decisions are made, whether in the corporate world, or in Washington, or even, in the world of global development projects in which I myself have spent so much of my time. Go to the World Bank with a mathematical model, and you will be welcomed. Go in with a story, and you are likely to be turned away.[1]

Martha C. Nussbaum is a prolific scholar of philosophy, literature, law, and feminist studies. Stoic philosophy and poetry, constitutional and international law, childhood development, and South Asian studies are just a sampling of her intellectual interests.[2] The remarks above, shared with graduates of an inner-city Chicago community college, reflect her unique world view and approach to social injustice. As a political philosopher Nussbaum attempts to make human flourishing, a topic that she considers to be the "substantive question of philosophy," the focus of public debate, particularly for those who formulate human-development policy.[3] "Economists are good at many things," she notes, "but arguing for a particular conception of the ultimate ends of human social life does not seem to me to be among them. And yet, they put forward ideas on this issue all the time, particularly in international development, and these ideas are enormously influential."[4]

Nussbaum recognizes the human implications of this disconnect in ways that implicitly echo the demands for a new approach to compassion outlined in the first chapter. For example, in order to resist an uncritical marriage between utilitarian or metaphysical philosophy and economic theory, she remains acutely aware that the majority of the world's population struggles with hand-to-mouth survival. Moreover, she recognizes *unjust suffering* so evident in a variety of situations of need, impairment, and what she calls "capability failure"—whether among poor women in India and China, young adults in inner-city Chicago, or even in the situation of her mentally disabled nephew, Arthur. She attributes her attuned perception of suffering to her love of the ancient Greek poets who argued that "tragedies show us plainly that even the wisest and best human beings encounter disaster . . . but they also show us, just as plainly, that many disasters are the result of human behavior."[5]

Nussbaum interprets the musings of the ancient Greeks as well as the narratives of women in economic collectives in India in order to find the answer to one of the most central questions in philosophy and ethics: What are the characteristics or qualities of our existence that make us recognize that existence as truly human? Or, said differently, What are the basics that make our lives truly livable? The wisdom inherent in these narratives cultivates a sense of shared vulnerability that arises when we seriously consider unjust suffering. In other words, rather than determine what it means to be human in ahistorical and abstract terms, she argues that her account of human nature "is the outcome of a process of self-interpretation and self-clarification that makes use of the story-telling imagination far more than the scientific intellect."[6]

In addition, Nussbaum seeks *encounters with others in contexts of radical inequality,* not only in her interdisciplinary work in the academy but also in the personal relationships that she has initiated with people around the world through her economic-development work with the United Nations. These encounters profoundly shape her questions, methodology, and conclusions. For example, personal relationships with poor women in India and her reliance on their narratives of suffering contributed to her intellectual divergence from Amartya Sen, another human-development philosopher with whom she once collaborated. These women's narratives call into question who sets the parameters in theories of justice or social contracts and who benefits from prevailing approaches to human development. In addition, her relationships with those who do not fall into the "normal" categories of personhood—whether as a result of extreme economic under-development or physical or intellectual impediments—have endowed her with a hermeneutic of suspicion that challenges notions of personhood narrowly defined by rationality or autonomy. She claims that encounters with different others can and should lead to self-examination and acknowledgment of shared humanity rooted in vulnerability.[7]

Nussbaum also acknowledges the need for universal or global ethics in order to *evaluate critically nations and cultures in this age of globalization.* She argues that because cultures and traditions are often socially constructed, we need to intervene on behalf of marginalized people, particularly women who suffer differently from men in culturally fueled conditions of poverty and oppression. Women's experiences of natural disasters, for example, are often colored by the additional pressures of physical and economic vulnerability, pregnancy, or care for dependents. Women's abilities to live fully human lives ought to set the "threshold" for flourishing in every culture. However, in making universal claims regarding flourishing, Nussbaum condemns "benevolent colonizing" on the part of intellectuals in the West that often unintentionally manages the needs of suffering others in paternalistic ways.[8] Rather, she proposes that those whose flourishing is threatened ought to have authority in identifying and securing life-sustaining activities, as well as in how they will express those activities in the context of their individual lives. Empowering them in this way shifts our response from the benevolent management of suffering to a more just dismantling of the causes of suffering. She suggests that we can resist benevolent colonizing through a "cosmopolitan citizenship" that features a life-sustaining allegiance within the worldwide community that is rooted in an understanding of all people as "rational and mutually dependent rather than as members of some particular nation."[9] Cosmopolitan citizens are able to recognize the increasing interdependence among persons and our responsibility to and for those outside national boundaries.

With these sensitivities in mind it is no wonder that compassion is an essential component of Nussbaum's philosophical and political ethics. She vehemently asserts that compassion is a basic social emotion that serves as a bridge to justice because it begins with self-interest and moves to altruism by means of an awareness of another's need and the connection of that other to our own flourishing. She defines compassion as a "painful emotion occasioned by an awareness of another person's undeserved misfortune," which differs from "egoistic reciprocity" and is often "linked with benevolent action."[10] More important for the continuing evolution of compassion in our contemporary global age, Nussbaum's recent writing on compassion reflects her awareness of her social location in the world's remaining superpower. Compassionate persons, in her estimation, ought to experience an *upheaval* in our self-understandings, our beliefs and values, and our world views in the process of our compassionate responses to others. These upheavals occur through an increased awareness of our direct or indirect involvement in or responsibility for others' dehumanizing affliction. Upheavals also arise through innovative strategies that bolster all person's capabilities for flourishing. Her ideas about the emotions, judgments, and practices associated with compassion, therefore, offer three insightful contributions to the Christian tradition of compassion: *perceiving suffering* with the help of Aristotelian sensibilities, *interpreting the causes of suffering* with the help of emotive reasoning, and *transforming suffering* through the capabilities approach to justice.

PERCEIVING REALITY: ARISTOTELIAN LIBERALISM FROM ANCIENT GREECE TO THE UNITED NATIONS

As a true ethicist, Nussbaum insists that the wisdom to ask the right questions is more important than the ability to formulate the correct answers to existing questions. "In short," she notes, "we need to ask *what* politics should be pursuing for each and every citizen, before we can think well about economic change. We need to ask *what* constraints there ought to be on economic growth, *what* the economy is supposed to be doing for people, and *what* all citizens are entitled to by virtue of being human."[11] Three elements of Nussbaum's Aristotelian philosophy enable her to ask the right ethical questions. They also assist us in asking how we might more effectively respond to those who unjustly suffer.

Tragedy and Tragic Questions

Nussbaum claims that the Greek philosophers and poets can help us to detect the hidden or disregarded contours of our contemporary social reality. Their perceptions shake us out of our "contemporary complacencies, whatever they are, and force us to approach problems from a different, unfamiliar angle."[12] The Greek poets, in particular, relied on the medium of tragedy to expand and sharpen perception. Plays such as Aeschylus' *Oresteia* or Sophocles' *Antigone* encouraged ancient audiences to surmount the socially constructed and biologically determined boundaries that separated people. Exposure to radically different others in the context of tragedy enables spectators to perceive a relationality among the members of humanity that the boundaries of gender, race, and economic class otherwise prevent. In addition, tragedy invites us to consider various aspects of the human condition from relatively unknown or marginalized perspectives. In so doing we move beyond the observable "facts" or preconceived notions of the situation of others and more precisely perceive the often-hidden implications of those facts in the context of their life.

Tragedy, therefore, does not primarily establish similarity among persons, although that is certainly the case when "tragic spectators" realize that we, like those we watch, are not immune to tragedy. Rather, tragedy's central role "is to challenge conventional wisdom and values" and "to disturb us."[13] Tragedy creates a more sympathetic understanding of the implications of difference among persons. Most notable among these differences are the varying levels of vulnerability within human experience. For example, tragedy instills a sense that unfortunate circumstances and vulnerability are disproportionately experienced, particularly by those who are often on the fringes of our circles of compassionate concern.

Nussbaum incorporates tragedy and tragic spectatorship in her development ethics. For instance, she notes that obvious answers to the question of what we should do—usually determined through utilitarian strategies or prima facie obligations—do not enable us to recognize the complexity of experiences of suffering. This complexity stems from human vulnerability, conflicts in human values, or competing interpretations of the same event. We would be better to follow the pensive Greeks and ask more tragic questions: Why do certain people suffer in this way? What can be done to prevent it? Tragic questions unleash our imaginative ability to perceive what is going on in our social reality and to create upheavals in our presumed innocence in the causes of unjust suffering in our world.

Tragic questions also create upheavals in contemporary approaches to justice, given an Aristotelian awareness of the gap between the good or virtuous person and that person's actual ability to flourish.[14] Tragic questions reveal that circumstances beyond their control, namely, birth location and gender, render many good persons' existence survival rather than actual flourishing. Tragedy and vulnerability ought to continue to disrupt contemporary thinking about the basic ingredients of a fully human life as well as provoke a compassionate response to those who struggle to survive. An awareness of the tragic aspects of the human condition brings the following to compassion:

- A willingness to ask difficult questions in order to better understand the situation at hand from a variety of perspectives;
- A series of upheavals in our frameworks of meaning that stem from an acknowledgment of human vulnerability and lack of control over many of the circumstances of our existence; and
- An awareness that the causes of suffering often lie outside of the control of those most affected by it and squarely in the hands of others.

An Anthropology of Flourishing

As a self-proclaimed neo-Aristotelian liberal, Nussbaum claims that all people are of equal worth and dignity regardless of their geographic, social, or cultural location or their physical, mental, or spiritual abilities. While rationality is certainly a source of that dignity, Nussbaum highlights what she sees as the three interrelated components of our relationality that expand our understanding of it as more than an isolated, intellectual, and metaphysical entity. She says that reason is shaped by (1) our capability for a rich array of life-sustaining activities that demand ongoing support, (2) our social nature, which requires meaningful connections with self and others, and (3) bodily needs that rely on care of self and others. With these ideas in mind, Nussbaum suggests that commitment to human dignity must "draw attention to areas of vulnerability" and not merely emphasize our capacity for autonomous individuality. It must cultivate a connection between "rationality and sociability" that understands reason as a function of our relationality. And human dignity demands symmetrical and asymmetrical relations, or associations with those most like us and most different from us, in order to sustain "truly human functioning."[15]

In addition, the primary source of our dignity is our power of moral choice or the ability to love according to our own evaluation of our own ends.[16] Nussbaum delineates a variety of capabilities—and not goods—that enable people to articulate and achieve their own ends. She prefers the "activity approach" to *eudaimonia*, or happiness. In other words, she views happiness or the good life as more than the pursuit and enjoyment of material goods or fortune, and more than the pursuit of stable, self-sufficient states of passive being. Rather, *eudaimonia* entails acting in a good way or pursuing excellence in a wide variety of activities that we recognize as central to a truly good human existence or functioning.[17] The driving ethical question, therefore, becomes not what a person has or whether a person is free to chose, but rather, what a person is actually able to do and to be.[18] Nussbaum uses Aristotle's emphasis on activity to define the livable life according to capacities for certain actions that we can recognize as constituting a good human life. These include capacities for practical reason, for affiliation, for health, and for play.

Nussbaum's Aristotelian anthropology provides two important insights for the role of compassion in more accurately perceiving both the complexity of our social reality and those in it. First, she sharpens compassionate perception by emphasizing vulnerability and fragility. However, she does not accentuate these features at the expense of autonomy and capability. As a feminist, she contends that human persons are capable by emphasizing activity-based flourishing. We have the distinct ability to choose and actively to pursue our own ends. However, all human capability is contingent on external conditions and relational goods. Compassionate persons cannot underestimate the significance of this provision. For example, each human being's good "must always be pursued as a system of complex relations of dependence between the agents and unstable items in the world such as friends, loved ones, food, water, a city of fellow citizens."[19] Therefore, we are vulnerable, fragile, or susceptible to tragic circumstances that lie beyond our control.

When we more accurately perceive this vulnerability, we more accurately address the impediments to flourishing faced by so many. This may be particularly true when we realize that while all persons are fragile, many suffer from excessive vulnerability caused by humanly created and sustained social structures. In other words, Nussbaum's insistence on the connection between goods and activity helps to establish a telling causal relationship between "being well-fed and being free, between bodily integrity and moral functioning."[20] Effectively "suffering with" these persons will entail a restoration of both life-sustaining goods and activities.

In addition, coupling vulnerability with capability reminds would-be compassionate persons that the goal of suffering with others ought to be empowerment. People are empowered through two specific capabilities—practical reason and affiliation. In many ways Nussbaum expresses a Kantian emphasis upon the importance of practical reason, or the ability to determine the direction of our own life. This capability is essential in order to protect us against domination at the hands of others. Practical reason, "being able to form a conception of the good and to engage in critical reflection about the planning of one's life," ensures that human persons are autonomous; in other words, that they are not treated as a means to another's end or as a "herd animal."[21] Practical reason also guarantees that we can make distinctions concerning certain human activities, such as the difference between starvation and the choice to fast, compulsive sexual mutilation and the choice of abstinence or celibacy, underemployment and the choice not to work.

Practical reason should not be limited to individuals. When debating development strategies, Nussbaum claims that Western governments and NGOs can avoid paternalistic or imperialistic dealings with under-developed nations by allowing those nations to conceive of and engage in critical reflection about strategies for their own development. This wisdom can be brought to bear on first-world approaches to the HIV/AIDS pandemic in Africa, for example. It shifts the focus from a top-down analysis of the distribution of resources, which often ignores recipients' perspectives, to a more grassroots evaluation of the ways those resources will be used. The former relies exclusively on the perspective of those not necessarily affected by the disease, while the latter depends completely on the wisdom of those infected.

Moreover, empowerment occurs when we bolster the capability for affiliation or voluntarily chosen relationships of love, friendship, or camaraderie. Affiliation places much-needed limits on unfettered individualism and autonomous isolation, which in turn shape the self-understandings and world views of the privileged minority who determine the "good life" for the majority. For example, the capability to live in relationships of love and care with others in a dignified and non-humiliating way takes center stage among Nussbaum's list of requirements for human flourishing. In other words, while we may be autonomous and separate, we cannot thrive if we are segregated or isolated from the wider human community or prevented from engaging in healthy relationships with self, others, and aspects of the world around us. As we have already seen in the previous chapters, relationships with others contribute to the vulnerability and dependency we experience as human persons—which is why Plato sought to avoid them and Rousseau encouraged them. Nussbaum's ideas support the much-needed sense that suffering with another enhances our under-developed capability for relationality with distant and different others. It is precisely in the context of relationship that compassion promises transformative possibilities for both the suffering and non-suffering persons:

- Compassion recognizes our inherent vulnerability, particularly vulnerabilities that lie outside the control of some but squarely under the control of others.
- Compassionate responses aim to empower us to overcome unjustly imposed vulnerabilities through increased capacity for relationship with self and others.
- Compassion can be the virtue that stimulates, evaluates, and directs transformative relationality, particularly on the global scale.

Goods and the Good Life

Nussbaum characterizes her Aristotelian liberalism by its breadth and depth, its "thick vague conception of the good," and its firm assertion that governments ought to support human thriving by ensuring capabilities for distinctively human activities.[22] These factors contribute to an understanding of the "good life" that can redress the flaws of contemporary compassion since they propose alternative perceptions of human flourishing.

Nussbaum's liberalism broadens the boundaries of those who are responsible for creating the good life, as well as those who are entitled to enjoy it. Her Aristotelian liberalism is broad in that it is not only concerned with the thriving of the elite, but also with the capabilities for all citizens, particularly women, to flourish. For example, when we make the family unit the focal point of social welfare or human development strategies, whether in the United States or in many of the other countries around the world, impediments to the flourishing of the family's female members often remain on the periphery of our social vision. Women's particular needs—for health, education, bodily integrity, living-wage employment—are often subsumed into the general needs of their families and, as a result, often go unmet. A rising family tide does not necessarily lift each member's boat. Nussbaum insists that these overlooked persons should become a focal point of human development strategies—whether in India or the south side of Chicago.

In *Frontiers of Justice* Nussbaum attempts to extend notions of the good life by means of the experiences of persons with disabilities as well as those of nonrational animals. In so doing, she broadens her notion of participants in the good life to include those who are assumed to enjoy the trappings of such a life but in many cases do not. Their experiences highlight the limits to what the good life entails when that life is construed exclusively by rational and normally abled inhabitants. These persons frequently claim that those who set the parameters of justice ought to possess "rationality, language, and roughly equal physical and mental capacities" and that "mutual advantage and reciprocity" ought to be the basic outcomes of justice.[23] The experiences of persons with disabilities, however, call our attention to the narrowness and shallowness of many social contract theories that have proposed notions of the good life and guided social behavior for centuries. They remind us of the many expressions of rationality, beyond merely logic or intellect, such as sociability, emotional attachments, and bodily needs. They help us to realize that societies are "held together by a wide range of attachments and concerns, only some of which concern productivity."[24] And they also suggest that the human capacity for care highlights a wide range of activities necessary for living a good life—whether one is cared for or a caregiver—including affiliation, self-respect, the ability to play and enjoy life, and the ability to have control over one's environment.[25]

Nussbaum's liberalism is also deep because it involves more than the accumulation of wealth or income. Goods are "just stuff until we begin to see how they are put to work in the context of human lives."[26] That kind of ethical evaluation is qualitative rather than quantitative; it prioritizes activities rather than goods, as well as each person's freedom to choose from among these activities in building a thriving life. Therefore, the good life requires what Nussbaum calls a "thick vague notion of the good." This notion of human thriving is thick because it "deals with human ends across all areas of life," but it is vague because "it deals with an outline sketch of the good life" that allows each individual to flush it out in that way that his or her practical reason dictates.[27]

Moreover, the "thickness" of Nussbaum's notion of the good life arises from the dialogical process that brings together in the public square many persons from a variety of cultural backgrounds, metaphysical views on the world, and frameworks in order to discuss these constantly evolving human capabilities for flourishing. In seeking "over-lapping consensus," an idea first articulated by political philosopher John Rawls, her process of understanding the good life creates upheavals in the prevailing world views and frameworks of meaning. Ideas, visions, and practices pertaining to the good life that come from those on the margins challenge the existing and incomplete ideas, visions, and practices of those at the center. Much like the interruptive or disturbing aspects of Greek tragedy, discussions about the good life—usually best engaged through the capabilities of practical reason and affiliation—enable us to perceive more accurately the realities of others, who bring with them knowledge that can disrupt our previously held perceptions. These cognitive upheavals are a communal experience, facilitated through a vibrant public discourse. They commission world citizens to bring their various relationships, represented by concentric circles, closer to the center of their concern and activity.[28]

This orientation to flourishing distinguishes Nussbaum's brand of liberalism from that of others that focus on measuring the good life by means of an accumulation of wealth, the distribution of wealth, maximizing preferences, or even the exercise of individual freedom.[29] In true Aristotelian fashion the driving question becomes not how much people have, but rather what they are able to do and be.[30] Therefore, in keeping with her anthropological claims, Nussbaum understands flourishing as the pursuit of activities by means of capabilities that make life truly human.[31] This is essential in order to perceive, understand, and respond to those with limited capabilities for thriving. For example, in the context of homelessness, we might begin to perceive the difference between "being housed"—having access to affordable housing—and "being at home"—converting that dwelling into the locus of a variety of life-sustaining activities. Or, in the case of disaster preparedness, we might perceive the conditions in which many live prior to disasters just as threatening to the good life as those experienced in the aftermath of any hurricane, tsunami, or earthquake. Therefore, this Aristotelian notion of the good life makes several contributions to the tradition of compassion:

- A thick and vague notion of the good life deepens our sense of human suffering as thwarted or stunted capabilities for distinctively human activities and not merely as limited access to material goods or exclusion from the "good life" narrowly construed by the values of free market capitalism. Compassion, therefore, focuses on restoring capabilities.
- A thick and vague notion of flourishing emphasizes central capabilities such as affiliation, recreation and play, and emotional expression. Compassion, therefore, empowers thriving persons to acknowledge vulnerability and the need for relationships.
- A thick and vague notion of the good life grows organically out of the collective and cosmopolitan process of discussing the good life. Compassion, therefore, cultivates consensus among divergent persons.

Concluding Remarks

Nussbaum's Aristotelian liberalism offers an important foundation for her ideas about compassion and for the evolution of compassion in a global age. For example, examining tragic narratives as a source of moral wisdom gives us insights to identify more precisely what is going on in our reality. As we will see in Chapter 6, listening to the stories of persons affected by natural disasters heightens our awareness of the disastrous living conditions many endure long before catastrophe stikes. In addition, Nussbaum's anthropological emphasis on vulnerability bridges the social, cultural, and geographical gaps among persons that fuel inaccurate perceptions and normative judgments that prevent us from either perceiving others' suffering or from understanding its significance in their lives. As we will see in Chapter 7, we can reverse many of the demoralizing effects of globalization on first-world persons by penetrating our false sense of invulnerability and unleashing our under-developed capabilities for relationality. Finally, her understanding of human development rooted in flourishing and characterized by life-defining activities attunes us to situations of suffering that otherwise might go unnoticed and offers creative alternatives to prevailing human-development strategies.

INTERPRETING REALITY: THE UPHEAVAL OF EMOTIONS

If notions of persons and the good life assist us in perceiving more accurately instances of suffering in our social reality, then the emotions—a uniquely human capability for making sense of that reality—become an important tool for interpretation. Nussbaum insists that the emotions are essential for individual and collective moral reasoning. She quotes Proust in describing emotions as "geological upheavals of thought" that mark the landscape of our lives as "uneven, uncertain, and prone to reversal."[32] She reveals her feminist and Aristotelian sensibilities when she claims that emotions ought to be incorporated into ethical theories precisely because they assist us in asking tragic questions and in interpreting conflicts in meaning.[33]

However, Nussbaum advocates a critical approach to the upheavals that emotions create since unreflective reliance on the values and beliefs that shape our emotions can negatively affect moral agents or moral theories that incorporate them. At least three aspects of Nussbaum's work with emotions—particularly the emotion of compassion—further the evolution of compassion among privileged Christians in our global age.

Emotion and Moral Reasoning

The Aristotelian tradition, which we examined in the previous chapter, contends that emotions differ from feelings, passions, "objectless moods," or appetites that merely push or pull a moral agent around in an irrational or unthinking manner. Rather, in Nussbaum's assessment, emotions are "intelligent responses to perceptions of value" that cannot be "sidelined" from ethical theories precisely because they are involved in judgments about and appraisals of flourishing.[34] More specifically, "emotions are not just the fuel that powers the psychological mechanism of a reasoning creature, they are parts, highly complex and messy parts, of this creature's reasoning itself."[35] Emotion "records that sense of vulnerability and imperfect control" we experience when we acknowledge this vulnerable aspect of our human existence, an aspect central to Nussbaum's anthropology and likewise to the continued evolution of compassion.[36] To that extent, emotions are "acknowledgments of neediness and lack of self-sufficiency."[37] In order to be an emotional person in the evaluative and cognitive sense of the word, we must acknowledge or assent to that sense of vulnerability. This ability to embrace vulnerability is a particularly human capability. In other words, it is a cultivated ability to "have attachments to things and people outside of ourselves" and "in general to love, to grieve, to experience longing, gratitude and justified anger."[38]

Two specific elements of Nussbaum's work in emotions, particularly the emotion of compassion, can bolster the efficacy of compassion in responding collectively to situations of injustice on a global scale.

Emotive Cognition

Emotions in general and compassion in particular are not merely "value-laden cognitive states" such as feelings with "rich intentional content" or bodily experiences of pleasure, pain, or passion.[39] Rather, they are cognitive evaluations that rely on values and beliefs in order to receive information and then process judgments that motivate certain behavior. Their cognitive feature arises from exactly what the Stoics found problematic about emotions, namely, that they compel us to "assent to" or to acknowledge voluntarily a perceived object—person, thing, dilemma—as it is. This first step of emotion entails "embracing a way of seeing something in the world, acknowledging it as true."[40]

For example, let's suggest that the object of my emotion is a woman sitting on the sidewalk surrounded by bags. Prior to any evaluation I make of her using the beliefs and values I may have, I must first acknowledge this woman. I must actually choose to see her and the self-evident particularities of her situation. I must assent at the very least to the fact that she is there, alone on the street, surrounded only by possessions that she herself can transport. So from the outset, emotions indicate to us that something or someone has moved from the periphery of my perspective to a position with closer proximity to the center of my line of vision. How I understand and respond to these newly visible objects will depend on a variety of factors, but emotion or an emotional response requires that at the very least I see or acknowledge or assent to the existence of these objects.

Emotions, therefore, enable us to acknowledge or assent to people, things, or situations that we otherwise might not see. In our global age, when we are bombarded with thousands of visual objects each day, we have a tremendous need to cultivate this kind of perception. We need to be more intentional in our focus on the human beings who pass in and out of our sight lines so that we not only see them but actually assent to their existence or acknowledge them. This emotional assent can be difficult, particularly when our acknowledgment of others interrupts prevailing social lenses, world views, or ways of understanding our relationship to them. For example, in order to acknowledge a homeless woman, at the very least I must recognize her as human being, as a female, and as a woman who shares a particular space and time with me. Assenting to the truth of these obvious facts can break through the false assumptions and stereotypes that often segregate persons in self-enclosed enclaves that are voluntarily and involuntarily constructed. In this case, assenting to this woman on the street can challenge socially constructed beliefs about homeless persons that release us from a sense of responsibility to them—that they are lazy, antisocial, potentially violent, and so on. In addition, these commonalities, when rightly evaluated, can provide the foundation for my response to this fellow human being.

Emotions and Evaluative Judgments

Nussbaum argues that emotions, particularly those that involve assenting to the existence of others, are eudaimonistically evaluative. In other words, they involve judgments about states of and conditions for flourishing and about connections between another person's flourishing and my own. Therefore, like all judgments, emotions involve interpretations and normative evaluations that underscore their cognitive quality. Three specific judgments arise in emotions connected to others' suffering. These reinforce the evaluative moral reasoning that goes into compassion, as well as the need for ongoing critical assessment of the beliefs and values that shape compassion's evaluative judgments.

First, the *judgment of seriousness* entails an evaluation of the size and gravity of the other's suffering. Compassion ought not be used for trivial suffering, even if that suffering is unpleasant both from the perspective of the onlooker and the perspective of the person experiencing it. Certainly, there is a significant element of subjectivity in ascertaining the seriousness of another's suffering. For example, if my beliefs and values are such that I judge the disappointment of not being able to own a home in a gated neighborhood to be dehumanizing, I might decide that compassion is an appropriate response to someone unable to afford such a home. Likewise, if my beliefs and values about homelessness are such that I judge the condition of homelessness to be uncomfortable but not necessarily life-threatening, I might withhold compassion from a person unable to afford any type of housing.

A failure to recognize the difference in these two circumstances of insecurities related to housing points to a central flaw in all three of compassion's evaluative judgments, particularly that of the judgment of seriousness. Compassion privileges the onlooker and the beliefs and values that inform that onlooker. Nussbaum acknowledges as much when she notes that "emotions look at the world from the subject's own viewpoint, mapping events onto the subject's own sense of personal importance or value."[41] As we discussed in the first chapter, critics of compassion argue that this kind of privileged perspective can easily lead to false assessments of suffering as well as paternalistic and condescending treatment of those who suffer. Leaving the assessment of another's suffering in the hands of the non-suffering onlooker can assault the sufferer's dignity, fail to call into question the erroneous values that shape the non-sufferer's perception of reality, and ultimately ignore the underlying causes of the affliction.

Nussbaum attends to these liabilities by proposing that flourishing—the capability to engage in a variety of rich, life-defining, and sustaining activities—serves as the optimal litmus test for judging the seriousness of another's suffering. She suggests that ten central capabilities constitute the good life and that a lack of any one of these capabilities constitutes serious suffering, for which compassion would be required.[42] This more objective evaluation of the seriousness of another's suffering, rooted in an assessment of life-defining activities rather than the subjective values and beliefs of potentially compassionate persons, expands our understanding of suffering to include experiences that might otherwise go unnoticed. These include housing insecurity, lack of access to health care, dependence on minimum-wage work, forced migration, and lack of control over reproductive health. We begin to reevaluate previously held beliefs about seriousness that erroneously served as the litmus test for our judgments and misdirected our compassionate response. Evaluating suffering according to the basic requirements of human flourishing makes us aware of situations of suffering that we might miss if we persist in evaluating flourishing according to either access to material goods or satisfaction of personal preferences. For example, when we begin to recognize the impact of homelessness upon other capabilities such as bodily integrity, affiliation, and practical reason, we can begin to understand the severity of this type of suffering and the various tangible and intangible goods necessary to resist this kind of suffering.

Moreover, when we root the judgment of seriousness in human flourishing, we also call into question the true severity of suffering situations that often preoccupy our compassionate attention or distract us from other situations of suffering. These might include anxieties that stem from dissatisfaction with physical appearance, lack of contentment with material possessions, fear of mortality, or decline in economic or social status. While certainly viable concerns, these expressions of suffering become serious and deserving of a compassionate response only when they threaten the ten central capabilities.

In addition, evaluating the seriousness of suffering in light of an activities-based approach to human flourishing protects suffering persons from potentially disrespectful and paternalistic treatment at the hands of those who, despite their good intentions, often misinterpret or ignore the complexity of the situation. Moreover, since an assessment of capabilities necessarily incorporates the perspective of those whose flourishing is threatened, this kind of evaluation empowers those who suffer to articulate the seriousness of their situation and to discern the most fitting response to bolster their capabilities. Often, these overlooked perspectives challenge onlookers to reassess their own beliefs about what constitutes serious suffering. A more complete understanding of the severity of suffering, in turn, enables a more accurate response, such as a shift from providing a homeless family with temporary housing to working with the family to create a more permanent state of being "at home" in the community.

Compassion's second judgment involves an *evaluation of desert,* that is, an assessment of whether or not others deserve or in some way have merited the suffering they experience. We tend to reserve compassion for those whose suffering we deem as undeserved or disproportionate to the actions that may have produced it. We generally do not have compassion for those we judge to have brought their suffering on themselves or for suffering that appears to be commiserate with particular actions. This judgment presents its own limitations to compassionate action in our global age. As was the case with seriousness, assessing desert and proportionality can be a narrowly subjective process, because this evaluation also stems from the values and beliefs of the potentially compassionate person. For example, some philanthropists suggest that our civic response to Hurricane Katrina was significantly less impressive than our response to the terrorist attacks of 9/11, given the number of private foundations created after 9/11 and the amount of money donated to them. They attribute this discrepancy in large part to judgments involving desert. Unlike the involuntary suffering of terrorism, Americans tend to consider poverty a voluntary state caused by individual bad choices. As a result, we respond with less compassion toward those suffering in "voluntary" conditions of poverty in the aftermath of a hurricane than to those involuntarily reeling in the aftermath of a terrorist attack.

In addition, the criterion of desert is problematic from the standpoint of Christian ethics because it allows people to shirk their compassionate responsibilities in many situations. As we discussed in the third chapter, the Christian tradition suggests that going and doing as he did requires that compassion to be extended to those for whom Jesus himself showed compassion—those found to be least deserving in his social milieu, including tax-collectors, non-Jews, adulterous women, and lepers. Diana Fritz Cates questions if judgment about whether people deserve their suffering ought to be included at all, noting that if it is, "compassion will be very rare" and or "forestalled indefinitely."[43]

However, when coupled with Nussbaum's anthropology and notion of tragedy, the judgment of desert might actually expand rather than narrow the circumstances for compassionate action. By proposing that persons are simultaneously vulnerable and capable, Nussbaum suggests that human agency—a significant component in assessing culpability and desert—is often tempered by tragic circumstances that lie outside a person's control. We must take these tragic circumstances into consideration in assigning culpability. In this way, evaluations of desert informed by vulnerability might shift our focus away from personal causes of suffering toward more structural and systemic causes. In other words, if we accept that tragic circumstances beyond an individual's control often cause the dehumanizing affliction of concentrated poverty, for example, then we must accept that much of this affliction is undeserved and as such demands our response. We might reassess our reactions to the suffering of drug-addicted homeless persons, for example, when we recognize the causal connection between concentrated poverty and drug abuse, or homelessness and a lack of affordable mental health care; or we may reevaluate our reaction to mothers with children in the shelter system when we discover the prevalence of domestic abuse.

Moreover, when coupled with Nussbaum's notion of tragedy, the judgment of desert can effectively shift responsibility for suffering away from those suffering and toward those who knowingly and unknowingly support the structural and social systems that threaten others' capabilities to flourish. In other words, responsibility for much of the social suffering in our global age arises from collective practices of flourishing people and not those struggling to survive. For instance, the connections between racism and segregated public education, or sexism and women's need for public assistance, or the culturally driven expectation of owning a single-family home in suburban neighborhoods and the concentration of poverty in urban areas all suggest that the causes of social inequity and the suffering it creates also lie with the privileged. Protecting parents' choice of where to send their children in the public school system does little to challenge the attitudes and preferences that shape the disparity among schools and districts. As a result, these attitudes and preferences perpetuate the status quo. This evaluative component of compassion brings a much needed self-critical awareness to our assessments of where others' suffering is deserved.

Finally, Aristotle proposes that compassion involves an *evaluation of similar possibility* that arises through a sense of vulnerability or a sense that what has happened to our suffering neighbor could easily happen to us. This evaluation often generates a fear that we may unexpectedly find ourselves in their shoes. This fear motivates us to respond.

Like the previous two judgments, the evaluation of similar possibility presents significant obstacles for cultivating the kind of compassion required in our global age. Aristotle believed that the judgment of similar possibility could exist only between relatively similar persons, which in and of itself has the capacity to narrow compassionate action, given the radical inequality that separates people in our contemporary reality. More important, this judgment fails to challenge sufficiently cultural attitudes and social structures that perpetuate divisions among persons. For example, Nussbaum notes that after 9/11 Americans showed boundless compassion to the families who lost loved ones in the terrorist attacks but were unable to extend it to the families of the terrorists who also lost loved ones.

In order to bridge this gap in our understanding of similarity, Nussbaum shifts Aristotle's understanding from a sense of similar possibility to shared notions of flourishing. In other words, in addition to recognizing the significance of suffering for the person enduring it, Nussbaum claims that compassion requires a eudaimonistic judgment in which we also perceive this suffering as significant for our own flourishing, or in which we sense that our own capabilities for full humanity are jeopardized insofar as those of another are also threatened. This eudaimonistic judgment, however, depends on our willingness to "make ourselves vulnerable in the person of another."[44] This vulnerability is different from the loss of control we might experience through Aristotle's fear of similar possibility. Rather, Nussbaum considers vulnerability a desire, an openness, and a willingness to make one's flourishing contingent upon that of another specifically for that other's sake.

When rooted in a desire for vulnerability, the eudaimonistic judgment provides the centripetal force that pulls more unrelated, distant, and different persons into the moral agent's center of moral concern. It is "the thing that makes the difference between viewing hungry peasants as beings whose sufferings matter and viewing them as distant objects whose experiences have nothing to do with one's own life."[45] It is also central to our "eudaimonistic imagination," which allows us to "wonder" about another's situation to the extent that the knowledge we gain in this imaginative identification throws our beliefs and values into an upheaval. Intimate knowledge of another's suffering makes us vulnerable.[46] The eudaimonistic judgment motivates the onlooker to act compassionately for the sake of the other. In other words, compassion's eudaimonistic judgment is what makes the suffering of the chronically homeless or the housing insecurity of poor families matter in our own scheme of flourishing. Nussbaum claims that we can reach that judgment through the cultivation of our understanding of others as united in our own vulnerability to tragedy and in our common capabilities for flourishing.

Emotions as Historically Conscious

Moral theologian Charles Curran defines historical consciousness as a way of viewing reality that "emphasizes the changing, developing, evolving and historical" aspects of the human condition and the world. This outlook, which emerged in everything from art and literature to theology and philosophy, is quite distinct from the more Platonic and classicist world view that underscores the "static, the immutable, the eternal, and the unchanging" features of the same. The historical world view celebrates "the individual traits that characterize the individual," including feelings, emotion, inductive reason, and conscience. This world view, therefore, highlights the constantly evolving human capability for knowledge of ourselves and our world and for individual and collective development. It also makes evident the changing demands of human relationality in light of ever-changing social circumstances and empowers us to "observe, experience and then tentatively proceed to conclusions" as to how we ought to engage in reality.[47] In short, historical consciousness suggests that change is possible and commissions individuals to use the wisdom of their experience to determine when and where that change can and should occur.

Emotions are an important aspect of the socially critical moral agency that accompanies this world view. For example, Nussbaum notes that part of the cognitive makeup of emotions stems from their foundation in the cultural attitudes, value systems, and beliefs of individuals that are reinforced by social relationships. In fact, as we have seen in compassion's three evaluative judgments, these undercurrents frequently contribute to the unpredictable, irrational, and unreliable reputation of emotions. We have already discussed the ways in which philosophers through the centuries cite the relationship between emotion and subjective beliefs in order to dismiss emotions as viable tools in moral reasoning. However, the fact that emotions arise from contextually or socially constructed beliefs points to the psychological, social, and relational depth of emotions. These dimensions suggest that emotions are not merely isolated or ahistorical means of interpreting reality, but rather historically conscious interpretations, rooted in the particularities of cultures and individual perceptions of concrete reality. As such, they offer an important means of unearthing and questioning the implicit value systems, tacit beliefs, and unspoken social conventions that accurately or erroneously inform the way we evaluate and ultimately respond to situations. In other words, attending to the cultural contexts of emotions can create new self-awareness and historical awareness in our understanding of self, others, and the world.

We noted in our discussion of compassion as a virtue that emotions are historical both in terms of their development in individuals, from infancy throughout adulthood, and in terms of their cultural and social construction. They are dynamic rather than static, dependent upon changing norms and values and open to critical and public examination. For example, sociologists have pointed out the ways in which varying beliefs regarding the state of racial discrimination in this country gave rise to quite different emotional evaluations of and responses to the natural disaster of Hurricane Katrina. Different pre-existing emotions regarding race gave rise to very different perceptions and responses to those affected by the same event. Some Americans perceived looters among those stranded in New Orleans after the levees broke and demanded restitution, while others saw those "looters" instead as resourceful citizens and celebrated their resilience. The difference in these emotional responses to others' suffering reinforces Nussbaum's claim that "the education of emotion, to succeed at all, needs to take place in a culture of ethical criticism, and especially self-criticism, in which ideas of equal respect for humanity will be active players in the effort to curtail the excesses of the greedy self."[48]

If emotions have roots in our history—both individual and cultural—then we might consider recognizing them as an important means of critically evaluating our social reality via historical consciousness. For example, emotions form a narrative that continuously evolves as a source of identity for individuals and institutions; emotions can reshape and refine our sense of self, our goals, and our understanding of flourishing. Consider, for example, the powerful emotions of patriotism cultivated by the story of the American struggle for independence that continues to fuel American domestic and foreign policy; or think about the emotions of unity fanned by the accumulated stories of the Olympic games, which cultivate peace around the world in unexpected ways.

In keeping with Rousseau's insistence that the young pupil Émile experience a variety of emotions as part of his educational development, the historical nature of emotions underscores the importance of self-critically and intentionally shaping our emotional history and identity. We can do this through exposure to new people, things, and situations that can evoke emotions with the potential to disrupt previously held beliefs and values. For example, encountering a homeless woman and developing our sense of relationality and vulnerability in the context of a relationship with her has great potential not only to stimulate a different emotional response to that particular woman, but also a different emotional response to the larger reality of homelessness. Volunteering for a week with congregants in a local church in New Orleans can challenge previously held beliefs regarding the structural causes of the Hurricane Katrina catastrophe in ways that simply making an online donation cannot. More important, both of these instances suggest that when we interrupt our previously held beliefs and values, we free our imagination to envision more creative responses to these situations. Often these responses transcend common wisdom or standard operating procedures.

In addition, Nussbaum contends that we need to become cognizant of the beliefs that shape all of our emotions, but particularly those beliefs that shape emotions that we are not even aware of experiencing most of the time. Background emotions are often unconsciously formed and operative throughout an individual's life and subtly affect interpretations of other objects. Part of the challenge of compassion in our global age involves questioning the inherent background emotions of the American subconscious, such as individualism, productivity, self-sufficiency, and consumerism, that shape so many of our emotional responses. If we can reshape our background beliefs about poverty and poor people, about mental illness and welfare dependency, about race and white privilege, or about development aid, then we might also be able to shape interpretations of the suffering of homeless persons, the suffering of natural disasters, and the human causes for tragic suffering in most circumstances of injustice. If we can change interpretations, we might ultimately change our emotive responses. This emotive commitment to self-awareness and self-criticism makes a valuable contribution to the evolution of compassion.

Concluding Remarks

Nussbaum's overarching theory of emotions and their connection to perceiving suffering accurately provides three bases for an approach to compassion. First, she recognizes that emotions are necessary for ethical evaluation, action, and moral development because they reveal information that might otherwise go unnoticed in our interpretations of the social reality: erroneous values and beliefs that shape our perception and interpretation, and the vulnerability of all persons to situations and circumstances we cannot control. Second, given their roots in deeply held and largely socially constructed beliefs and values, emotions offer an element of historical consciousness to moral reasoning as well as much needed self- and social criticism on the part of moral agents in acknowledging that they are historically conditioned and in need of constant refinement. Finally, through the process of assenting to another's reality, emotions generate important upheavals in our ways of perceiving self, others, and the world and thus spark new moral questions and imagination.

However, precisely because emotions are connected to beliefs, beliefs that are usually culturally and socially constructed and influenced, emotions themselves can and ought to be critically evaluated. Compassion can serve as the optimal emotion for assessing beliefs and transforming those beliefs when they erroneously prevent us from perceiving, evaluating, and responding to another's suffering.

- Assent to or acknowledgment of the existence of a suffering other creates a vulnerability in compassionate persons that arises when we perceive these persons and ourselves quite differently.
- When rooted in vulnerability, compassion's evaluative judgments of seriousness, desert, and similar possibility interrogate erroneous beliefs and values regarding flourishing, desert, and similarity among persons and as a result increase our responsibility for responding to suffering persons.
- Exposure to stories and narratives of suffering helps us reevaluate prevailing beliefs and values that often prevent us from accurately perceiving and responding to others' suffering.

TRANSFORMING REALITY:
THE CAPABILITY APPROACH TO JUSTICE

Nussbaum's capabilities approach to human development offers a global approach to responding to those who do not truly flourish, even those who live in the developed and over-developed countries of the world. In many ways the theory epitomizes her.[49] It reflects her political and public approach to her vocation as a philosopher, her ardent claims that we can think about persons in a cross-cultural way, her insistence that we acknowledge vulnerability and capability, the experiences that shape her ideas about securing human development, and her cosmopolitan charge to citizens, educators, and national governments. In addition, the capabilities approach reflects Nussbaum's attempts to take seriously the signs of the times—suffering, encountering others in situations of gross inequality, and globalization. For example, personal encounters with poor women significantly changed her thinking about conditions of flourishing. In fact, she weaves narratives of two Indian women—Vasanti and Jayama—into her presentation of the approach, which reinforces ideas about particular conditions and universal claims for flourishing. Moreover, the capabilities approach intentionally fills a void in global ethics. Nussbaum notes that "especially in an era of rapid economic globalization, the capabilities approach is urgently needed to give moral substance and moral constraints to processes that are occurring all around us without sufficient moral reflection."[50]

The theory relies on narrative accounts of particular tragic circumstances as well as accounts of what constitutes a human life in order to propose a list of ten "central human functional human capabilities." An abbreviated version of these capabilities follows: (1) life, (2) bodily health, (3) bodily integrity, (4) senses, imagination, and thought, (5) emotions, (6) practical reason, (7) affiliation, (8) other species, (9) play, and (10) control over one's environment.[51] One capability cannot be suppressed with the intention of better achieving another. Two "internal capabilities" in particular—practical reason and affiliation—give shape to the others and ensure that persons not be treated as a means to another's end by creating and protecting real choice, or the ability to be a self-determining agent in a variety of spheres of activity and relationship.[52] These internal capabilities combine with external conditions that support human functioning to create "combined capabilities" such as bodily health, play, and control over one's environment.

The goal of the approach is not mere functioning, but rather the capability to function in certain ways should a moral agent so choose. "Otherwise promising approaches [to justice] have frequently gone wrong by ignoring the problems women actually face. But the capabilities approach directs us to examine real lives in their material and social settings," Nussbaum argues. "The central question asked by the capabilities approach is not, 'How satisfied is Vasanti?' or even 'How much in the way of resources is she able to command?' It is, instead, 'What is Vansanti actually able to do and to be?'"[53]

This line of ethical questioning reflects the orientation of virtue ethics and thus necessarily incorporates virtues such as compassion into its methodology. Nussbaum implicitly incorporates compassion into her capabilities approach to justice, underscoring four ways that compassionately suffering with others goes hand in hand with actively undoing the causes of social injustice.

Tragic Questions and Human Development

Tragic questions lie at the heart of the capabilities approach, since this kind of inquiry unearths what people are actually able to do with the resources and freedoms they possess. In other words, Nussbaum contends that human development cannot begin with assessments of material wealth or income, or even the protection of basic freedoms. Rather, we must begin with an evaluation of another's satisfaction and contentment in the context of a variety of rich human activities. Nussbaum's continued personal experiences with poor women in India led her to see the problems women actually faced. Often, these are tragic problems such as illiteracy, lack of employment, financial and social dependence on abusive men, no access to political processes, unsanitary living conditions, and little if any access to health care. Given the intractable nature of many of these problems and their impact on what women are able to do with the limited resources at their disposal, Nussbaum recommends that human development strategists need to begin with the previously mentioned "tragic question," namely, "*Why* [do] people have to face [these problems], and what can institutional and political change do to make sure that they don't face this again?"[54]

Her insistence on the importance of tragic questions in human-development strategies compelled her to part ways with leading human-development philosopher Amartya Sen. She found that his emphasis on securing human development by bolstering human freedom missed the intractable and tragic nature of many social problems.[55] Human freedom is not always the best indicator of levels of human development because freedom can only be fully expressed or actualized in a variety of activities that empower individuals to envision and seek after their own destinies. For example, a woman might be free from impediments in voting, in divorcing her husband, or in going to school, but unless she is empowered to translate these freedoms—to vote, to divorce her husband, or to receive an education—into capabilities to think for herself, to be in control of her body, or to participate in recreational activities, they do not ensure that she will thrive. In addition, many people erroneously equate freedom with choice or preference, both of which are frequently socially constructed. Often, culturally contrived preferences do not support the ten central capabilities, as is the case in many cultures where religious values dictate women's choices about their bodies, their relationships, and their engagement in public life. Tragic questions that ask what people are able to do in various circumstances interrogate these socially constructed preferences and reveal a lack of real freedom behind many "choices" in these cultures.

Nussbaum also differs from Sen in insisting that tragic questions better illuminate humanly created and sustained correlations between over-development and under-development, between excessive wealth and concentrated poverty, between progress for progress's sake and decline for progress's sake. When we ask why certain people suffer the way they do, we are better able to recognize that many of the world's injustices are not caused by unavoidable natural conditions, nor are they the coincidental byproducts of living in a global age. Rather, illiteracy, hunger, disease, child mortality, and homelessness tragically arise from avoidable and often intentionally sustained circumstances. Unlike in previous centuries, people today do not have to suffer in this way. We tragically allow them to do so.

Moreover, when we ask what people are able to do with the freedom and resources they possess, we might discover that most who live comfortably in developed or over-developed countries actually lack many of the basic capabilities necessary for authentic human thriving. For instance, a hyper-individualized, materialistic, consumer-driven, and fear-obsessed culture threatens first-world citizens' capabilities for affiliation, emotion, creative imagining and recreation. Therefore, tragic questions challenge the visions of human progress or development held by good-intentioned persons that often erroneously serve as the benchmark for other persons' thriving. Attention to tragic questions more closely connects compassion to social change.

- Compassionate responses begin with a line of inquiry that exposes the causes of suffering and not just what might be required in terms of immediate relief.
- Compassionate responses have a political orientation because they focus on what people are able to become in the context of community, rather than simply what individual persons do or do not possess at a particular time.

Activity-based Human Development

The capabilities approach challenges prevailing models of human development or theories of justice with its simultaneous emphasis on human vulnerability and capability, as well as its thick and deep notion of the good life. Answers to tragic questions as to why people suffer the way they do point us away from an assessment of access to material goods or even applications of abstract theories of justice and toward a rich variety of activities that define existence as distinctively human. The inability to choose even one of these activities—from bodily integrity to practical reason—calls the very humanness of life into question. These human activities ensure that we always treat all persons as an end and never as an instrumental means, not only in behind-closed-door policy development meetings or high-profile international summits on human rights or global poverty but also in our day-to-day interactions. Nussbaum says that "without such an inquiry into the goodness and full happiness of various types of functioning, and into the special obstacles faced by deprived persons, the most valuable sort of social change could not have begun. Simply making enough things available was not enough."[56]

For example, when we focus exclusively on either gender or economic injustice in the context of homelessness, we fail to address the complexity of women's lives where economic capabilities and sexual capabilities are intertwined and where sexual and economic oppression reinforce one another. It makes little sense to work with a single mother and her children to find affordable housing if she continues to be stalked by an abusive partner or does not earn a living wage. Empowering a woman left homeless by a natural disaster will entail more than the material good of a roof over her head. It will require a legal system that protects her from abusers, a health-care system that enables her to take care of herself both mentally and physically, and a minimum wage that enables her family to engage in activity-based flourishing. Approaching human flourishing with an emphasis on activities more closely connects compassion to social change in several ways:

- Compassionate responses perceive the ways that social problems threaten central human capabilities and thus debilitate individuals, families, and communities.
- Compassionate responses aim to empower people to participate more fully in life in community by bolstering a variety of life-defining activities.
- Compassionate responses reverse social problems by an emphasis on human activity, not simply material goods or access to opportunity.

Self-criticism and Social Criticism in Human Development

Nussbaum notes, "If we really do believe that all human beings are created equal and endowed with certain inalienable rights, we are morally required to think about what that conception requires us to do with and for the rest of the world."[57] The capabilities approach, therefore, requires those above the threshold to acknowledge those who are very distant from us and to assent to their reality. The capabilities approach presents several opportunities for this kind of assent.

For example, the bottom-up nature of the capabilities approach, which begins with basic activities that define human flourishing in all countries and cultural contexts, avoids the pitfalls inherent in many top-down approaches to human development fostered by international agencies, think tanks, and institutions such as the International Monetary Fund, the World Bank, and even the American Red Cross. Often these entities fail to interrupt cultural and political divisions that erroneously and dangerously separate persons. These divisions, between lender and debtor or developer and developed, reinforce national identities, religious affiliations, and political allegiances. Moreover, they keep us from recognizing our shared human characteristics and the need for goods that serve as a common denominator in the human experience as well as the importance of maintaining a critical engagement with our own nation, religious tradition, and political group. They also prevent us from expanding circles of concern.

In addition, the capabilities approach not only entails an honest appraisal of the capabilities of those below the threshold of human flourishing and our connection to the tragic causes of their suffering, but it also critically evaluates the life-defining activities of those *above* the threshold. While Nussbaum intended the capabilities approach as a *positive comparison*—highlighting what needs to be done to bring people up to and over the threshold—when coupled with compassion, her approach can also provide a *negative comparison* that highlights the inaccuracies in what is considered to be the threshold according to first-world perspectives. This negative comparison can turn prevailing notions of compassion and flourishing on their heads.

For example, by challenging consumerist notions of flourishing rooted in the desire for material goods with an emphasis on what people are actually able to do with these material goods, the capabilities approach helps us to differentiate between basic needs such as bodily integrity desired by people in the developing world and cultural desires for bodily enhancements desired by people in the super-developed United States. It can help us understand the difference between embodied affiliation or relationality desired by those who are marginalized from the common good and the desire for isolated connectivity on the part of those who already thrive within the common good. Or it illuminates the difference between life-sustaining work desired by the chronically under-employed and over-productivity desired by success-obsessed cultural elites.

The capabilities approach might also highlight the disconnect between needs as they are perceived by those in a position to offer aid and needs as they are experienced by those who receive aid. For example, with capabilities as a benchmark for flourishing, we can identify the difference between being housed and being at home, between emergency and preventative medicine, between voluntary and involuntary immigration, and between meaningful work and demoralizing labor. Ultimately, this might lead us to understand the difference between compassionate disaster relief in the aftermath of our most recent national disasters and compassionate development aid. The former emphasizes the immediate distribution of material goods with the intention to return victims to pre-disaster levels of flourishing. The levels themselves, as well as the values, beliefs, and practices that reinforce them, go unchallenged. The latter approach, however, relies on a critical examination of what people are actually able to become, with the intention of empowering people to climb above previous levels of flourishing. In this scenario, what it means to flourish—as well as the values, beliefs, and practices that reinforce that notion—is called into question.

Finally, a more eudaimonistic sense of flourishing rooted in activities such as affiliation, bodily health, and control over one's environment suggests that materialism, production, and individualism are dehumanizing standards of human existence for those *above and below* the threshold of flourishing. In other words, an activities-based understanding of the good life might interrogate what Mary Elizabeth Hobgood has identified as the values of North Americans that set the standards for the rest of the world. These include "obsessiveness about work, managerial control over work, and restrictions on friendships, intimacy, and community."[58] All of these values threaten the basic capabilities of those who supposedly thrive in the world's remaining superpower, including affiliation, recreation, emotional health, and bodily integrity. Therefore, an activities-based approach to human flourishing critically challenges first-world notions of what it means to thrive. This links compassion more closely to social transformation in the following ways:

- Compassionate responses ought to focus on development aid that bolsters future capabilities and not simply on disaster relief that sustains people at low levels of flourishing.
- Compassionate responses to others' suffering cannot uncritically rely on a limited notion of what restoration might entail but must incorporate the perspectives and wisdom of those suffering.
- Compassionate responses ought to reinforce everyone's capability for flourishing—both the sufferers and the compassionate.

The Moral Imagination and Human Development

Lastly, the capabilities approach offers a creatively constructive method for social transformation that features an emphasis on narrative, consensus, and humility. Narratives of those who suffer and a willingness to listen to them provide the distinctive method of the approach. This orientation recognizes that even in attempts to make universal claims about flourishing, we need to pay attention to particular people, to their specific circumstances, and to the concrete impediments to their flourishing if we want these claims to make a difference in the lives of actual people. To that end, Nussbaum's approach underscores the importance of ethnography in ethics, an approach that those of us in the Christian tradition are just beginning to embrace. The stories and perspectives of those on the underside of history are necessary for imagining a new future.

Nussbaum transforms this attention to narrative into a method of building "overlapping consensus" on ideas about human functions and flourishing. In other words, consensus about what it means to thrive lies in the common denominators of human *experience* and not necessarily in the social values or cultural world views that often dictate these experiences. In this way the experiences of persons might challenge political, ethical, and religious principles that often positively and negatively shape their experiences. The process of building this organic consensus from the bottom up requires an ongoing commitment to attend to narratives and people's experiences of flourishing. It also requires a willingness to reflect honestly on the reality of others, particularly distant others, in order to bridge gaps between their experience and our own.

The list of capabilities requires ongoing reflection and revision if it is to remain consistent with and complementary to human experience. In this way the capabilities approach employs important reflexive equilibrium—a commitment to constant questioning of our intuitions about human persons and flourishing so that it is more in touch with the "modern world" rather than a "timeless" list.[59] This approach to human development contains an element of humility or self-doubt insofar as we recognize that the activities that some might see as central might not necessarily be so in the experience of others. We gain that realization only when we make honest attempts to listen deeply to others' stories, allow them to correct our self-understanding and world views, and then imagine with them alternative possibilities. When integrated with the imagination, compassion creates innovative alternatives for social transformation:

- It celebrates humility as an attribute necessary for better seeing, understanding, and changing the world.
- It liberates people from entrenched social enclaves and limited epistemologies through deep listening and dialogue, both of which can transform persons and empower them for social change.
- It highlights stories and narratives both as sources of wisdom for the future and compelling ways to shape new communal identities.

Concluding Remarks

To some extent, Nussbaum's understanding of human development echoes current trajectories in Christian ethics. Generally speaking, the capabilities approach does not seek material wealth or measure growth according to income but rather suggests satisfaction and contentment in the context of a variety of rich human activities. More specifically,

- Nussbaum's Aristotelian anthropology resonates with Christian ethics, particularly as it is articulated by feminists who have consistently argued for the importance of individual dignity *and* sociality, autonomy *and* relationality, reason *and* emotion.[60]
- Nussbaum's notion of development echoes that of John Paul II who suggests that life is more than mere functioning but rather ought to be defined by a variety of meaningful activities that allow for relationships with others and God.
- Her attentiveness to tragedy in human development, instances where persons are forced to choose among equally bad or immoral options, is consistent with the Christian emphasis upon focusing development efforts upon those who are most marginalized—in other words, the preferential option for the poor.
- Her emphasis on the importance of empowerment, rather than paternalistic charity, echoes Catholic themes of social justice entailing participation and contribution to the common good.

Moreover, Nussbaum's capabilities approach solidifies the connection between compassion and social justice in our global age. Engaging the capabilities approach in order to recognize the dignity and equal worth of persons will require a new approach to compassion. Its new features include an ability to perceive the suffering others and ourselves as equally human, to interpret their reality in a way that privileges their narratives, and to transform us and their reality by a commitment to bolstering life-sustaining capabilities and empowering them in the context of relationships. In other words, compassion is implicit in the following aspects of the capabilities approach:

- Compassion is critical for asking tragic questions that explore the depth of others' suffering, or for attempting to suffer with others in order to better understand their situation rather than moving to solve the situation without a full understanding of what is going on.

- Compassion can become a tool for not only more accurately understanding another's suffering, but more important, for exploring our connections to it.

The capabilities approach offers several correctives to the often misguided values and beliefs that lead to misguided evaluative judgments and often undercut compassion's efficacy in human development strategies:

- Compassion requires an attention to a set of human capabilities for flourishing and not merely material goods or political freedoms.
- Compassion involves reshaping the perspectives, beliefs, and values of those who flourish; justice for the marginalized will not be complete or effective if the beliefs and values of those within the margins go unchanged.
- Compassion requires a desire to work in conjunction with those who suffer in order to empower persons in practically every aspect of their lives, not merely the temporary mitigation of suffering.

POLITICAL COMPASSION
AS PERSONAL AND SOCIAL UPHEAVAL

In Martha Nussbaum we find an important resource for understanding compassion as an emotion that facilitates much-needed individual moral development as well as collective socioeconomic development. Given their cognitive, historical, and interruptive nature, emotions are an invaluable source of moral reasoning. Moreover, like all emotions, compassion engages certain capabilities that make for a constitutively human life, such as practical reason, affiliation with others, control over our environment, and the imagination. However, when directed by tragic questions and anchored in an openness to vulnerability, compassion critically challenges many of the values and beliefs that fuel first-world emotional responses to the tragic suffering in our global age. Recall, for example, that emotions involve assent and "the very act of assent itself is a tearing of my self-sufficient condition. Knowing can be violent, given the truths that are there to be known."[61]

Nussbaum's work in the emotions and *eudaimonia* in human development reveals that compassion creates a variety of upheavals in the way we understand and interpret the world around us and those who suffer within in it. For example, the human capability for emotion itself creates an upheaval in prevailing theological and philosophical anthropologies that define human beings as independent, self-sufficient, and rational. In addition, emotions potentially spark an important realization of our interrelatedness to all human beings when we see ourselves as vulnerable through the value we place on others. Compassion, in particular, continuously raises awareness of our vulnerabilities and the vulnerabilities of others as well as our imaginative capability to address them. In other words, moral development involves the ability to think perceptively, evaluatively, cognitively, and constructively about things and persons beyond our control.

Ultimately, compassion entails a self-critical "assent" to the reality and perspective of other persons. This new perspective exposes potentially compassionate persons to a new view of the world and of themselves. It is from this perspective that moral agents can and should examine our respective internal values, beliefs, and conditions for flourishing in light of the reality of the other who interrupts us. Assent creates the possibility of tragic questions—the series of whys that cannot always be neatly answered or explained away but rather require ongoing emotive cognition, evaluation, and response. These dangerously uncomfortable questions have the potential to reveal our complicity in another's suffering—whether indirectly, through ignorance, misguided values, and erroneous beliefs, or directly, through participation in structures of dehumanizing oppression and marginalization. They interrupt our own "cognitive-makeup" or our own sense of what it means to flourish.

Nussbaum's ideas resonate with Diana Fritz Cates's argument about the importance of this type of choice in compassion when Nussbaum writes: "Choosing to feel compassion's complacency [in another], in particular, involves choosing repeatedly, inside and outside of situations in which we are actually confronted with those who suffer, to be and to become the sorts of people who are characteristically attuned to what other people are going through, ready and even eager to take in, or be taken in by their experience."[62] Most important, these interruptions can motivate moral action. In Nussbaum's estimation, emotions or "emotions,"[63] as Cates calls them, entail an experience of being moved by something and being pulled in certain directions.

Nussbaum's perception of the good life—constituted by a wide range of capabilities—enables us to envision a different approach to responding to the suffering of others, one that ultimately seeks their empowerment. Through the capabilities approach Nussbaum offers a constructive means for transforming the social reality that does not rely on nation states alone, but rather on individual and institutional commitment to ensuring a wide range of capabilities. Compassion is necessary in order to perceive instances when these capabilities are threatened and to respond in a way that restores suffering persons to a series of interrelated life-sustaining and defining activities.

Perhaps most invaluable for the evolution of compassion in our global age are the possibilities the capabilities approach presents for critically addressing the over-development of certain peoples, and for interrogating our preferences for limited understandings of human flourishing on the basic capabilities of others. For example, compassion's evaluative judgments compel us to acknowledge our connections to those whose flourishing is in some way threatened—whether through common experiences of vulnerability, through culpability for the structural causes of their affliction, or through a renewed sense that human flourishing is an exercise in human interdependence. Moreover, with its reliance on vulnerability and practical reason, compassion helps us to recognize that notions of the good life rooted in individualism, materialism, consumerism, and fear threaten the central capabilities of others and of ourselves to flourish. We must call into question values and beliefs that deny emotional health, the viability of play, the imagination, and our ability to enter into deep relationships with people similar to and different from ourselves. As a result of the upheavals it creates in our self-understanding and world view, compassion unleashes the moral imagination to think collectively with others, often in the context of shared narratives, about innovative alternatives to the way things are. Compassion empowers people to work together to resist the causes of social injustices, and not just its symptoms.

In short, Nussbaum helps us to realize that compassion entails perceiving the absence of certain activities necessary for flourishing, judging that absence as a serious and undeserved cause of suffering, and acting to empower those who suffer by bolstering their capabilities for life-defining and sustaining activities.

5

Compassion as "Interruption"
in the Political Theology
of Johann Baptist Metz

Compassion sends us to the front lines of social and cultural conflicts in today's world. For perceiving and articulating others' suffering is the unconditional prerequisite of any future politics of peace, of every new form of social solidarity in the face of the widening gap between rich and poor, and of every promising interchange between different cultural and religious worlds.[1]

This statement captures the centrality of compassion in Johann Baptist Metz's theological method and reflects the unique orientation of his vocation as a theologian. He contends that the theologian's central task is the ongoing "effort to formulate the eschatological message of Christianity in the conditions of present-day society."[2] Certainly, social conditions have changed dramatically in Metz's lifetime. What was once the paralyzing silence of the German churches in the decades following the Holocaust has become the divisive clamor between secular humanism and religious fundamentalism in the European Union of the new millennium. However, Metz has not wavered in his commitment to understanding the ongoing significance of the memory of the crucified and resurrected Christ—what he calls the *memoria passionis* and *memoria resurrectionis*—in the lives of disciples.

"I happen to see [political theology] as a critical corrective to contemporary theology's tendency to concentrate on the private individual," Metz explains, "and at the same time as a positive attempt to formulate the eschatological message in the circumstances of our present society." This eschatological content of the Christian tradition, recognizable in Yahweh's covenantal promises to the Israelites or Christ's signs and symbols of the reign of God, point toward "freedom, peace, justice and reconciliation."[3] This message does not condone "passive waiting where the Christian lounges around in lackadaisical boredom until God opens the door of his office and allows the Christian to enter." Nor does it concentrate on "what is private." Rather, Metz argues that theology "must place itself in communication with the prevailing political, social, and technical utopias and with the contemporary maturing promises of a universal peace and justice."[4] In short, political theology seeks to "de-privatize" Christianity.

120

This orientation makes Metz an essential resource for Christians who attempt to live the moral imperatives of the memories of Christ in a global age. His theology challenges American disciples in particular to perceive accurately and articulate the memories of those who suffer in our own history and present reality. In addition, he argues for a political approach to compassion that encourages us to enter into relationships with those on the margins, rather than to participate in a kind of charity that is "almost obviously private and stripped of all political meaning."[5]

For instance, although he does not explicitly name it as such, Metz's political theology provides a critical framework that first-world Christians can use in order to examine the complexities of privilege and its impact on the way we perceive, interpret, and respond to the afflictions of our neighbors.[6] He provocatively voiced concerns about Christian comfortability and complicity in social suffering in the decades immediately following World War II. In fact, he asked his mentor and the "father of his faith," Karl Rahner, one of the greatest Catholic theologians of the twentieth century, "why is it that Auschwitz never shows up in [German] theology."[7] Metz also says, "I was disturbed by the conspicuous amount of apathy in theology, by its astonishing and obdurate befuddlement."[8] Rahner's failure to wrestle with the Holocaust still leaves Metz with the impression that "his [Rahner's] transcendental concept is in the final analysis ahistorical, too removed from history."[9]

Our own theology and faith remain dangerously private, bourgeois, and removed from history so long as we, as persons of privilege, fail to recognize the ways in which our privilege protects us from being thoroughly interrupted or upended by situations of injustice, whether our colonial history of genocide, our national "original sin" of racism, or our obsession with personal and national security.

Moreover, although Metz has not written extensively on the subject of compassion, his attention as a theologian and person of faith to the suffering of the world and the political and mystical features of his theology offer important channels that can move American Christians from a merely believed in and therefore "bourgeois" compassion toward an active and therefore political compassion. In fact, Metz calls compassion "political empathy" because compassion is the primary disposition of a God who is not concerned primarily with human sinfulness and redemption but rather with "unjust and innocent" human suffering and the justice it demands. In other words, we cannot engage in God-talk, one of Metz's pithy definitions of theology, without also examining the comprehensive justice of God and its ramifications for social living. We cannot be believers in the God of Jesus unless we practice the compassion of Jesus' God.

In his political theology we can find the resources to argue that compassion entails deeply mystical encounters with self, God, and others in the context of unjust suffering, as well as political commitments to take active responsibility for suffering persons by participating in God's ongoing just action in the world. Compassion, therefore, is a deeply personal experience of suffering with others in which we discover new things about our reality; it is never a private experience that keeps us at a safe distance from the front lines of justice.[10] With Metz's help, we can begin to understand compassion, or suffering with others, in innovative ways:

- as a public and political commitment rather than a private and personal conviction;
- as a dangerous participation in justice rather than a comfortable expression of charity;
- as an ongoing process of conversion rather than a series of unrelated acts of kindness; and
- as a transformative relationship between giver and receiver rather than an unreciprocated gift of self.

FACING THE SUFFERING PEOPLE

Metz's theology implicitly addresses the three signs of the times that first-world Christians must take seriously in our attempts to suffer effectively with others: (1) the prevalence of unjust suffering, (2) encounters with others in contexts of radical inequality, and (3) globalization. Certainly, like other theologians who came of theological age during Vatican II, Metz embraces the outward-gazing orientation encouraged by the council. However, Metz is concerned that first-world Christians are often inescapably self-referential and self-exonerating when we follow the imperative of *Gaudium et Spes* to "scrutinize the signs of the times and interpret them in light of the Gospel" (nos. 3, 4).[11] In other words, he worries that first-world Christians rarely see reality as it truly is. Rather, we tend to see reality as we would like to see it, and we see ourselves as we would like to be seen. He provocatively asks, "Do we believe in God? or do we believe in our beliefs in God and, in so doing, perhaps really believe only in ourselves or in what we would like to think about ourselves?"[12]

This myopia presents a significant obstacle for compassionate action in our contemporary global age. Contemporary technology bombards us with the signs of the times—practically as they occur. However, we can conveniently select which signs of the times we prefer to scrutinize. Moreover, we can do so without leaving the comfort zones of our homes, offices, schools, gyms, community libraries, faith communities, or lifestyle enclaves, and without any real relationship with the people we scrutinize. In our global age we have gradually become voyeurs of others' hardships, briefly captivated by the drama of their circumstances but rarely moved to enter into the chaos they experience.

This orientation to our social reality, made possible and sustained by privilege, perpetuates unilateral, paternalistic, and unreciprocated connectivity with others. As such, it offers little opportunity for critical self-reflection about our connections to others' suffering or our complicity in its unjust causes. We can easily remain unaffected by the gross inequities that separate those of us who are privileged enough to read in comfort about the times from those who desperately struggle to survive them. And we can remain comfortably unaware of the web of structural sin that simultaneously connects us and fuels the socioeconomic divisions among us.

Therefore, rather than passively, comfortably, and discriminatingly reading the signs of the times, Metz recommends that we actively, uncomfortably, and intentionally *face the suffering people* of the times. This orientation arises from his concerns about Christian complicity in the Holocaust, as well as from his personal commitment "not be talked out of" his own difficult experiences as a teenage soldier in the German army, so that we might courageously "bring them to the Church . . . in order to believe in God and talk about God. In fact, he claims that he tries to do his theology for and facing people like himself who "have always in some sense felt God's absence" or "who have no intact, undamaged images of home, or whose childhood dreams have fallen apart."[13]

In the case of Jewish-Christian ecumenism after Auschwitz, the context in which Metz first articulated this orientation, facing suffering people requires that we do not "offer" the victims an opportunity to dialogue but rather place ourselves at their disposal in order to listen to them. It requires that we resist the temptation to draw comparisons between our experiences so that theirs might thoroughly challenge any preconceived notions we might have. It expects that we refuse to explain our indifference to their suffering in order to interrogate ourselves about the triumphalism inherent in our faith, social status, and cultural privilege, or about our willingness to conform to rather than resist the status quo.

This orientation to the world can help us to remove the social blinders of privilege that keep us from seeing the suffering on the periphery of our circles of concern or trap us in ineffective cycles of charity. It serves as an antidote to bourgeois American Christianity and extracts a more authentic approach to compassion from those of us who have gradually become anesthetized to the radical suffering in our reality. It requires a disruptive "about face"—physically, cognitively, and spiritually—so that we might encounter and perhaps enter into relationship with those who suffer from the times we attempt to scrutinize. It interrupts the logic we use to make sense of our reality—a logic often influenced by values of individualism, free-market capitalism, and autonomous rationality—with new images, memories, and narratives that convey a different worldly wisdom in different ways.

An "about face" orientation to homelessness, for example, encourages us to face, meet eye to eye, converse with, and come to care about actual homeless persons and not just the abstract sociological problem of homelessness. In the context of disaster response, it entails making efforts to introduce ourselves to individuals, families, neighborhood associations, and faith communities in devastated areas and to work with them toward restoration rather than simply donating money to them online. In terms of the campaign against global poverty, it demands that we tune out the sound bites of policymakers and celebrities in order to listen carefully to the messages of the poor communicated in nontraditional media outlets and in unconventional ways.

Facing the signs of the times in this way helps us to resist the temptation to see ourselves as we would like to see ourselves in our social reality—as dutiful disciples, as communities committed to justice, or as compassionate in times of disaster. Rather, it requires that we meet the gaze of people who most likely see us quite differently than we see ourselves—as quiet hypocrites, as insatiable consumers, or as a cult of "do gooders." Metz insists that turning to face those who suffer allows us to see *ourselves* in their faces. This perspective has tremendous potential to interrupt our complacency, to disclose our self-deception, and to spark the sense of responsibility we have to others by virtue of our shared humanity. It assists us in developing a "moral awareness" of the ways in which we as individuals, as communities of faith, and as members of religious traditions and institutions have contributed to the history of domination of others as a result of a failure to remain critical of power.[14]

When we face suffering persons, we receive new insights about the three signs of the times that face first-world Christians who desire to respond to neighbors in need with authentic compassion.

The Face of Unjust Suffering

The socially critical edge of Metz's theology, which in turn imbues his approach to compassion with similar social criticism, arises from his deliberate commitment to face the people who lived and died at Auschwitz. Auschwitz shapes Metz's understanding of what it means to suffer and eventually opened his eyes to similar expressions of suffering in a variety of contexts around the globe. He associates suffering with the inability to establish relationships with self, others, and God. In other words, suffering includes all experiences of the inability to become a "human subject," a person capable of loving both self and others. This often happens as a result of threats to individual and collective identity, domination at the hands of others, or denial of the meaning-making activities of memory and narrative.

Moreover, the event of Auschwitz and the suffering inflicted and endured in that place and time is an "ultimatum" that centers Metz's God-talk and informs his self-understanding as a Christian.[15] It serves as his touchstone for authentic Christian theology, faith, and practice. He constantly returns to it; in fact, he chases after its evolving significance in Christian theology. To that end he calls his fundamental practical theology a theology "after Auschwitz." Said differently, and in the words of Rev. James Forbes, a senior minister emeritus of Riverside Church in New York City, Metz wants to ensure that "what matters to him, matters to God."[16] Metz is convinced that what matters to God is not human sinfulness but unjust human suffering. Therefore, his entire theological project has been one of directing himself and the Christian community away from obsession with personal salvation and redemption and back to serious concern with the kind of unjust suffering with which Yahweh and Christ concerned themselves.

Through this ongoing commitment to face suffering persons Metz has discovered that faith concerned only with doctrinal certitude, with surviving the challenges of modernism and rationlism, or with the salvation of individual believers quickly becomes spiritually, socially, and politically irrelevant. He found an antidote to this crisis of relevance by turning his face toward the Jews—both those who suffered at the hands of German Christians and those who waited on

God's justice in the biblical narratives. In them he discovered the political significance of a faith that actively hungers and thirsts for God's justice in the world and refuses to be pacified with or distracted by anything less. He identifies the Jews and the Jewish biblical tradition as the touchstone for authentic Christianity.

Metz contends that suffering persons are frequently in the optimal position to disclose the ways that privileged persons' uncritical participation in the systems and structures of globalization "contribute to the erosion of values in our society."[17] Moreover, they remind us that while "we may not immediately and directly agree on the positive meaning of freedom, peace, and justice, we all share a long-standing and common experience of what these things are *not*."[18] Often these negative experiences become the cornerstones of more constructive frameworks for human rights, national budgets, and peace treaties. Therefore, Metz attempts to protect the "authority of the experiences of suffering" as an invaluable source of social criticism. However, in order to tap this resource we must "begin really listening" to what these persons are saying about themselves and about us.[19]

Facing Others in Contexts of Radical Inequality

Metz's anthropology, with its emphasis on the human subject as an inherently relational being, reflects the importance of encounters and relationships with others as the most basic element of human happiness. He insists on replacing an anthropology of domination with "an anthropology guided by acknowledgment and acceptance."[20] In his estimation the process of becoming human subjects entails entering into and maintaining relationships with others and God despite social forces that oppose these life-giving relationships. It requires a commitment to "ruthlessly unmask the myths of self-exculpation and the mechanisms of trivialization" that we rely on in order to navigate the difficult encounters with those who suffer in this world.[21]

In addition, Metz's theological method necessarily involves encountering others in contexts of asymmetry, most frequently the kind of asymmetry that exists between those who do and those who do not suffer. He insists on acknowledging "the other as other, and endeavoring to uncover the traces of God in the experience of the other's alterity" or encountering the mystery of the other in their otherness.[22] In addition to a preferential option for the poor, we "must adopt the 'option for the other in their otherness.'"[23] He suggests that encounters with radically different others—particularly suffering others—spark mystical experiences that have the potential to interrupt privatized and comfortable experiences of faith and to sharpen our focus on the political warrants of the "kindom" of God in the current reality.

In our age of growing religious, political, and cultural pluralism, the decision to turn and face those who suffer leads Christian communities to recognize those who suffer injustice as an important source of moral authority that can guide us through the complexities of multiculturalism. "In my view," he says, "there is only one authority recognized by all great cultures and religious: the authority of those who suffer. Respecting the suffering of strangers is a precondition for every culture; articulating others' suffering is the presupposition of all claims to truth."[24] For example, they remind us that war and hunger negatively affect people in similar ways, regardless of geographical location or cultural identity, or that power and wealth often cloud the judgment of those in positions of political and social influence.

In addition, Metz suggests that encounters with suffering others invite us to participate in a self-emptying "suffering unto God." This mystical experience entails a desperate longing for God, an attempt to grapple with the meaning of God in the context of suffering, and an urgent demand that God enter into our experiences of suffering and take responsibility for it. Metz adamantly claims this approach is not synonymous with "suffering *in* God," which implies a passive acceptance of suffering or even a glorification of suffering. Rather, as a lament of resistance similar to Christ's cry of abandonment from the cross or the Israelite's grumblings in the desert, "suffering unto God" urgently demands God's presence in the midst of experiences of abandonment.[25] Wailing mothers, wives, daughters, and sisters in Baghdad, Camp Pendleton, Khartoum, San Salvador, or Karachi offer contemporary examples of this urgent demand for God's consoling presence.

When we encounter these persons we are exposed to their desire for God and discover that their passion for God fans the often dwindling flame of our own desire to participate in and with God in creating a more just reality. Encounters with suffering others, particularly with their memories and narratives, serve as a catalyst for the transformation of non-suffering persons from bourgeois to political understandings of self, world, and faith. Encounters with suffering others break open private, quiet, and self-referential understandings of our reality with a politically and mystically disruptive other-centered orientation. These political understandings—including political compassion—are colored by an openness to self-interrogation, a decision to "experience and define ourselves" with our faces turned toward other subjects, and a willingness for self-critique.[26]

Facing Others in the Context of Globalization

Metz implicitly acknowledges that the reality of globalization continues to shift his own gaze beyond Auschwitz to other genocidal contexts around the world. He notes that any attempt to articulate the Christian defense of hope that does not take "the global aspect into consideration will only be dubiously abstract."[27] Since he did much of his writing on this subject in the 1980s, Metz does not use the term *globalization;* however, his ideas about "hominization" and "polycentricism" reflect many aspects of globalization that we discussed in the first chapter. By *hominization* Metz refers to the shift from a cosmocentric to anthroprocentric world view, or what Charles Taylor refers to as the transition from an enchanted to disenchanted sensibility, in which human beings actively construct, harness, and control our environment and ourselves.[28] Metz uses polycentrism in his observation that "the Church is in the process of moving from being a culturally more or less uniform, that is, a culturally monocentric, European (and North American) church to becoming a world church with a diversity of cultural roots."[29] In addition, like the liberation theologians, he recognizes that "the Church no longer simply 'has' a Third World Church but 'is' a Third World Church."[30]

Metz espouses a mixed view of this phenomenon. As a theologian who came of age on the cusp of post-modernism, he optimistically approaches the relationship between Christianity and modernity, or between religious pluralism and secularism. In fact, he suggests that many features of our current reality "emerged not simply against, but precisely *through* Christianity"[31] as a result of Christian confidence in and celebration of the human person rooted in the doctrine of the incarnation, an anthropocentric gospel message, a belief in an immanent God at work in human history, and doctrines of human freedom. This lens highlights globalization's positive attributes: we more easily engage different people and cultures and recognize our mutual interdependence; we have opportunities to experience and define ourselves from their perspective; and we experience God's ongoing presence and revelation in human history in the religious praxis of different religious communities.

However, Metz also associates globalization with death for so many of the world's people who struggle to survive under the threat of increasing oppression, exploitation, racism, and Western inculturation. He holds Christianity particularly responsible for globalization's negative effects, given its tendencies toward "bourgeois (merely believed in rather than practiced) faith," as well as its capitulation to an anthropology of subjugation in which by subjugating we subjugate others, nature, knowledge. He contends that the drive to become human by dominating others contributes to "the massive helplessness and fear," the "apathy and resignation," and the "contagious fears of survival" that now dominate first-world consciousness.[32]

Metz claims that the reciprocal task of theology and discipleship, particularly in this age of globalization, "is to protect remembering and retelling [memories of suffering] from suspicion of reductionism and homogenization and to develop their communicative value, indeed superiority, for intercultural exchange."[33] Memories of suffering remind us of what we would like to forget: a history of domination of peoples in this country, support of despotic dictatorships in other nations, and the widows and orphans of our military invasions. In addition, these memories provide an indisputable authority to address global injustices.

Metz also argues for the importance of experiences of guilt in the project of humanizing globalization. He redefines guilt by emphasizing its connection to the social reality of human *suffering* rather than its longstanding association with individual *sinful acts*. "A religion originally sensitive to suffering became a religion emphatically sensitive to sin—indeed I might say hypersensitive to sin," says Metz of the Christian tradition today. "This has had serious consequences in our time. . . . A person's capacity for guilt, which in the biblical traditions is virtually *the* mark of human freedom, now has become the antipode to the concept of freedom."[34] He points to the memory of Christ, whose encounters with others focused not on their sins but on their sufferings at the hand of social, economic, and religious systems and whose basic moral imperative demanded that we love these persons as he did. "Go and do likewise," Christ tells us at the conclusion of the parable of the good Samaritan.

A liberating and productive guilt creates the possibility of moving beyond paralyzing obsession with private failings to a potentially galvanizing acknowledgment of collective responsibility. Liberating guilt interrupts our "exculpation mechanisms" that relegate those who suffer unjustly to a "faceless distance" and prevents the transformative move from self-criticism to social critique.[35] Moreover, productive guilt implies the capability to take responsibility for our connections to suffering. It serves as a necessary first step in "the concrete and fundamental revision of our consciousness" on which wider social transformation hinges.[36]

In the context of globalization a productive sense of guilt, one that does not paralyze us with self-absorbed negativity, helps us to perceive more accurately what is going on in the world. For example, it helps us acknowledge that the peoples of the Third World are not necessarily "un-developed" or "under-developed" but, rather, are victims of those in the developed world.[37] It helps us to acknowledge that the suffering of natural disasters has significant human causes. It liberates us to accept that most urban poverty is not the result of individual choices.

When we perceive our connections to suffering reality in this way, we shift the burden of responsibility for social change from the backs of those least capable of securing it and onto the shoulders of those who have the resources to create change but no will to do so. Responsibility lies with us, the victimizers of innocent people in war zones; with us, who augment natural disasters such as hurricanes or famines with levels of consumption that destroy the environment; with us, who segregate ourselves in communities of privilege that sustain neighborhoods of concentrated poverty; with us, who value private property to the extent that we privatize elements of the common good such as health care, energy, and prisons.

Concluding Remarks

Metz's commitment to face the suffering peoples of our times makes several contributions to the continued evolution of compassion in our global context:
- As compassionate persons we must turn and face those affected by our times with a willingness to perceive reality and ourselves more accurately from their perspective.
- If suffering involves the inability to enter into and sustain important relationships, then the goal of compassion ought to include resisting systems, institutions, and relationships of domination and non-identity. Compassion also seeks to restore relationships among distant and different peoples and within transnational institutions.
- Globalization challenges us, as compassionate people, to free ourselves for the experience of productive guilt that sparks social responsibility.

PERCEIVING REALITY: COMPASSION AS POLITICAL

Metz suggests that the "political" nature of his theology creates the "positive" or "constructive" aspect of his God-talk because "it aims at reassessing the relation between religion and society, between the Church and public society, between eschatological faith and social life."[38] J. Matthew Ashley contends that Metz's political theology, with its distinct emphasis on human "subjects" in the context of his discourse about God, attempts to explain the relevance of the gospel message in light of the historical reality of individuals, churches, and societies.[39] To do this, Metz engages the word of God either from the context of the human struggle for genuine relationality in the midst of dehumanizing domination and oppression, or with his face turned toward those engaged in the struggle against dehumanization and oppression. This gives his theology its second purpose, namely, a hermeneutics of belief after Auschwitz or the ongoing attempt to explain and then interpret the practical significance of belief in God in the midst of a long history of human suffering.[40] These goals render Metz's political theology simultaneously outwardly political in its turn toward a suffering reality, and inwardly mystical in its talk about God and self in light of that reality.

Two particular aspects of the political nature of Metz's theology, a theology that "no longer presents its explanations of the world and its interpretations of human existence in closed, asituational systems"—assist us in more accurately perceiving reality.[41] These components include Metz's understanding of what constitutes the "political" aspects of human existence and the role of historical consciousness in our perception of what's going on in our world. Both expand and deepen our perception of the social reality and shed light on our relationship to it. As such, they are critical to the evolution of compassion.

"The Political"

Metz's theology perceives the social reality—not metaphysical anthropology, the church, revelation, or even religious truths—as the location for encountering and understanding God, for engaging gospel imperatives, and for discerning what it means to be a disciple.[42] His political theology sets as its focal point the social, public, and political human subject, who is constituted by relationship with self, God, and others, and who participates in salvation history as it continues to unfold. John Downey puts it this way: "Metz uses the word 'political' to remind us to attend to concrete social circumstances. . . . Human life is value laden, and this theology simply asks what sort of person those deep values reflect and create."[43] According to Metz, "The *terminus a quo* of the Christian mission should be the secular society."[44]

Metz rightly reminds us of the Aristotelian use of the term *political* by suggesting that politics is best understood as a collective activity of human subjects who are engaged in the project of rightly ordering the social aspects of our lives or our life in common. He connects political activity to questions of human development and flourishing. This "political" focal point contributes to the evolution of compassion, because it helps us to perceive the political nature of persons as well as the constructive relationship between faith and politics.

Metz's notion of the political expands what has become a dangerously limited understanding of this idea in the American context. We tend to relegate everything related to the noun *politics* to notions of government, and the adjective *political* to activities related to elections, legislating, organizing, or protesting. Metz reminds us that *politics* is best understood as a verb—the process of collectively discerning, identifying, and supporting the values and practices that shape and sustain social life or life in community.

In addition, Metz unequivocally reasserts the political dimensions of revelation and subsequent imperatives for Christian discipleship and brings clarity to a contentious concept in theological circles. Little consensus exists among biblical scholars, systematic theologians, and ethicists as to whether God's action in human history reveals any conclusive divine interest in the "political" life of humanity, or whether the life and teachings of Christ can be understood as directing disciples how to organize or operate in the public square. However, Metz insists that "the scandal and promise of [Christ's] salvation are both equally public," since Christ insisted—to the point of execution—that salvation is not a private or an individual experience. Rather, Christ's salvation is "concerned with the world, not in the natural cosmological sense, but in the social and political sense. . . . The eschatological promises of the biblical tradition—freedom, peace, justice, reconciliation—cannot be reduced to a private matter. They constantly force themselves into a sense of social responsibility."[45]

Therefore, Metz's ideas transcend the increasingly polarized impasse between faith and politics in the American context. In the midst of this polarized atmosphere faith is often associated with a narrow understanding of "the political" and is often easily manipulated or politicized to serve the limited or narrow ends of a particular political group or ideology. This politicization further privatizes faith and dilutes its socially critical edge, fatally isolating the church in a ghetto or "micro-society" or an "ideological protective shell." However, when integrated with "the political" more broadly construed, faith becomes an avenue to explore the demands of social living, to articulate alternative values and visions, and to cultivate practices that contribute to a more just society. In his words, "[Christianity] should be the liberating and critical force of the one society."[46]

In short, "the political" aspect of Metz's theology provides an antidote for privatization and passivity, two morally numbing phenomena of American bourgeois Christianity. Political theology resists bourgeois self-referential perceptions of God and the social reality that pay little attention to unjust suffering, much less to the human complicity in its causes. Negatively or critically, this emphasis on "the political" resists any attempt to perceive theology as pertaining only to the private and personal sphere and rather inextricably connects religious belief to experiences of unjust suffering. For example, political theology expands the scope of Christian concern and witness beyond private and narrow concerns with personal salvation or intra-ecclesial obsessions with doctrinal orthodoxy. It even expands Christian ethical evaluation beyond issues that fall under the rubric of personal control.

With these ideas in mind, Christian faith entails the ability to perceive those who suffer unjustly in the world and to recognize more accurately our connections to their suffering, if only by means of our passive apathy. Therefore, the practical orientation of Metz's political theology encourages observers to engage in the social reality with a liberating freedom for self-critique (guilt) and social responsibility. Ashley sees this hermeneutical process as political—and dangerous—because the struggle for meaning Metz endorses ultimately implies the transformation of social relationships, social structures, and social development that currently control models and means of meaning.[47]

Historical Consciousness

This emphasis on "the political" necessitates historical consciousness as a crucial component of Metz's theological method. In other words, in his approach to God-talk he privileges the dynamic and unfolding aspects of the social reality and human nature over their static and immutable aspects, the particular insights of human experience over abstract claims to universal truths, the historically conditioned and contextual nature of knowledge over ahistorical and metaphysical epistemologies, and inductive reasoning over deductive reasoning. "The orientation toward the promise of peace and justice changes every time our historical presence changes," says Metz. As a result, "the parables of Jesus are parables of the Kingdom of God and *at the same time* parables that put us into a new critical relationship with the world that surrounds us."[48]

Like Marx, Metz asserts that history is the location of human self-realization and discovery as well as a medium of revelation and salvation. "In distinction to all the other great religions," explains Metz, "Christianity is guided by a vision of God and history or God in history." Historical consciousness reveals that human history, therefore, is also salvation history—an idea that later becomes the bedrock of liberation theology and protects against what Metz calls a Hellenistic-Greek tendency toward ahistorical dualism.[49] This understanding indivisibly integrates personal and social salvation by asserting that salvation is an ongoing historical process and not merely an individual one, or that our world is truly a "historical world, insofar as it is a world 'arising toward God's promises' made clear in biblical revelation."[50]

In addition, Metz recognizes the church as a historical institution, constituted in and by the social reality, not standing "by the side of" or "above it." Therefore, the church should be "an institution of social criticism" that seeks "the historical affirmation of salvation for all." It should defend individuals against social progress that dehumanizes them, guarding against political ideologies that place exclusive claims on truth, and practice a type of love that embodied an "unconditional commitment to justice, freedom, and peace *for others*."[51] To accomplish this, Metz believes the church will need to take seriously nontheological and experiential wisdom, speak in hypothetical and provisional ways, engage in practices of public criticism within the institution, cooperate with non-Christian institutions, and put forward a doctrine of social criticism.

These actions serve as important prerequisites for first-world Christians who attempt to take seriously Jesus' command to "go and do likewise." Furthermore, Metz's approach to historical consciousness reveals invaluable information regarding God, self, and others that can help first-world Christians to acknowledge our responsibility to all people as well as our complicity in others' suffering as we attempt to compassionately respond to them.

Perceptions of God

Metz proposes history, particularly the history of those who struggle against non-identity and domination in order to become subjects, as the ideal context for exploring God's ongoing relationship with humanity. For instance, through biblical history we come to understand *who* God is: one who faithfully seeks relationship with humanity, one who dramatically liberates individuals and communities from situations of dehumanization, one who doggedly maintains a special presence among those who suffer injustice.

We also come to know *where* God is: with those who suffer as well as with those who work with them to resist that suffering. We can see in biblical history examples of God's compassionate action in human history, action that resists systems of domination and empowers those who suffer. Moreover, the event of the incarnation—God's ultimate entrance into human history—imbues that history with a concrete, practical, and undeniable anthropocentric orientation rather than a metaphysical or cosmocentric focus.

In addition, Metz contends that the Christ of salvation history, the ultimate source of moral authority for today's disciples, integrated the salvation of individuals with social transformation. For example, in answering the popular question, What would Jesus do? Metz might hypothetically answer that Christ drew attention to the social causes of those who were suffering in his own historical reality: harmful beliefs and values about women or religious practices, and righteous living that denied some full participation in community or threatened their capacity for relationships. In remembering his relationships with those ostracized in society—lepers, tax collectors, divorced women, Samaritans—we are commanded to "go and do likewise" in the context of our reality by calling into question our erroneous attitudes and beliefs in order to spark the gradual process of personal and social change.

Perceptions of Others

Metz's understanding of human beings as historical subjects "in the world" underscores his claim that to be human is to be in relationship with self, God, and others. We are inextricably connected to others—directly and indirectly, consciously and unconsciously, living and dead—through the deep roots of our shared human history and the branches of our shared future. Honest intellectual, spiritual, and practical grappling with the gift and responsibility of this relationality lies at the heart of what it means to become a fully human person. The process of becoming more and more authentically human involves being able to perceive our relatedness to those of our past or present whom we do not know and yet whose flourishing is connected to our own. It entails being able to acknowledge our unavoidable entanglement in situations of injustice throughout human history. It requires the ability to break through our desire to dominate others or the natural world in order to "see and judge [ourselves] through the eyes of [our] victims."[52]

Perceiving others with historical consciousness also reveals that non-identity and domination are the most serious threats to human "subject-hood" because they threaten and destroy relationality and capacities for the making of meaning. Therefore, historical consciousness expands our understandings of what it means to suffer and integrates experiences of suffering into theories of theological anthropology that exclusively emphasize rationality, autonomous separateness, or even sociability. For example, we perceive attacks on human relationality as a common denominator of many social problems such as sweatshop labor, drug addiction, deportation of undocumented workers, urban youth violence, or sexual slavery. When we fail to consider this type of suffering in terms of what it actually does to people, we risk understanding others in merely abstract or metaphysical ways, and we risk missing the connections among those caught in webs of social sin. Metz notes with "a kind of objective cynicism, we speak frequently today of so-called underdeveloped people. When we look more closely, it is often a question of peoples whose cultures we have subjugated, devastated, and exploited."[53] If we miss the mark when it comes to perceiving suffering accurately then we will inevitably miss the mark in rectifying it.

Perceptions of Self
Historical consciousness reveals the connection of flourishing persons to the suffering of others by viewing all of human history from the perspective of those who suffer. This perspective bursts the bubble of bourgeois Christianity that enables us to examine issues at a safe distance, or to reassure ourselves constantly with a variety of myths that we construct about our social circumstances: that individual salvation in the next life is more important than transforming this one, that we are not really responsible to our suffering neighbors who find themselves dealing with the consequences of a series of bad personal choices, or that the United States is a land of freedom and equal opportunity. Metz would consider these the trappings of a "bourgeois religion" or "the kind of Christianity [that] does not live discipleship but only believes in discipleship, and, under the cover of merely believed-in discipleship, goes its own way." This believed-in discipleship gives rise to equally believed-in compassion that "cultivates an apathy that allowed us Christians to continue our untroubled believing and praying with our backs to Auschwitz."[54]

Historical consciousness of ourselves as people who individually and collectively perpetuate social injustices—whether intentionally or unknowingly—creates what Metz calls a "moral awareness of tradition" that uncovers the way in which privileged members of religious traditions have contributed to the history of domination of people.[55] For example, we might consider how ecclesial racism facilitated the cultural imperialism and genocides of the colonial era as well the church's current withdrawal from inner-city neighborhoods, or how attitudes regarding women's leadership roles in the church also silence their voices in other spheres of influence, or how the doctrinal adherence to magisterial teaching on contraception contributes to the pandemic of HIV/AIDS in the townships of Johannesburg.

Metz suggests that only by acknowledging the connection between our personal beliefs and values and the dehumanizing aspects of our culture will we be capable of the difficult task of self-criticism and social criticism. This self-reflection reveals our connections to others' suffering and as such frees us to take individual and collective responsibility for that suffering, if only through awareness of our connections to its causes. He calls this self-reflection or self-examen a "mysticism of open eyes." This wide-eyed perception "makes visible all invisible and inconvenient suffering, and—convenient or not—pays attention to it and takes responsibility for it."[56] It sparks a new moral imagination that can better resist suffering by replacing our drive to subjugate others with a desire for vulnerability. This vulnerability interrupts the domino effect of social sin because, in Metz's estimation, "only when people themselves remain capable of suffering do they refrain from forcing suffering arbitrarily upon others, and are able and ready in their own way to share in the sufferings of others and become active in the liberation struggles of the tortured and exploited."[57]

A compassion that perceives reality with this "mysticism of open eyes" resists an inherent tendency to distance ourselves from the causes of another's suffering, to see history and ourselves as we would prefer, and to fall back on responses to that suffering that fail to address effectively its causes. In other words, compassion involves more than serving food at a local soup kitchen; we must also question the relationship between our overabundance of food and its scarcity for others. Compassion entails more than evaluating the seriousness of injustices caused by natural disasters; it demands that we situate such events in the long history of the humanly caused social disaster of concentrated poverty. This self-critical mysticism of open eyes, and the new understandings of self it generates, can liberate non-suffering subjects from our prevailing values, beliefs, and logic that deny all people—even us—our full humanity.

In addition, this historically conscious perspective redirects history's "winners" in our process of becoming human subjects or what Metz calls the struggle within ourselves to resist our anthropological need to dominate others. Historical consciousness therefore becomes an essential ingredient for human autonomy through its connections to liberating guilt and responsibility. In other words, to be truly free and capable of relationships, we need to be able to accept our culpability in situations of suffering rather than shy away from or isolate ourselves from this uncomfortable realization. This also is true for institutions such as the church, which frequently fail to consider critically their impact upon the lives of suffering people. Historical consciousness enables collectives and institutions to perceive themselves and their engagement in the world through the eyes of those they directly and indirectly victimize. This perspective clearly reveals unjust practices as well as means of rectifying them.

Concluding Remarks

Several of Metz's ideas concerning "the political" and historical consciousness have implications for the much-needed evolution of compassion in our global age. By expanding the scope of Christian concern to include the current political reality, Metz also expands compassion beyond concern with individual situations of suffering and beyond individual responses to it rooted in private, interpersonal exchanges. This expansion brings the following features to our understanding of compassion:

- Compassionate people recognize that all suffering is socially constituted and that we must respond to social conditions as well as to the suffering persons; this is a political process rather than a private one.
- Compassionate people ask questions—such as, What's going on?—that reveal the historical conditions of suffering and enable us to understand the causes of suffering and respond with political justice rather than individualized and private charity.
- Compassion entails a willingness to view history and ourselves from the perspective of those who suffer and with a "mysticism of open eyes" that sees more accurately our connections to others' afflictions.
- Compassion is a necessary component of first-world Christians' struggle against our culturally constructed and sustained desire to dominate others. It is just as important for our own liberation as it is for the liberation of our neighbors.

INTERPRETING REALITY: COMPASSION AS MYSTICAL

Mysticism, quite simply, involves "consciousness of the experience of uncreated grace and self-communication of the triune God"[58] or "processes resulting from that experience of God"[59] that influence the way we think about, converse with and participate in the divine. In many ways Metz's mysticism is rather traditional and reflects the sensibilities of those throughout history who have expressed a deep longing for communion with God. For example, James Matthew Ashley notes that, much like Rahner in his fundamental theology, Metz insists on integrating spirituality and theology in the "mystical biography of the ordinary, average person."[60]

However, the distinctive qualities of Metz's biography—his experiences as a conscripted teenage soldier in the German army and his "after Auschwitz" restlessness in the theological academy—make his mysticism particularly helpful for cultivating a spirituality that can nourish the kind of compassion we need in our age of globalization. For example, Ashley notes that where Rahner defines human experiences of God through the symbol of the ever-present but always-beyond-reach infinite horizon, Metz encounters God within the finite confines of human experiences of suffering. This spirituality descends into the dark depths of human experience where we often feel most isolated from God; this contrasts with a spirituality that ascends to the glorious peaks where union with God is practically palpable. It draws believers to the very limits of our ability and willingness to believe because it inevitably raises questions that we rarely dare to ask for fear of the answers we might receive: What kind of God allows this suffering to happen? Who is this God that fails to intervene on the behalf of the afflicted? How can I continue to believe in such a God as this? "What is really at stake," Metz explains, "is the question of how one is to speak about God at all in the face of the abysmal histories of suffering in the world, in 'his' world."[61]

Ashley notes that Metz resonates with elements of "apocalyptic spirituality" within the Christian tradition, epitomized in the interrogation, protests, and laments of the biblical Job or the Christ of the cross. Mystical experiences of God that ask God difficult questions about God's relationship to situations and experiences of human suffering courageously encourage us to resist actively rather than to accept passively unjust suffering. Through them we challenge critically rather than accept blindly God's will, or cultivate lived commitments rather than articulate verbal convictions of faith.

By refusing to shy away from difficult questions about God's responsibility for unjust suffering, Metz reinforces the practical and political significance of belief in God in our increasingly secular age where conditions of massive unjust suffering challenge the reasonableness of such belief. This "mystical" component of his theology, therefore, resists privatization and passivity by cultivating a socially critical and edgy Christian spirituality. This edginess arises from the close attention Metz pays, both intellectually and emotionally, to God's relationship to human suffering. This persistent questioning also interrupts traditional ways of understanding *human* responsibility for suffering.

The source of Metz's mysticism lies with a willingness to ask these questions—which always have the potential to undermine rather than reinforce faith. His spirituality provides the method for a socially critical approach to compassion that refuses to disavow God's role in human suffering, and that replaces the modern and post-modern dismissals of God's relevance with an insatiable desire for God and an equally urgent desire to participate God's justice. The question, therefore, is not, What does our history of suffering say about *God*? but rather, What does this history say about *us*? Metz's mysticism assists non-suffering persons in more accurately understanding or interpreting ourselves, God, and the world in the context of unjust suffering. Two salient features of his mysticism facilitate these interruptive interpretations and provide the methodological tools for a more evolved approach to compassion in our global age.

Theodicy

The "theodicy question"—the question of God's connection to human suffering—resists bourgeois Christianity and bourgeois compassion because it places the issue of responsibility for suffering at the forefront of Christian consciousness. More specifically, theodicy interrupts prevailing ideas regarding who God is and who we are in light of suffering. Theodicy is an interruption that cultivates aspects of Metz's political theology that are essential for his notion of compassion as "political empathy," including historical consciousness, vulnerability and relationality, anthropodicy, and freedom for guilt.

Theodicy emerged as Metz became increasingly irritated by Christian complicity in the Holocaust. He concurs with Holocaust survivor Elie Wiesel's observation that "the thoughtful Christian knows that it was not the Jewish people that died in Auschwitz, but rather Christianity."[62] The cause of that death can be traced to a failure to understand Christianity not necessarily as a discourse about God but rather as a conversation *with* God, and in particular with a God who appears to be absent from a human history of suffering. Metz suggests that this kind of relational discourse "always examines and *calls into question* our preconceived notions about life and existence, our interests, our memories, our experiences."[63] The conversation begins with basic questions such as, Who is God? But given the predominance of suffering in human history, it quickly moves to the more demanding and challenging question, *Where* is God?

In asking "Where is God" in situations of suffering, as opposed to who God is in light of them, we are more likely to discover that God is in fact not detached, distant from or unaffected by human suffering. Rather, God is present with human subjects in that suffering. God suffers with those who suffer unjustly and resists their suffering through acts of justice. "God is not merely an inescapable mystery beyond the horizons of thought," Metz explains. "God is the liberator of history, choosing to be on the side of the oppressed, on the side of those who suffer history."[64] Mysticism, therefore, involves discovering God's vulnerable presence among the suffering in human history.

Moreover, God is not only present in unjust suffering, but God also condemns it. This is evident in the context of God's compassionate interventions into human history on behalf of the oppressed. Consider Yahweh, who hears the cries of the Israelites in Egypt and liberates them from slavery, or Christ's encounters with the hemorrhaging woman, or the blind man, or the lepers that result in life-giving miracles of healing. These interventions are necessarily political since they restore persons and communities to full relationship with self, God, and others.

If in this conversation we discover where God is and how God responds to suffering, an even more pressing question remains. "Where was *God* in Auschwitz?" evolves into "Where was *humanity* in Auschwitz?"[65] The latter question—the anthropodicy question—ultimately defines Metz's theology and underscores its political-ethical significance. The anthropodicy question creates an invaluable opportunity for interruptive self-reflection and criticism in light of the suffering of others. In other words, the disruption of the anthropodicy question encourages responsible Christian *engagement in* the complexities of the social reality rather than an apathetic or guilt-ridden *withdrawal from it.*

In fact, the anthropodicy question makes important contributions to our understanding of responsibility and guilt. Its self-reflective pause can spark a productive sense of guilt that actively takes responsibility for the causes of suffering rather than egotistically obsessing about individual sinfulness. In the context of our conversation with God, productive guilt enables us not merely to ask *God* to do something about injustice—which ultimately exonerates us from social responsibility—but also to demand that God enable *us* to address injustice ourselves. This type of conversation or prayer keeps us from "giving in to the web of excuses we weave around ourselves" and stirs up our emotions so that we can "react against" the aspects of our lives that keep us from perceiving how our actions affect others, or from perceiving others on the periphery of our social concern, or from perceiving the narrative of Christ in those who suffer around us.[66]

Passion for God

Conversation with God that arises from concern with evil creates a "passion for God" or a deep desire to experience God's presence in the process of resisting injustice. Metz suggests that this passion creates and protects the most fundamental way of being human. And it redirects our attention to the central biblical question "about justice for innocent sufferers," which we have erroneously contorted into a preoccupation with "redemption for the guilty."[67] As such, it is important for both suffering and non-suffering persons.

For those who experience dehumanizing suffering, passion for God galvanizes prophetic resistance to injustice. Passion for God resists any attempts at easy consolation, empty solutions, or false platitudes that try to smooth over the disruptiveness of suffering and that keep us from asking the interruptive questions of theodicy and anthropodicy. This refusal to be placated by anything less than God's presence gives suffering persons a unique capacity for God. Consider, for example, the Israelites' constant grumbling in the desert—they refused to be satisfied with anything less than what was promised to them by Yahweh in the covenant and demanded that Yahweh keep the divine end of the bargain. Or consider Martha and Mary, who refuse to accept that Jesus will not come to heal their brother, Lazarus, and steadfastly await his healing presence even after Lazarus has been buried. These faithful persons reflect a passion for God in the midst of their suffering, a passion that trusts in God's dramatic work on their behalf in order to break through systems of oppression or experiences of isolating suffering. To that extent they became a people of memory—memory of God's promises of justice in the covenant—and a people of expectation who long for God to be present with them in the context of their suffering, whether in Egypt, the desert, Auschwitz, or New Orleans.

The capacity for this kind of passion for God is also central for the liberation of non-suffering persons. This desire for complete dependency on God allows us to move beyond a believed-in faith in ourselves or in the finite things that we make ultimate—possessions, health, or security, for example—toward a radically active faith in the God of suffering. Passion for God breaks through the myopia of first-world bourgeois Christianity by encouraging a hunger for something that promises the type of fulfillment that we erroneously seek in so many other places and things. Recall that in the Sermon on the Mount Jesus reminded the wealthy among his table fellowship to respond to God's love for them with justice, that is, a deep commitment to upholding all persons' abilities for full relationship with God, self, and others. This commitment brings deep contentment: "Blessed are they who hunger and thirst for righteousness. For they shall be filled" (Mt 5:6).

Passion for God has the power to challenge the various "isms," such as materialism, consumerism, or moral therapeutic deism, that promise a false contentment and, in so doing, perpetuate anxious unfulfillment. Passion for God reminds us that when we desire God's justice we experience a purposeful contentment that liberates us for a more authentic relationship with God, self, and others. This passion for God, while certainly individualized in its focus on personal discourse with God, is never individual or private. Passion for God does not focus on individual salvation but on the full flourishing of all. It is a political passion.

Mystical passion for God is essential for all persons—suffering and non-suffering—to become fully human persons. Metz claims that "only through poverty of spirit do we draw near to God; only through it does God draw near to us."[68] To that end, a praxis of suffering unto God and a poverty of spirit refuse to be satisfied with development strategies or planning that seek to manage or ameliorate social suffering rather than eradicate it. Rather, it demands an approach to social justice that restores the relationality all of persons.

Concluding Remarks

The components of Metz's mysticism work in concert to resist the privatization of Christian faith and to maintain a socially critical awareness when it comes to understanding God, ourselves, and the social reality in light of unjust suffering. Metz's mysticism instills a "character of corrective" within Christian theology and compassion.[69] This interruptive and uncomfortable mysticism replaces privatized and individualized piety—the latter creates an equally privatized and individualized compassion—with a spirituality of questioning, protesting, and lamenting. This "character of corrective" nourishes new expressions of compassion that interrupt privatized experiences of faith and responses to unjust suffering:

- Compassionate people are engaged in a conversation with God concerning the causes of suffering and our connection to them; we remember, imagine, and imitate God's presence with suffering people throughout history.
- Compassionate people ask the most central question of Christian discipleship—not who or where God is in times of acute suffering or injustice, but rather, who and where *we* are during these times.
- Compassionate people overcome the paralyzing notions of guilt and a self-help approach to Christianity with a liberating freedom for social responsibility that takes seriously our contributions to the social conditions of sin.
- Compassionate persons seek a humble poverty of spirit and an urgent desire for God that arise from a historically conscious awareness of our connection to the causes of unjust suffering.
- Compassion is a prerequisite for first-world people who wish to become more fully human subjects.

TRANSFORMING REALITY:
AN ANTHROPOLOGY OF THE POLITICAL SUBJECT

Metz suggests that theology can be defined in one word, namely, interruption. This stems from an attuned ability to perceive and interpret the social reality, particularly a reality of suffering, in a way that interrupts the day-to-day beliefs and actions of flourishing, first-world Christians with the demands of those who stand on the brink of a premature and apocalyptic death. Informed by their perspectives and critical interpretations of us and the social reality, our central task as people of faith is not to interpret the social reality but rather to transform it. Therefore, Christian disciples are commanded to interrupt things as they are and transform them in light of a vision of what might be: "The Christian is a 'co-worker' in bringing the promised universal era of peace and justice," Metz argues. "The orthodoxy of a Christian's faith must constantly *make itself* true in the 'orthopraxy' of his actions, actions oriented toward the final future, because the promised truth is a *truth* which must be *made*."[70]

The transformation of the world begins, in Metz's opinion, with the transformation of individuals—both those who thrive and those who struggle to survive—into fully human *Subjekts*, a German word that has no real equivalent in English. Metz attempts to explain his idea by suggesting that it is "not equivalent to 'person' or 'individual'" but rather "connotes the person insofar as it is individualized by means of social and historical intersubjectivity," which in turn implies "constitutional and chronic vulnerability." In other words, "experiences of solidarity with, antagonism toward, liberation from, and anxiety about other subjects form an essential part of the constitution of the religious subject."[71]

The absence of dehumanizing suffering does not necessarily guarantee that individuals are fully human subjects. For those of us who are not consumed with the struggle for survival, Metz claims the process of becoming a human person is somewhat different but no less urgent. It includes mystical experiences of conversion through transformative encounters with those who suffer as well as attention to memories of suffering. It entails liberating ourselves from false ideologies and perceptions so that we can share the narrative of others' suffering in the public sphere. Becoming human subjects demands that we take responsibility for our contributions to the suffering reality through active solidarity with those who suffer. To that extent, justice entails evaluating what it means to be a human person, what it means to flourish, and what it means to develop as a community from the perspective of those who suffer.

That perspective levels a provocative and uncomfortable criticism at those of us who traditionally have set the standards for flourishing or dictated the frameworks for justice. The struggle for meaning in light of these criticisms is synonymous with our struggle to become fully human. In other words, the transformation of the social reality is dependent upon the ability of those who already flourish to become fully human.

Three distinct components of Metz's anthropology—memory, narrative, and solidarity—highlight relational mutuality as the feature of human "subject-hood."

They form the basis for his understanding of compassion as a first-world response to a social reality defined by suffering and provide provocative approaches to justice and human development. These facets of the human subject also serve as an important bridge between his theology and his more recent writings on compassion in light of his claim that all effective revolutions begin with a change of heart.

Memory and Transformation

Metz's conceptual category of memory serves as the hub of his anthropology. His distinctive ideas of persons and faith radiate from his approach to memory. He notes that "Christian faith can be understood as that stance in which a person remembers the promises of the past and the hopes out of which people lived because of those promises, and binds herself or himself to these memories in a life-determining way."[72] To that end, faith is not primarily concerned with catechisms or with moral guidelines. Rather, discipleship entails the active process of remembering or actually "remembrancing" the life of Christ and his promise of the "kin-dom" of God.

Memory is a particular act or expression of human freedom that affirms identity and makes sense out of our historical reality. For example, enslavement, colonization, and totalitarianism all share a similar end goal: they deny individual dignity and collective identity by denying memories and the right to remember. The ability to remember, to bring events of the past into focus in the present, is indeed interpretive and, as such, integral to the ongoing process of becoming human. Remembering memories of suffering is humanity's only means of resisting the technical, scientific, and seemingly subject-less process of human progress. To that end, memory becomes a source of freedom when it enables us to perceive ourselves, our relationships with others, and our historical realities from a distinctive perspective, a perspective that calls into question technical reason, the dictates of social progress, and the forces of the market.

Metz argues that this kind of remembering "lifts up the insights garnered from past experience and in this way destabilizes all those things that are taken for granted in the present."[73] In many ways, memory becomes the great equalizer, expanding our acknowledgment of those beyond Western or European circles to include all persons who are subjects of history.

In addition, Metz envisions the freedom of memory precisely as a "socially emancipatory action" through the freedom for social criticism.[74] This is the case when memories of suffering or *memorias passionis* are integrated with the "already but not yet" eschatological proviso of Christianity. In other words, these memories of the past make the vision of the future a more pressing reality in the present. Using the central rhetorical strategy in his famous "I Have a Dream" speech, Martin Luther King, Jr., does as much when he causes the black community's memories of the past to point more clearly and prophetically toward an urgent vision or dream of the future. Metz suggests that a dangerous memory "harries the past and problematizes since it remembers the past in terms of a future that is still outstanding."[75] It is precisely this dialectic of the "future of the memory of suffering" that allows memory to become the link between history and reason. It retells history from the perspective of its victims, so they might become the subjects of history, authorities empowered to build a universal justice for the future.

Finally, the anthropological category of memory provides Metz's theology with an innovative approach to reason. Reason rooted in memory becomes the defense against what he calls the culture of amnesia that pervades our modern consciousness. In other words, reason informed by memory and not merely logic challenges strictly abstract, rational, or cognitive thinking by relying on emotions, imagination, and human relationships to make sense of reality and to guide our moral choices. Anamnestic reason recalls the dangerous memory of Christ, as well as those who have suffered throughout human history, in order to challenge mythical and uncritically optimistic notions of human progress.

Given its connection to what Metz calls "remembrancing,"anamnestic reason is a political and communal activity. Rooted in the liturgical "do this in memory of me," remembrancing protects the prophetic wisdom of memories of suffering and allows them to interrupt ideologies, social values, and strategies of human progress or development that do not turn and face those who suffer unjustly so that *all* might become more fully human.[76] In addition, those memories stimulate our imagination for social and political action that creatively resists the processes of domination and non-identity. We remember that Jesus liberated people by liberating their imaginations with stories, parables, and images of a different way of being. To "go and do likewise" demands a similar approach to moral reasoning and Christian living.

Narrative and Transformation

Narrative reminds the community of faith of those forgotten memories as well as of our underutilized capacities for emotion and imagination. Even in the midst of the post-modern suspicion of meta-narratives, stories can be more than "artificial, private constructions." They serve, rather, as "narratives with a stimulating effect aimed at social criticism." In addition narrative becomes an important means of communicating the wisdom of lived experience in the contexts of relational encounters. For example, Metz argues for a strong connection between biography and dogmatic theology in order to protect theology from becoming "a natural science of the divine," which in its own way denies the subjecthood of disciples.[77] Several elements of Metz's narrative anthropology cultivate a compassion that seeks after social transformation.

For instance, the ability to tell stories, to translate one's memories into narrative, is a distinctive human capability that reinforces *the process of becoming subjects* both for those whose identity is threatened by unjust suffering and those who do not suffer. For the former, narrative involves the active process of articulating their self-understanding and memories "against time" or in the face of a culture of amnesia and evolutionary progress. Doing so resists the domination that causes suffering. For example, the success of truth and reconciliation commissions in places such as South Africa, Rwanda, and even the Gulf Coast of the

United States point to the importance of storytelling for restoring individuals and societies.

For those whose identity is not threatened by the prospect of unjust suffering, narrative entails rewriting human history to include the forgotten memories of the dead and defeated. This gives storytelling its practical and critical edge, largely because it lifts up details often overlooked by those privileged enough to record history's disasters rather than to experience them. This too is a dangerous act of resistance that calls the comfortable status quo into question. For example, the Christian narrative of Christ's life is not intended primarily to build up or reinforce a sense of group identity as much as to challenge false identities or exclusive associations that have failed to acknowledge the "subject-hood" of all persons.

For instance, when he entered into relationships with others, Jesus focused upon their suffering rather than their sinfulness. Christ dangerously criticized social, political, and religious attitudes and structures that either denied relationality among persons or refused to uphold the dignity of the least well off among us. In fact, this is the moral lesson of the parable of the good Samaritan. Narrative, therefore, becomes a means of interrupting bourgeois Christianity, particularly when it is expressed as a life-affirming sacramental quality that joins the stories of suffering subjects to the defining narrative of the Christian community, namely, the narrative of Christ.

In addition, narrative saves history and the future from declining into an empty historicism that does not have human subjects at it center. In other words, narrative reminds us that the abolition movement was not about ending slavery as much as about liberating the enslaved, that the civil rights movement was not about rejecting Jim Crow as much as about supporting the full equality of persons, that health care reform is not about expanding access to a system as much as about caring for the uninsured, that immigration policy is not about economic theory or national security as much as about the dignity of people from neighboring nations. Narrative protects the activity of meaning-making in human existence. More specifically, it lifts up stories of human history that we have long forgotten, stories that capture the listeners' imagination and compel them to engage the world from the perspective of the suffering subject of the narrative.

Narrative, therefore, is related to Metz's mysticism of open eyes that allows the memories of suffering to critique the social reality. The narrative of Christ in the New Testament transforms listeners by calling them to encounter the marginalized of history with an ear for their condemnation of the systems and social attitudes that silence them and prevent them from becoming subjects. This capability to hear other narratives of unjust suffering within the narrative of Christ enables listeners to respond more fully to Jesus' invitation to do as he did and to resist dehumanizing structures and attitudes. "These discipleship stories are in themselves appellative and imperative. They try in the very telling to transform the subject who is hearing them and to dispose him or her for discipleship."[78]

The dangerous narrative of Christ's life is pivotal for informing and transforming the collective identity and engagement of the Christian community.

These components of the Christian narrative provide the basis for a more public and political understanding of compassion. Narrative transforms the listener from merely a *hearer* of the word to a *doer* of the word, from passive reception to active engagement.[79] As communicable and sharable, narratives become creative discourse about "what we hold to be true about the human person and what we hope for."[80] In other words, narrative engenders social transformation.

Finally, narrative preserves the prophetic content of memories of suffering. In fact, narrative is the "original form" of theological reasoning. The Christian community is not primarily a "reasoning community but a storytelling community."[81] Narrative resonates with the wisdom of lived experience and embodiment frequently ignored in strictly logical or rational approaches to reason. At the same time, narrative pushes theologians and philosophers to acknowledge the importance of storytelling and to cultivate stories of incommensurable suffering as modes of reasoning and rational thinking. Narratives of suffering remind us of the incommensurability of experiences of suffering, the inability for many to make meaning of their lives within traditional frameworks or paradigms, and the ineffectiveness of logic and reason alone as constructs for meaning. "These stories break through the spell of a total reconstruction of history by abstract-instrumental reason. . . . They show that human consciousness is a 'consciousness involved in stories.'"[82] To that extent, narrative is a necessary means for integrating the concepts of history and salvation and for transforming history from a subject-less, Godless construct to a subject-based salvation history that reveals God's ongoing saving action.

Solidarity and Transformation

Metz integrates solidarity with memory and narrative in order to create a distinctively relational posture toward suffering subjects in the social reality. Solidarity is "a category of assistance, of supporting and encouraging the subject in the face of that which threatens him or her most acutely and in the face of his or her suffering."[83] As noted in the first chapter, various notions of solidarity pervade Catholic social ethics: from the liberation theologians who insist that solidarity is a physical and emotional alignment with the poor to John Paul II's sense of solidarity as a firm and preserving commitment to the good of all for all. Metz agrees with these definitions but also offers three distinct elements given his audience of first-world Christians and that audience's connections to the suffering in the world

For example, solidarity is not a bond forged among like-minded persons, or even persons who share similar social historical circumstances. Rather, it is a human response to those whose existence is "threatened" by unjust suffering that attempts to create relationships among otherwise disparate persons. Therefore, relationships that are ahistorical, apolitical, disembodied, or based on reciprocal exchange among equal and sympathetic partners do not fall under the umbrella of solidarity. Even though they may attempt to respond to injustice, these relationships do not meet the requirements of the solidarity litmus test because they are not critically engaged in the social reality, because they fail to listen to the memories of narratives of distant others, and because they fail to encourage a self-critical reflection on our connection to others' suffering. Ultimately, these kinds of relationships might be more concerned with mutual protectionism or the advantage of the reciprocal parties.

True solidarity, on the other hand, involves freely entering into relationships with subjects whose very humanity is on the brink of destruction and doing so in a way that empowers them and liberates us. In fact, Metz's approach to solidarity challenges models of equal exchange or alliances between equal partners by suggesting that "something might be lost" in authentic relationships of solidarity, namely, our dependency on the various "isms" that dominate us. In addition, solidarity is uniquely comprehensive. If solidarity is directed toward those who suffer, then it cannot be reserved only for the living but most also be shared with the dead who have been left behind in the march of progress. Their memories offer a dangerous critique of the cadence and direction of progress.

Moreover, solidarity involves the individual and communal imitation of Christ, whose death was political. Doing as Christ did involves the danger of raising up threatened people. As a political praxis, solidarity ensures the ability of each human person to become a subject in the context of communion with others. It means resisting the sources of injustice that threaten people's ability to be the focal point of their own histories or to explore their self-understandings through relationships with others.

Precisely because solidarity entails a special relationships with those who suffer—those subjects who are threatened by oppression and injustice—Metz claims that it includes a "pathic" praxis that features emotive responses to suffering. Solidarity is emotively practiced in mourning and lament as well as in gratitude and joy. It is an essential category of our understanding of non-suffering persons. It is the means by which we ensure that all persons can be subjects in a human history defined by subjects.

Concluding Remarks

Metz's theological anthropology, with its three components of memory, narrative, and solidarity, constructs a viable framework for social transformation since each component is a necessary, life-sustaining capability and a community-building capability of human persons. Together, they point to a dynamic approach to becoming human that is particularly valuable for first-world Christians whose capabilities for memory, narrative, and solidarity are increasingly threatened in our global age. Metz reminds us that the process of becoming human involves a struggle against ourselves, an ongoing commitment to becoming poor in spirit so that we might more accurately perceive the world around us, and a willingness to be in solidarity with those who suffer.

- Compassion is an active expression of the kind of relationality that makes us all fully human subjects, as well as an expression of social criticism that lifts up dangerous memories and narratives of suffering to direct strategies for human development.

- Compassion employs anamnestic reason to complement, or even interrupt, prevailing models of logic that perpetuate anthropologies of domination and cycles of dehumanizing oppression. It places the authority of those who suffer in direct conversation with God and discussions about justice.
- Compassion can be understood as an ongoing process of readjusting our understandings of self, others, and the world in order to make more accurate judgments about others' suffering.

POLITICAL COMPASSION
AS A FIRST-WORLD INTERRUPTION

"[Christianity] is mystical and political at the same time," Metz contends, "and it leads us into a responsibility, not only for what we fail to do but also for what we allow to happen to others in our presence, before our eyes."[84] If nothing else, Metz's political theology demands that we stop intellectualizing about social injustice and turn to face the people who suffer. The political and mystical experiences that might arise with our faces turned in this direction interrupt a variety of first-world tendencies that limit our compassion. For example, they interrupt our tendency to privatize our personal relationship with God and expressions of love of neighbor; to focus our moral sensibilities on human sinfulness rather than on human suffering; to relegate events such as Auschwitz to the past and fail to see them reincarnated in so many contemporary human catastrophes; to make God the scapegoat for these disasters rather than to take responsibility for our own culpability; to forget the historical conditions of suffering in which we are deeply embedded.

This interruption brings much needed critical and constructive elements to Christian compassion. For example, Metz's political compassion gives Christian ethics a two-pronged approach. We cannot simply ask suffering persons what they are able to do or to become. We must also ask those who do not suffer how we are to become more fully human so that the suffering other might also become more fully human. It is not enough simply to evaluate what people are able to become without asking ourselves how we keep them from doing so through our lifestyles. Compassion is a difficult, disruptive, and uncomfortable process that sharpens first-world understandings of anthropology, suffering, and even flourishing. It allows us to see ourselves from the perspective of the victims of social injustice. This sheds an unflattering light on our need to dominate others and our collusion in the structural causes of unjust suffering.

And yet, with Metz's political theology, compassion is also innovatively constructive. For example, with our faces turned toward people who suffer, we experience a liberating freedom from guilt and a hope-filled resistance. We incorporate anamnestic reason into our deliberations about justice and human development, an intuitive and imaginative approach to reason that unleashes new creative possibilities for building a more just world. We become more fully human ourselves by creating relationships of solidarity that cooperate with suffering people in order to resist the sources of social injustice.

Metz's understanding of compassion as "political empathy" offers three general contributions to the Christian tradition and our attempts to evoke innovative ways of suffering with others:

1. Compassion is a mystical experience that involves a self-critical conversion necessary for first-world persons to become subjects;

2. Compassion moves beyond contractual, reciprocal exchanges among private individuals to more collective and historically conscious relationships with particular suffering persons; and

3. Compassion is best understood as a mystical-political interruption of self- and world-understandings that is dangerous in terms of the social upheaval it demands and promises.

6

Christian Ethics after Katrina

Political Compassion in Social Disasters

On 29 August 2005, Hurricane Katrina, which had been building strength for weeks in the Atlantic Ocean and Gulf of Mexico, made landfall along the Gulf Coasts of Alabama, Louisiana, and Mississippi. Meteorologists called it a "perfect storm." Once there, it collided with another "perfect storm" that had been brewing for at least three decades in most communities of this region, perhaps even since the colonial settlement of the Gulf Coast. Sociologists called this equally life-threatening storm "concentrated poverty," and its conditions in many Gulf Coast neighborhoods included hyper-segregation, high unemployment, low high-school graduation rates, and income levels well below the national poverty line of $19,000 for a family of four.

When the deadly meteorological conditions in the sea and sky mixed with the dire socioeconomic conditions in these parishes and wards, Hurricane Katrina became more than one of the most devastating natural disasters in American history. The storm was, and continues to be—as the inexcusably slow recovery process attests—a catastrophic *"social* disaster" or "a disaster predicated upon and exacerbated by structural inequality and human decision-making."[1] Even more than four years later, with thousands of Katrina's diaspora still spread throughout the community and many who have returned struggling to survive amid a crippled physical and social infrastructure, American citizens have yet to respond effectively to the suffering it caused.

As a social disaster, the human event of Hurricane Katrina offers a provocative lens through which we can view any number of social ills that have reached pandemic proportions in this country and that contribute to unjust suffering: racism, classism, ageism, sexism, social welfarism, Nimby(not in my back yard)-ism, suburbanization, and environmental degradation. Moreover, Katrina prophetically exposes the all-too-familiar values that we celebrate as constitutive of our American identity, values with connections to these entrenched social problems that we simultaneously ignore: individualism, autonomous self-sufficiency, consumerism, materialism, productivity, and the privilege of whiteness. Many scholars have already begun to examine the intersection of these values with the causes, impacts, and possible solutions to the human disaster of Katrina.[2] However, only a small portion of this scholarship examines this social disaster from a theological perspective or with attention to its implications for faith traditions

148

and communities that place love of the suffering neighbor at the center of their identities.[3]

Johann Baptist Metz would have a problem with this lacuna. "Ask yourselves if the theology you are learning is such that it could remain unchanged before and after Auschwitz," he provocatively challenges his students so that they remain aware of the impact of this human catastrophe on their talk about God and discipleship. "If this is the case," he says, "be on your guard!"[4]

Metz might pose a similar question to us after the natural and social disasters of Katrina. Is the way we practice our compassion such that it could remain unchanged before and after Katrina? If so, and there is compelling evidence to suggest that this is indeed the case, then we too need to be on our guard!

The state of many communities along the Gulf Coast four years after the hurricane, and the experiences of millions who continue to be affected by it, prophetically tell us that our compassion cannot be the same after Katrina. Post-Katrina compassion not only must be more effective in responding to the ongoing social disaster that Katrina made evident in communities along the Gulf Coast, but it also must more effectively expose similar social disasters in urban communities around the country. Compassion after Katrina must continue to evolve into a more "political" expression of love of neighbor that is able to see, interpret, and respond to the type of dehumanizing suffering that social disasters create.

The people who continue to suffer in the wake of Katrina expose our national need for an approach to compassion that not only sees the often-hidden examples of human suffering that we prefer not to acknowledge, but also perceives the relationship between this suffering and our own complacency. Katrina also urges us to practice a type of compassion that interprets situations of suffering with often unexplored tools and sources of wisdom such as emotion, memory, narrative, and imagination. This national social disaster also underscores the need for an approach to compassion that transforms realities of suffering by empowering people for more complete relationality—whether we find ourselves on the margins of society or at its very center. In short, we need to devise an "ethics *after* Katrina" that places a political approach to compassion at its very center.

Note the double-entendre here. Living in post-Katrina America demands that we reflect critically on the ways that we suffer with others, placing this at the heart of our evaluations of the moral life, whether we reflect on the moral life of individuals or of communities. Moreover, seeking after the meaning of Katrina or attempting to understand its significance for the American experience, whether secular or religious, must also involve more critical attention to the ways in which we respond—effectively and ineffectively—to the reality of suffering in this country.

Critical examination of the ways that Americans responded to the suffering people of the Gulf Coast reveals the need for reconstructed compassion and a case study of how this new approach to suffering with others might look, feel, sound like, and what it might actually accomplish "on the ground." After a brief overview of some the tragic circumstances that contribute to our understanding of Katrina as a social disaster, we consider the ways in which the three-part praxis of political compassion—perception, interpretation, and response to suffering—might enable us to love more effectively those of our neighbors reeling from the social disaster of concentrated poverty along the Gulf Coast, as well as in other disaster zones of concentrated poverty around the country.

THE MASSIVELY UNEVEN TRAGEDIES OF A SOCIAL DISASTER

In its October 2005 report "New Orleans after the Storm: Lessons from the Past, a Plan for the Future," the Brookings Institution characterized the impact of Hurricane Katrina as *"massive and uneven."* And just months after Katrina hit, the Congressional Research Service reported that "the 700,000 people acutely affected by Katrina were more than likely overall to be poor; minority (most often African-American); less likely to be connected to the work force; and more likely to be educationally disadvantaged (i.e., not having completed a high school education)."[5] David Dante Troutt reiterates this more provocatively, "Because Katrina did not curve off in time, the science of storms and ecosystems met the dynamics of race, space and marginalization in a generation's single most profound spectacle of cumulative black disadvantage."[6]

Massively Uneven Levels of Flourishing Pre-Katrina

Relying on statistics provided in the months immediately following the storm by the Brookings Institution, the Center on Budget and Political Priorities, the Congressional Research Service, and the Urban Institute, we could easily spend most of this chapter exploring the massive and uneven distribution of poverty long before the storm made landfall:

- Of the 5.8 million people who lived in areas affected the storm, more than one million or one in five lived in poverty;
- Mississippi and Louisiana boasted the highest and second highest poverty rates in the nation, 21.6 percent and 19.4 percent respectively, compared with the national average of 13 percent;
- At least 28 percent of the 1.3 million people living in New Orleans struggled to survive in isolated neighborhoods of concentrated poverty before Katrina veered toward the coast;
- As of the 2000 census, New Orleans had forty-seven tracts of concentrated poverty with fifty thousand people living in them;
- The average African American in New Orleans lived in a neighborhood where 82 percent of the population was black; 84 percent of the city's poor were black;
- Between 1970 and 2000 the city lost 18 percent of its population to suburban sprawl expanding into the city's natural hurricane buffer areas;
- Twenty-five percent of New Orleans workers made less than $7.15 an hour in a sluggish local economy dependent upon a low-wage service industry;
- New Orleans ranked eightieth in college attainment rate out of the nation's one hundred largest metropolitan areas;

- The child poverty rate for areas acutely damaged by the storm was 30 percent, nearly twice the national average of 16 percent;
- The 55 percent rate of homeownership in hurricane-impacted areas was lower than the national average of 66 percent; however, of those homeowners, 29 percent had lived in their homes for more than twenty years. This statistic exceeds the national "nativity" average of 23 percent and exacerbated the emotional impact of displacement on many of Katrina's diaspora.[7]

Massively Uneven Experiences of Katrina

In light of these facts it is difficult to deny that the devastation of the disaster was not evenly experienced by the 2.5 million people affected by the storm. For example, the following statistics reported by the Congressional Research Service in November 2005 detail the demographics of the 700,000 people "acutely" affected by Katrina, "based on geographical analysis of Federal Emergency Management Agency (FEMA) flood and damage assessments and year 2000 Census data"[8]:

- Half of the people displaced by the storm in the 100-mile radius that marked its landfall lived in New Orleans;
- Orleans and St. Bernard parishes in Louisiana took the heaviest beating of the eighty-eight counties federally designated as disaster zones in the 100-mile radius of the storm's landfall;
- Roughly 90 percent of those acutely affected by the storm, or 657,000 people, experienced flooding as a result of structural damage to levees; most of those people lived in three parishes in and around New Orleans;
- Of those affected in Orleans parish, 272,000 black persons were displaced, compared with 101,000 non-blacks; among blacks, 34 percent (or 89,000 people) were considered by Census Bureau standards to be poor, compared with 14 percent of non-black residents who were displaced;
- One-fifth of those displaced, or 144,000 people, were "likely to have been poor" and lived with poverty rates that far exceeded the national average—21 percent compared with 12.1 percent;
- Thirty percent of this group of 144,000 had incomes below one-and-one-half times the poverty line (approximately $29,000 for a family of four or $14,500 for an individual) and over 40 percent had incomes below twice the poverty line ($38,600 for a family of four or a little over $19,000 for an individual);
- Forty-four percent of the storm's 1,000 victims were African American;
- An estimated 88,000 elderly persons (or 12.8 percent of the entire population affected by the storm), many having lived in New Orleans for the entirety of their lives, were displaced;
- More than half of the 183,000 schoolchildren who were displaced were African American (55 percent), and many of them (45 percent) were poor.

Massively Uneven Rates of Recovery

Nor were the benefits of recovery efforts evenly shared. A *New York Times* article on the third anniversary of Katrina, "The Patchy Return of New Orleans," notes that while some estimate that 70 percent of the city's original population had returned from "exile" by August 2005, its poorest neighborhoods, such as the Lower Ninth Ward and sections of Gentilly, "still have just a fraction of their pre-Katrina populations."[9] In fact, the Brookings Institution, which has monitored recovery in New Orleans since December 2005, reports that 52 percent of those who have returned to the city on the third anniversary of the storm now reside in neighborhoods that were least affected by the storm; these areas previously housed only 39 percent of the population.[10] Furthermore "affluent areas with the highest pre-storm house values" received the largest grants of the $3.3 billion Road Home initiative, the largest housing program in American history, despite the fact that 300,000 (70 percent) of the homes affected by the storm throughout the region were occupied by low-income persons and families.[11]

In its 2008 report the Brookings Institution also notes that while "New Orleans approaches its fourth year of recovery in a position of strength, many recovery trends have slowed or stagnated" as a result of thousands of still blighted properties, lack of affordable housing for those directly involved in the recovery process, "thin public services," particularly public transportation, and a failure to employ a "coastal restoration plan" that would replace reliance on the levees to protect against future storms. Oxfam America, an international relief and development organization that operates in 120 countries around the world to find viable solutions to hunger, poverty, and injustice, offers a rather prophetic view of the Gulf region three years after the storm: "Workers living along the Gulf coast have been hit by a double injustice," the organization states. "On the one hand they cannot afford the rising costs of rent, housing, insurance and utilities. On the other hand, they can't find the kind of jobs to offset those increased expenses."[12]

Consider the following indicators—gathered from a three-year analysis by *The New York Times*, the Brookings Institution, and Oxfam America—that capture the unevenness of recovery rates on the three-year anniversary of Katrina:

- The city still must deal with 71,657 blighted or vacant properties, or a vacancy rate of 33 percent. This far exceeds Detroit, which has the next highest non-occupancy rate at 18 percent.
- Only half of the $7 billion that FEMA designated for infrastructural repairs and debris removal has reached the targeted communities; the hardest hit and poorest neighborhoods, particularly Plaquemines and Orleans parishes, have received only 26 percent and 41 percent respectively.
- According to Oxfam, thirty-seven thousand people throughout the Gulf Coast still live in FEMA trailers three years after the storm; one third of these are disabled or elderly.
- More than thirty thousand persons are not qualified for various forms of government assistance, particularly Road Home grants;

- Rents on average are 46 percent higher than they were before the storm; for example, in 2008 a two-bedroom apartment in the region rented for an average of $990, up from $676 in 2005. This increase disproportionately affects the working poor who have returned to the city.
- Oxfam reports that the number of homeless in New Orleans has doubled since Katrina, and currently totals twelve thousand persons.
- The New Orleans metro area lost 30 percent of its jobs (178,000 jobs) to Katrina. As of May 2008, it had recovered 98,000, many in the professions connected to reconstruction and hospitality.
- The Occupational Safety and Health Administration waived a variety of safety and fair labor precautions in the months following the storm, according to Oxfam. As a result, more than half of the construction workers in New Orleans at one point were undocumented migrants. Federal contractors were not required to pay prevailing wages or to include an affirmative-action hiring plan in their federal bids. These conditions created disincentives for African Americans to return to the Gulf Coast, as well as divisive anti-immigrant sentiments in many communities.
- Oxfam America reports that only 12 percent of African Americans returning to the city have been able to find work; 65 percent of whites have been successful in that regard.
- There is a need for more workers, but the infrastructure to support them does not exist.
- Only 43 percent (117 of 275) of the city's child-care centers are operational; there are even fewer child-care centers in St. Bernard parish, where the rate of reopening is only 31 percent.
- While the use of public transportation grew by 45 percent between 2007 and 2008, the city public buses operate at 21 percent of their pre-storm level. In other words, only 76 of the pre-storm 368 buses are in operation. This affects low-income persons without cars.
- Only 50 percent of the city's supermarkets are open—19 stores compared to 38 prior to the storm. Even pre-storm levels were insufficient to support healthy communities.
- The number of students attending public and private schools in New Orleans is only half of its pre-storm level, and only 79 of the city's pre-storm 128 public schools are functional; however, enrollment of Hispanic students in schools in the metro area has increased by nearly 6 percent, which creates new challenges in the education system.

Massively Uneven Responses to Katrina

We can also apply the Brookings Institution's characteristics of "massive and uneven" to Americans' response to Katrina. In one respect our charitable response was *massive*. The *Chronicle of Philanthropy* in August 2007 reported that Americans had donated $3.7 billion in cash to charities connected to hurricane relief, a figure whose significance only increases when one considers the

$2.2 billion raised to support 9/11 families, previously the high water mark in American philanthropy, and the $2 billion donated to tsunami relief almost a year prior to Katrina.[13] Compassion did not take only the form of financial donations. The *Chronicle of Philanthropy* reports that in addition major charities received nearly $615 million worth of products, supplies, and services. Moreover, people around the region and the nation opened rooms in their homes and college administrators opened their classrooms and residence halls to many caught in the largest forced exile in the nation's history. And in the nearly three years since the water receded, more than one million volunteers have made pilgrimages to the Gulf Coast through various church-based work camps and creative collaboration among internationally recognized organizations such as Habitat for Humanity. In fact, faith-based charities and associations have been credited with contributing 56 percent of all financial and material donations to hurricane relief.[14] Certainly these examples reinforce the sense that compassion remains a central civic and Christian virtue in American self- and communal understanding.

No matter how massive the charitable response, however, there are several indications that our compassion both pre- and post-Katrina is also dangerously *uneven*—historically, financially. and relationally.

Historically Uneven Responses

The fact that conditions of concentrated poverty persisted in New Orleans for at least three decades—with little public outcry—speaks to the uneven nature of our compassion. That it took a disaster of this magnitude to raise the veil on the suffering of urban America—suffering that exists right now in neighborhoods in every major city in the country—ought to temper our satisfaction with our response to this tragedy.

"Hurricane Katrina affected among the most vulnerable people in America," said Neal Denton of the American Red Cross in a round table discussion among relief agencies. "In so many circumstances we were providing care for those who needed the assistance even before they were affected by Katrina."[15] Ashley Tsongas, policy advisor at Oxfam America, a non-profit that raised more than $6 million, calls the gap between need and government resources a "Grand Canyon" that "non-profits are never going to be able to fill."[16]

Our failure to provide that assistance to the people of the Gulf, and others like them in pockets of concentrated poverty around the country, speaks to a significant flaw in our understanding of what compassion requires. Pablo Eisenberg, a senior fellow at the Georgetown Public Policy Institute, challenges our self-understanding as a generous people when he notes that Americans pay the third lowest amount of tax of any developed country in the world and are increasingly unwilling to support government spending on "human and infrastructure needs" through taxes.[17]

Moreover, philanthropic analysts point to a "relatively low level of public and private support for social welfare agencies" that focus on meeting basic human needs in this country. Instead, we prefer to fund more creative projects, such as searching for medicinal cures, education, or the arts.[18] For example, while Americans donate approximately $250 billion a year to all charities, only $19 billion of those funds are earmarked to meet human needs for food, clothing, shelter, medical and legal services, and so on. One study that examined eight thousand gifts of $1 million or more to non-profits in 2007 revealed that social service groups received only 5 percent of those donations.[19]

The City of New Orleans offers a provocative microcosm of this national trend. Analysts note that in 2003 donations to the United Way of Greater New Orleans—one of the nation's largest social welfare agencies with local chapters in cities around the country—declined by 5.5 percent.[20] The chapter raised $18 million in one of the critical years before the hurricane, compared with the $54 million raised by the United Way of Columbus, an agency serving a comparable city, in the same year. The decline in this type of charitable giving ought to raise several red flags about American compassion. For example, either we are unable to assess accurately the various situations in American communities where basic needs are not being met, or we increasingly blame people for their need.

Furthermore, we ought to be particularly troubled by the fact that most Americans view charitable organizations as agencies that fill in the gap between what the market and government can do to affect people on the margins in a positive way. This mindset does not sufficiently interrogate economic systems and government policies that continue to broaden and deepen that gap. In the case of New Orleans, that gulf between the safety net of the market and the government was far greater than most non-profit charitable organizations were able to fill. What's more, in an age of designer philanthropy, donors and not agency administrators increasingly indicate how we would like our contributions to be used. Given the drift in national public policy and philanthropic trends away from supporting basic needs, many charitable organizations are expected to fill that dramatic gap but with increasingly restricted funds. Both circumstances contribute to an ineffective cycle of charity in which needs never end because the model of giving does not encourage critical reflection on or response to the causes of these needs.

Finally, this blind spot in our giving patterns points to a flaw in our understanding of compassion, considering that poverty has been on the rise nationally for four consecutive years. Effective rebuilding of the city of New Orleans will require a more accurate awareness of and attention to human need.

Financially Uneven Responses

Americans directed 85 percent of the $3.3 billion we donated to national "brand-name charities" such as the American Red Cross ($2.1 billion), the Salvation Army ($363 million), and Catholic Charities USA ($146 million). Debate continues about the effectiveness of the American Red Cross, the front runner in that group of organizations. It has a top-heavy bureaucracy that lacks relationships with existing social service agencies and networks on the ground. This greatly hindered the delivery of aid to those most in need.[21] Moreover, the deluge of funds directed toward brand-name charities during times of crisis diverts essential funding, potentially beneficial national attention, and opportunities for empowerment away from established agencies, non-profits, and other more local charities attempting to address the causes of social and economic vulnerability.

As brand-name coffers are nearly depleted and federal housing-support evaporates, the burden of recovery will fall upon these local groups. Moreover, the financial unevenness of our compassion is even more clearly evident in the responses of private foundations to the hurricane. The *Chronicle of Philanthropy* reports that foundations pledged $557 million toward hurricane related needs, compared with more than $1 billion dedicated to 9/11–related efforts and charities. This discrepancy might point to a flawed moral reasoning involved in any of compassion's three judgments—seriousness, desert, and similar possibility. Perhaps Americans gave more generously to the victims of 9/11 because we perceived a more serious type of suffering or tragedy surrounding that event. Or perhaps we detected a moral innocence among the victims caught off guard in their places of employment on 9/11 that was not evident in the forewarned victims stranded on the roofs of their homes in August 2005. Or perhaps we were able to identify more easily with the victims of terrorists attacks in the Twin Towers in New York rather than those caught in the twin storms of poverty and Katrina in New Orleans.

Michael Eric Dyson prophetically captures this disconnect in noting that "tragically, the victims of 8/29 are widely seen as undeserving of the respect and cultural empathy that go to the victims of 9/11. . . . There is also the widespread belief that the black poor basically got what they deserved because they were too stubborn or stupid to leave."[22]

Relationally Uneven Responses

American responses to Katrina reflect a *relational unevenness* in our compassion that ultimately traps all of us in seemingly endless cycles of charity. Although many Americans were willing to provide aid, we were not necessarily ready to enter into relationships with those who suffered from Katrina in the process of offering it. For example, Neal Denton of the American Red Cross, speaking at the Charity Navigator round table, acknowledged that part of the agency's ineffectiveness in responding to the crisis stemmed from its lack of connection to social-service agencies on the ground in the months prior to the storm, as well as a relative unwillingness to collaborate with these groups in Katrina's aftermath. Denton attributes the Red Cross's "go it alone" mentality to the American value of self-sufficiency, which shapes the ethos and mission of the organization widely seen as responsible for raising and distributing the most funds for hurricane relief.

Further, on an individual basis, the prevailing models of disaster response through online donations and celebrity telethons increasingly facilitate one-way, unreciprocated "charity from a distance." These strategies, while obviously successful in quickly raising substantial funds, inadvertently silence the voices of those affected by social suffering, do little to foster a sense of neighborliness or community, and enable those who so generously give to remain untransformed by the suffering experiences of others. The fact that a significant number of Americans who donated to the brand-name charities had little confidence in the organizations' ability to use the money effectively underscores the significance of this relational disconnect in our compassion.

In many ways this type of immediate, un-relational, and strictly charitable compassion comfortably and safely enables *someone else* to treat the symptoms of individual suffering rather than demanding that we participate in the uncomfortable process of taking responsibility for the causes of social suffering. It only reinforces the perceptions and attitudes that raise the humanly created boundaries that segregate people in pockets of poverty in not-too-distant neighborhoods. It insulates some people in pockets of privilege that perpetuate voluntary ignorance of the reality beyond these enclaves, and it isolates others in pockets of poverty that prevent them from participating in civil society. Comfortable compassion traps all Americans in cycles of charity since our philanthropic responses do little to explore why significant gaps in the safety nets of the market and government exist, and they offer little room for more creative responses that are both critical of this gap and constructive in narrowing it. In short, the relational unevenness of our compassion suggests that we do not associate it with justice.

The proof of this persists in the disaster zone today. Four years after Katrina made landfall, we have spent \$2.7 billion of our compassionate dollars as well as \$110 billion in federal dollars on relief. The experiences of Katrina's diaspora suggest that many have little to show for it. Disaster relief that addresses the immediate symptoms of the crisis conveniently forgets the more demanding and ongoing task of compassion, namely, the restoration of individuals, communities, and the nation.

Therefore, as compassionate persons we need to wrestle with the social causes of Katrina's suffering, many of which stem from problematic values that shape the American way of life, our personal and communal participation in those values (direct or indirect), and what we as Christian citizens of this nation are going to do about the persistent social sins of poverty and racism. A failure to address these questions will make it impossible to rebuild the city of New Orleans and other Gulf Coast communities. With this daunting task in mind, we can now apply the three-part praxis of political compassion that compassion after Katrina must employ.

PERCEIVING SOCIAL DISASTERS
THROUGH RELATIONAL ANTHROPOLOGY

In an interview with news anchor Jim Lehrer on public television's News Hour on 1 September 2005, then–FEMA director Michael Brown made the following now infamous statement regarding the rescue efforts in New Orleans, which at that point had been under way for several days:

> I think, again, the American people understand how fascinating and unusual this is—that we're seeing people that we didn't know exist that suddenly are showing up on bridges or showing up on overpasses or parts of the interstate that aren't inundated, and that now we're trying to get to

them by Coast Guard helicopter to at least get them some immediate relief so we can start airlifting them out.

Problematic Perceptions of the Social Disaster

Brown's telling statement underscores on several levels the necessity of perceiving a social disaster accurately before attempting to respond to it. First, in the days and weeks following Katrina, Americans were continually bombarded with provocative images from the Gulf Coast, many of which portrayed the roughly fifty thousand people to whom Brown referred in his comment. Many of us, like Brown, were shocked by the seemingly endless barrage of raw photographs and video footage of suffering people and the harrowing conditions from which they could not escape. However, in their analysis of media coverage of Katrina, Benjamin R. Bates and Rukhsana Ahmed note that the people in these images were not "engaged as interlocutors"; rather, they remained little more than visual objects, "victims, refugees, looters—for the home viewer's consumption." Because they were presented in this fashion, Americans were discouraged from relating to them as fellow human beings and instead engaged them with a voyeuristic curiosity akin to "disaster pornography."[23] For example, Bates and Ahmed observe that news coverage of the objects of Katrina's wrath appealed to the observers' "thanototic interest" or fascination with death and destruction.

Moreover, these images lacked critical value and most were rarely accompanied by any dialogue or meaning-making on the part of those depicted. In fact, Bates and Ahmed aptly reference philosopher Martin Buber in pointing out the implications of perceiving the "other" as an "it" to be experienced in a dramatic fashion, rather than as a "thou" to be encountered and understood in more relational ways. In the weeks following Katrina, Americans saw a barrage of "its" in devastated communities along the coast, but few of us truly connected with "thous"—real people with names, stories, and experiential wisdom to share with us. In short, "instead of seeking a deep understanding of the other, media coverage allows us to observe the other from afar and keep ourselves out of moments of relationship with them as valued others."[24]

Clearly, a voyeuristic way of perceiving the aftermath of the hurricane created an equally voyeuristic approach to compassion. Many Americans tuned in to fundraising telethons, followed the activities of celebrity volunteers in gossip magazines, and made online donations to charity websites as part of our response to these seemingly anonymous, voiceless, and powerless "its" of Katrina. To the extent that we did not see them as fellow human beings with a perspective on the situation and a story to tell, as citizens to whom we have a mutual responsibility, or as members who make up our collective body of Christ, we did not really perceive Katrina at all.

In addition, Brown's comments reveal the gaps inherent in the perspectives of those of us who do not immediately experience such events or who do not have firsthand knowledge of their impact. They illustrate the fact that it is often difficult for those who enjoy the benefits of certain American values such as autonomy, self-reliance, or whiteness to see the negative impact of these values on people in our peripheral vision. Those who are comfortable in this country often are not attuned to those who are uncomfortable or to the contexts in which they struggle, whether as a result of racism, the social causes of poverty, or the impact of voluntary white segregation. Many of us, like Brown, simply don't know that these persons and conditions exist.

Further, many of us fail to see the people who struggle in the midst of suffering realities—such as those who seemed to appear mysteriously on rooftops and overpasses along the Gulf Coast after Katrina—because it is easier for us to deny their existence than to acknowledge the uncomfortable challenges they pose to our integrity as American citizens and Christian disciples. Their very presence among us calls into question our commitment to the American values of opportunity, freedom, and equality for all. These persons interrogate Christian commitments to love our neighbor, to show concern for the least among us, and even to offer the compassion embodied by the good Samaritan. The struggle of millions of Americans to survive in the midst of the "perfect storm" of concentrated poverty remains largely invisible and renders us no more compassionate than the priest and the Levite who passed the man in the ditch along the road to Jericho.

Political Compassion and Perception of Social Disasters

Brown's comment, therefore, underscores the first distinctive characteristic of political compassion after Katrina. This kind of compassion necessitates that we turn to face suffering individuals, and not simply the "signs of the times" in which we may find them. We need to seek them.

Facing Suffering Persons, Not Social Problems

Compassion after Katrina demands that we turn to face the suffering people in order to resist our tendency to further dehumanize those who suffer by reducing their afflictions to abstract sociological phenomena or events rather than engaging them as acute, embodied, and contextual instances of dehumanization. When we perceive suffering situationally rather than personally, the actual persons who suffer and their experiences, insights, narratives, and prophetic truths simply—and conveniently—disappear. They become sociological statistics, one-dimensional images, or nameless victims of sociological phenomena such as poverty, gun violence, or hurricanes. The effectiveness of our response is immediately undermined. Frequently, we are overwhelmed by the thought of tackling a complex social problem such as racially motivated housing discrimination. We are often unable to understand what that problem has to do with us. Or, if we are moved to respond, we may focus on addressing the problem in an intellectual or rational way, using prevailing patterns of logic and existing civic and political channels.

However, with our faces turned to suffering persons, people become the focal point of our compassionate concern and just action. Rather than intellectually engaging the problem of housing discrimination, we may be compelled to work with actual individuals who grapple with housing insecurity. Our relationships to these persons—who have memories, narratives, vision, and wisdom—inseparably link us to this social problem. With them, we might incorporate intuition, relationality, and imagination in order to create new avenues to dismantle this injustice. In this kind of compassion after Katrina, overwhelming despair or detachment is replaced with energizing empowerment and responsible commitment to others.

Recall that Nussbaum and Metz distinguished their approach from those of their peers in their insistence that social responsibility begins with actually engaging suffering persons in order to lift up the wisdom of their experiences and to learn from them about our social reality and ourselves. Both scholars agree that the perspectives of suffering persons—whether Indian women engaged in micro-lending initiatives, survivors of Auschwitz, or those struggling to recover after Katrina—expand the purview of our social concern by calling our attention to the tragic nature of their suffering. With our faces turned to suffering persons we discover that their suffering is often the result of situations of injustice that are created by human beings and experienced by human beings as well.

We might wonder whether the citizens of the communities affected by Katrina would have "suddenly shown up" on bridges and overpasses had we made a concerted effort to turn and face them over a period of three generations rather than ineffectively and disinterestedly "reading the signs of the times" in which they were trapped. Had we made a concerted effort to turn and face them, and others like them in our own cities and neighborhoods, we would have learned from them about their struggles to keep their heads above water for decades before Katrina. We would have learned that recovery after Katrina requires that we as members of civil society attend to tragic circumstances that lie beyond the individual control of fellow Americans treading water in our global economy—tragedies such as less-than-adequate public services from garbage removal to public education, health care that is financially out of reach, lack of meaningful work that pays a living wage, racially motivated obstacles to homeownership, and a prison industrial complex fueled by a racially biased criminal-justice system.

Perceiving Ourselves through the Eyes of Others

In addition, turning to face the people who suffer *because of* the signs of the times rather than simply the signs themselves offers a much needed critical perspective on ourselves. Recall Metz's claim that facing suffering people can interrupt "merely believed-in discipleship," which remains largely unaffected by suffering and "cultivates that apathy which allows us Christians to continue our untroubled believing and praying with our backs turned."[25] In turning to face suffering others we are given a chance to see ourselves as they might see us, something that we crave in our self-centered culture but only when their perspectives reinforce our preconceived notions of ourselves. We resist when others' perspectives contradict our self-understandings. With our faces turned to those who suffer, it might become more difficult to ignore the many contradictions that surface in our self-understanding.

For example, we might realize that our commitment to human dignity is not as inclusive as we like to think, that our attempts to suffer with others actually cause more affliction, that our good intentions do not always motivate good actions, and that our personal appeals to color-blindness do not negate systemic racism. Michael Eric Dyson notes, "It is not all about what we saw. . . . It is also about what they, the poor, saw in us, or didn't see there. . . . It is their surprise, not ours that should most concern us and inform us."[26] In short, we begin to perceive ourselves critically or suspiciously, a point of view that frees us for a variety of new ways of seeing a situation of suffering and, more important, our connections to it. Anthropologist Virginia Dominguez captures this when she notes that "seeing doesn't just happen. We learn to see things in certain ways. . . . And once we're accustomed to it we just do it, largely without noticing. To see ourselves seeing others in particular ways—to allow ourselves to learn from an experience such as the Katrina disaster—we have to work hard to catch ourselves doing it."[27]

Perceiving ourselves as others see us takes hard work, but it is a necessary component of accurate compassion. For example, in turning to face these previously unknown persons stranded on rooftops and overpasses, we, like Michael Brown, may have begun to perceive ourselves as many along the Gulf Coast saw us in the weeks that followed Brown's comment—perhaps well-intentioned but irreparably handicapped by ignorance of the actual people we sought to assist and hindered by a culture that privileges whiteness. In other words, facing those who continue to struggle with the social disaster that brewed before the storm and continues to rage three years after it might provocatively reveal the bourgeois nature of our compassion.

For example, through a compassion that makes visible the "invisible backpack of white privilege," we might realize that as a result of our voluntary segregation from those who are different from us, many of us cannot count poor persons among our neighbors—in both the literal and the figurative sense. We might discover that as a result of our unquestioned acceptance of American individualism, many of us are blind to social conditions that generate injustices and to our collective participation in these injustices through our desire to maintain that individualism. Or we might learn that as a result of our preference for a tolerant and comfortable Christianity we make God the scapegoat for natural disasters such as Katrina rather than interrogate ourselves for allowing social disasters to continue to wreak havoc in the lives of the poor.

Dominguez notes that "these are not comfortable thoughts but they are necessary ones if any good is to come of the disaster and its aftermath."[28] This self-critical perception that political compassion might spark can help us unload the privileges we unknowingly accumulate in order to devise new ways of evaluating and responding to persons who still struggle after Katrina. This is the central lesson of the parable of the good Samaritan and Jesus' imperative to "go and do likewise." We must remove the blinders of privilege to see as the Samaritan and Christ did—with a keen attention to those on the periphery, with an eye for conditions of human suffering rather than sinfulness, and with disregard for the socially constructed divisions that keep people immune to each other's pain.

In addition, political compassion demands that we recognize experiences of non-identity, incapacity for relationship, or obstacles to the human capability to make meaning of our lives as the litmus test or bench mark for experiences of serious suffering. This expands our perception of suffering to include situations that we might otherwise neglect or that would remain invisible if we were to rely on other bench marks such as desert, or socioeconomic status, or similarities between "us" and "them." These situations might include a lack of meaningful work, addiction, domestic or sexual abuse, disenfranchisement in local government, an inability to share personal stories of survival, and the denial of the right to remember history differently.

Moreover, despite its very personal or individual expression (the inability for individuals to be in relationship with self, God, or others), this definition of suffering moves us beyond perceiving suffering in individual terms, particularly according to categories of deserved and undeserved suffering. This shift is possible only if we recognize the complex social, economic, and cultural conditions necessary for meaningful relationality with self, God, and others. These conditions might include freedom from extreme material want, an inclusive rather than exclusive civil society willing to engage in different stories and memories, and control over the circumstances that shape one's personal choices. In short, seeing this kind of suffering enables us to see the many ways in which the causes of others' suffering lie beyond their control and are more closely under our own spheres of influence.

A lack of critical perception of others' suffering leads to a less critical analysis of it and even a less effective response to it. Political compassion can rectify this. Turning to face those who continue to suffer from Hurricane Katrina ensures that we move beyond shock-value engagement with the images of suffering toward a more relational exposure to the experiential, embodied, and living wisdom these individuals have to offer us. Their "real world" perspective ensures that we do not miss the opportunity to become more informed about the human implications of this storm, or the chance to become critical about ourselves and the limits in our perception, or the chance to see more clearly the social causes of the social disasters that dominate our national landscape.

For example, rather than perceive victims of Katrina "as denizens of the Third World"[29]—which problematically suggests that this social disaster occurred in a distant place to distant people with no connection to ordinary Americans, or that these sorts of disasters are par for the course in the Third World—a political compassion helps us to see them as fellow citizens of this country, to see ourselves as somehow connected to the cultural values and systems that keep them invisible, and perhaps to see those same values from a different and more self-critical perspective.

Political compassion, therefore, also enables us to become more critical in our response to Katrina. Rather than simply engaging in a voyeuristic compassion that entails knee-jerk reactions to images of disaster selected for their temporary shock value, political compassion espouses a response that takes seriously the social disaster of Katrina, or in other words, the structural factors that exacerbated the deadly impact of the hurricane.

INTERPRETING SOCIAL DISASTERS THROUGH INTERRUPTIONS

In reflecting on the situation of twenty-three thousand people stranded for at least four days in New Orlean's Superdome, sociologist Sheryll Chashin comments that "most whites were of the view that the gut-wrenching delays in FEMA's response had nothing to do with race whereas most black people felt in their bones that this delay would not have happened if the majority of the people stranded at the Superdome or NO Convention Center had been white."[30] Findings from a Pew Research Center study on race and Katrina in fact confirmed Cashin's observation: 68 percent of African Americans thought the response would have been faster if those in the Superdome had been white, while 77 percent of whites felt it would have been the same.[31] Other disparities in interpretations of events revolved around whether those who did not evacuate had a choice, whether those who made it through the storm were resourceful survivors or thuggish looters, and what type of New Orleans might be rebuilt in the weeks following the storm.[32]

This stark contrast in the interpretations of the situation in New Orleans in the days after Katrina underscores the value of accuracy in interpreting and evaluating suffering. If political compassion begins with perceiving reality differently, it also distinguishes itself from less effective means of suffering with others in its method of interpretation and tools for critical analysis. This method and its analytical tools deepen the self-critical and socially critical approach to compassion initiated when we turn to face those who suffer. It does so by insisting on an interruptive line of ethical questioning, often overlooked sources of moral authority, and nontraditional ways of moral reasoning

Political compassion demands that we ask why these people suffered as they did, that we listen to their stories as starting places for evaluation, and that we incorporate emotion and narrative into our moral reasoning about this situation.

Interruptive Questioning

The interpretative process of political compassion begins with asking two specific questions, one ethical and the other theological. If you recall, Nussbaum insisted on the importance of "tragic questions" in devising human development strategies. Questions about why people suffer the way they do ought to be the first in a series of questions aimed at determining what a person might need to flourish. Note, the first question is not *who* is this person, or *what* can we do to help, or *what* material goods does this person need, or *how* can we alleviate his or her pain. Rather, compassion begins by asking *why* our neighbors suffer as they do.

This might not seem like an interruptive question, but it ought to give us pause if only because this is rarely an easy line of inquiry. In the process of discovering why individuals suffer we might discover information previously unknown or disregarded, information that challenges our previously held assumptions about them or the features of their conditions that often prevent us from responding. We might discover that the causes of their suffering can be traced to a mixture of bad individual decision-making and circumstances beyond their control. More important, we might discover, tragically, that these same circumstances are actually under the control of others who have failed to address them. These evaluations challenge our perception of the social reality as one defined by equal opportunity, pull-yourself-up-by-your-bootstraps self-sufficiency, and freedom. Rather, we come to understand more fully the tragedies of our reality—the sense that much of the worst human suffering happens unnecessarily at the hands of other human beings.

For example, in the case of the botched recovery efforts at the Superdome, political compassion encourages us to ask a series of why questions: Why did so many people fail to evacuate the city? Why were some able to leave and others not able to do so? Why did it take so long for aid to reach the people stranded in the Superdome or Convention Center, their homes, or hospitals? In trying to answer these tragic questions we might discover information that shifts the responsibility of the social disaster away from individual citizens and onto the wider community—both local and national. For example, if we ask these why questions, we might discover that many failed to evacuate the city because their resources were too limited for them to do so: 35 percent of black families in New Orleans and 59 percent of poor black households did not have a car,[33] and most poor families had insufficient discretionary funds for indeterminate stays in hotels. If we ask why aid was slow in coming we might discover that the storm destroyed an infrastructure and civil society already decimated and fractured by multiple consecutive decades of concentrated poverty. This deterioration of the common good in some of the hardest hit communities comes into sharp focus if we examine the rankings of Mississippi and Louisiana on various Census Bureau lists, for example, among the states with the highest rates of poverty or among the states with the lowest high-school graduation rates.

When we ask why people were stranded in their homes or the Convention Center for days on end, we discover that local, state, and federal officials chose "law and order" as their initial response to the crisis, which often inhibited if not trumped the necessary humanitarian search-and-rescue operations. In short, political compassion recommends that we ask these tragic questions in order to understand more fully Katrina as a social and "unnatural" disaster. Moreover, we begin to understand the significant demands that recovery from this storm and preparation for future hurricanes make on the nation as a whole. Political compassion explicitly surfaces the factors of concentrated poverty in our analysis of Katrina.

In more explicit theological terms, the method of political compassion relies on Metz's theodicy question to evaluate situations of suffering. Recall that Metz argues that theodicy is the primary line of theological inquiry in a post-Auschwitz world. Likewise, theodicy ought to be a central theological question after Katrina: Where was God during Hurricane Katrina? However, we should not stop there, lest we primarily understand this natural disaster as an act of God for which we have no responsibility. Metz reminds us that we ask the theodicy question because of the important link it offers to the anthropodicy question, or the analysis of human connection to situations of suffering: Where were you and I during Katrina?

The theodicy question resists Christians' temptation to understand God as either completely removed from and unmoved by human history or as solely responsible for its catastrophes. Rather, through the anthropodicy question we turn the critical gaze back on ourselves. Compassionate people must evaluate our own culpability in others' suffering, whether through our participation in structural violence, social sin, or merely our voluntary choice to remain ignorant. David Bentley Hart makes a poignant observation in his reflections on theodicy after the Indian Ocean tsunami that killed more than a quarter of a million people just twenty months before Katrina. He notes that "humanity is no less a part of the natural order than earthquakes and floods, and the human propensity for malice should be no less a scandal to the conscience of the metaphysical optimist than the most violence convulsions of the physical world."[34] In other words, the real tragedy of Katrina is the human contributions to the suffering. Compassion after Katrina must take seriously these contributions to suffering.

New Sources of Moral Authority

In order to answer the difficult tragic questions of why people suffer or the anthropodicy questions regarding our connections to others' suffering, political compassion turns to memories and narratives of suffering. These accounts are an essential and often under-utilized source of moral wisdom. Our own national history and the way we collectively recall it attests to our reluctance to acknowledge such memories, much less critically engage them. Therefore, when it comes to suffering with others, memories and narratives of suffering uncomfortably interrupt our patriotic nostalgia, confidence in government and non-profit organizations, and pride in civic virtue with a very different perspective on our shared past and present reality. In addition, an emphasis on memory and narrative affords those portrayed in Katrina's now iconic images a chance to share the stories that can fill out or deepen the one-dimensional images that we see. This is an essential step in empowering those whose voices have long been ignored.

For example, the memories and narratives of Katrina's diaspora challenge American myths of individual self-sufficiency, equal access to and participation in the common good, and confidence in our claims that we live in a color-blind society—simplistic attributions we frequently use to justify unnatural or unjust suffering or our limited responses to it. They challenge stereotypes of "victim" or "refugee" or even "low income" that so frequently shape our judgments regarding the desert and seriousness of suffering. Likewise, they challenge any plans for rebuilding New Orleans that do not incorporate their perspective, their wisdom, their vision of what a flourishing community might look like.

Recall Metz's central claim that memories of suffering provide a moral authority precisely because the people to whom they belong have been able to resist the wider society's willingness to forget the underside of human history. As such, they offer prophetic perspectives and insights from the margins of society and history that have yet to be taken seriously by those in the center. Both Nussbaum and Metz attempt to preserve the incommensurability and even prophetic sacredness of these memories of suffering because of their socially critical and potentially transformative capabilities. In other words, these memories have the ability to transform those who articulate memories of suffering, those who listen to them, and communities who take these memories seriously. The incommensurability of these memories or the sense that their content cannot be easily reconciled with the way that history's "winners" remember certain events or situations offers a more complete and even more accurate understanding of the past. And with a more accurate understanding of the past we gain a better sense of what is required to bring people above a threshold of flourishing as we move forward.

For example, Bates and Ahmed recommend that images of those affected by disasters be accompanied by information that calls into question uncritical ideologies that might otherwise be protected by even the most interruptive of pictures. They note that "although Katrina may have shocked the audience into pity, in the absence of proper information and critical knowledge, chances become slim for transforming that compassion into action for social justice."[35] Memories of suffering are interruptive because they physically, emotionally, imaginatively, and sensually embody the brokenness of social relationships, the dehumanizing impact of many social structures, and the limits of human progress that does not consider those on the margins. The perspectives of suffering people are privileged because as the experts who can identify precisely what human dignity means and requires in certain circumstances, they are essentially catalysts for social change. As we will see shortly, this privilege equates to empowerment, which becomes an important part of restoring suffering persons' capabilities for relationality.

Incorporating memory and narrative into compassion corrects the relational unevenness of contemporary responses to natural disasters. It suggests that rebuilding might best begin with a commitment to listening to memories and narratives of Katrina and being transformed by the wisdom they contain. In the case of Katrina, political compassion demands that we become more willing to listen to stories that present themselves in new forms of communication.

For example, in his analysis of the official transcripts from the Congressional Select Committee hearings on 6 December 2005, Terrence Check notes that a significant number of testimonies from the five survivors selected to testify were either truncated or eliminated on the grounds that the analysis they presented was too racially biased or motivated. Check argues that it was easier for Congress to "dismiss" these survivors rather than "confront" the claims they raise. In his estimation, dismissing their testimony makes "systemic change impossible."[36]

Check's observations underscore the importance of political compassion in engaging memories of suffering. For example, this approach to compassion suggests that Congressional hearings might not be the optimal setting for unearthing the moral authority of memories of suffering, given their tendency toward defensive argument rather than open dialogue, as well as the entrenched dynamics of power inherent in such events. Alternatives might include smaller town hall meetings, ecumenical faith-sharing groups, university conferences, and art exhibits that privilege voices that regularly go unheard in our public conversations. Consider the interfaith Katrina National Justice Commission, a coalition of black ministers and community leaders who travel the country and conduct public hearings with Katrina survivors. According to Iva E. Carruthers, the commission's general secretary, the group was organized "to hear, honor and memorialize those hurricane stories, and to identify the responses, both those that were inadequate and sufficient." This listening process has the power to transform all who participate—both storyteller and listeners—so long as we acknowledge what Metz would call the moral authority of those who suffer. It reflects the kind of compassionate privileging of memories of suffering that we need after Katrina.

In addition, political compassion underscores the need for listeners to become vulnerable in these exchanges by shedding preconceived interpretations or assumptions in order to listen to others. It requires an Augustinian humility on the part of the listener. Acknowledging that we might not be right or might not fully understand a situation enables us to move beyond the personal and cultural obstacles that prevent us from truly hearing what the suffering other is telling us. Racial and economic stereotypes, fear of difference, or paralyzing guilt all keep suffering others and their difficult memories at a safe and therefore manageable distance. Humble encounters with others' stories, however, open the possibility for new perspectives, new understandings, and new responses to some of the oldest social problems we face as citizens and disciples. Dyson encourages America's black faith communities to "wage memory warfare" that "pits us against the forces of cultural, racial and class amnesia."[37] Political compassion wages this kind of warfare by refusing to envision the future without paying close attention to the socially critical memories of the past.

Furthermore, political compassion demands that we listen to memories in a variety of vernaculars and communicative forms. Memories communicated in popular music or the visual or performing arts evoke the emotions, intuitions, and energies necessary to motivate difficult and demanding commitments to social change. Moreover, the very process of creating these artistic memories contributes to the restoration of individuals and communities. For example, artists in Bay St. Louis, Mississippi, have created provocative pieces with the debris of the hurricane that somehow survived the vast destruction of homes and lives —everyday objects such as dominoes, Mardi Gras king cake figurines, and carvings in leafless trees—in an attempt to capture the "energy" of the place that remains, even if people are still in exile. Reliquaries of other mundane objects—toys, toilets, and lawn ornaments—have "created a momentum of their own" in the restoration process that, in the words of Janet Densmore, an artist and Katrina survivor from Bay St. Louis, captures a "survivor's spirituality in a way that is physically very real."[38] Exhibits of this disaster art have traveled around the country, often telling a different, more hopeful story of the storm and providing nonverbal ways of examining the existential questions that the storm raised, whether about the purpose of existence, the nature of God, or what is required of human beings in the face of suffering.

New Tools for Ethical Analysis

Finally, political compassion uses nontraditional tools as part of our attempts to interpret and evaluate others' suffering. These include emotions and anamnestic reason, which break through the prevailing logic about the causes and responses to this natural and social disaster. Nussbaum reminds us that our emotions disclose our undeniable vulnerability and encumberedness through a variety of levels of relationality. As an "e-motive" approach to moral reasoning, our emotions and the intuitive sensibilities they uncover connect us to others' affliction, lift up information about the seriousness of their situation that we might otherwise miss, and uncover a shared sense of all persons' vulnerability to conditions that lie beyond our control. Each of these aspects of emotions challenges a strictly logical, theoretical, ahistorical, or rational approach to moral reasoning.

In support of his insistence on the moral authority of suffering, Metz's calls for anamnestic reason or remembering, which takes seriously the wisdom gained through close attention to stories or memories of suffering. This type of reasoning incorporates historical consciousness, which refuses to separate an individual's personal affliction from the social, economic, and cultural reality in which all human beings are participants. In the case of Katrina we are speaking about a reality dictated by values of individualism, security, whiteness, and consumerism that shape our beliefs about others and our responses to them. Anamnestic reason breaks through the forgetfulness that accompanies these values by instilling in us a self-critical realization of our connection to others, if only through the commonness of our shared history. By taking seriously the socially critical memories of those who suffer, anamnestic reason unleashes the moral imagination so that we might think creatively of new ways of being in the future.

For example, using anamnestic reason after Katrina would enable Americans to listen willingly and to reflect self-critically on the memories of suffering shared at congressional hearings rather than simply dismiss the speakers as radical, extreme, biased, or unreasonable. Anamnestic reason would make it possible for Americans to listen deeply to what Check calls the "historical narrative of institutional racism," a story shared by many Americans of the Gulf Coast that calls into question our national self-understanding as the land of the free or of equal opportunity. Memories of discrimination in housing, employment, health care, and public education have deep roots in the memory of social inequities connected to the institution of slavery, a part of our national narrative that white Americans are reluctant to hear.

Political compassion might also tap into a variety of emotional responses to Katrina's suffering—anger, disappointment, shame, and guilt—and harness the creative energy they create in order to inspire innovative responses to the social disaster that, at the very least, acknowledge the situations of Katrina's living and dead. Rage and anger, for example, are important emotions for resisting perceived injustices in the distribution of federal housing grants, or for demanding that national insurance providers overhaul their policies for communities living below sea level.

Finally, compassion after Katrina can support various ethnographical initiatives to capture the memories and narratives of the storm so that their wisdom can continue to teach us about the causes of social disasters and appropriate responses. The Katrina Narrative Project, an initiative of the University of New Orleans, has gathered more than a thousand narrative accounts of personal experiences of the storm, thirty of which have been published.[39] "We knew already that there would be histories written that would tell us how many breaches there were, how deep the water was, why it happened, how it could have been prevented," said Rick Burton, who initiated the project. "But the real human part of the story could only be preserved if we made an effort to get as many individual accounts down as we could."[40] Here we can continue to find a source of moral authority that can shape our compassion after Katrina.

TRANSFORMING SOCIAL DISASTERS THROUGH EMPOWERMENT, HUMILITY, AND SOLIDARITY

As we saw in the second and third chapters, the traditional aim of compassion as practiced in the Christian tradition is to empower those who languish in the ditch to get back on their feet and continue their respective journeys down to Jericho. However, a compassion rooted in political theology reminds us of two other critical entities, often overlooked in the tradition of compassion, that also need to be radically changed.

First, compassionate persons need to be changed, transformed, and even restored. We need to examine critically our values, our sensibilities regarding human flourishing, and our capacity for relationships if we hope to restore and revive the communities of the Gulf Coast and others like them around the country. Whether we acknowledge it or not, the central values of North American culture have detrimental effects on us as well as those we encounter in the proverbial ditch. Individualism, self-sufficient autonomy, consumerism, and whiteness have taken their toll on our ability for authentic relationships with self, God, and others. They have negatively affected our ability to be moved by the dehumanizing impact of concentrated poverty on our neighbors, to be more than merely entertained by the destructive power of natural disasters, to recognize our own vulnerabilities in the suffering of others, or to imagine alternatives to the way things are.

Second, the negative impact of globalization on the Jericho road suggests that we also need to transform our understandings of human flourishing and the paths to achieve it. For example, unfettered free-market capitalism narrows the road to flourishing in an age of globalization. It promises over-development to a limited few who carry certain unearned traveling privileges—whether as a result of the geographic location of their birth, their race, or gender—while sustaining the vast majority in conditions of under-development. For example, much of the Gulf Coast has been reconstructed by migrant laborers willing to work for a wage that does little to lift them or their dependent families throughout Latin

America out of poverty. Their employers undercut the pay-scale for Gulf Coast natives, who find themselves struggling with increasingly expensive costs of living. These persons have been robbed by corporate and private interests on the long road home to recovery.

Furthermore, since the Jericho road is largely paved by the competitive institutions and systems of free-market capitalism, globalization strangles or chokes other paths or access routes to human flourishing and leaves travelers with fewer and fewer options. For instance, when recovery decisions are dictated by the profit margins of major contractors outside of the region, rather than by a local commitment to generating meaningful and viable employment, then families who wish to return to their neighborhoods and homes are unable to do so due to a lack of affordable housing, basic infrastructure, and decent wages. They remain at a standstill—in communities far from home, or in FEMA trailers adjacent to their still storm-damaged homes. Or when undocumented workers bolster corporate bottom lines by taking dangerous and low-paying jobs, they make little headway in achieving "the American dream" of homeownership, health care, college, and retirement funds.

Finally, globalization narrowly construes indicators for human flourishing or recovery according to the objective or quantifiable standards set by those outside of the devastated region or those with little personal experience of the disaster. We do not get an accurate sense of what people are able to do with the resources available to them when the vitality of neighborhoods and cities is measured by employment rates or tax revenues, both of which have been on the rise in much of the Gulf Coast region. This gives a false impression that economies, neighborhoods, and actual people are thriving. When we measure flourishing according to often intangible goods of the social infrastructure that only those "on the ground" can assess—goods such as public transportation, child care, public schooling and safety, and operational supermarkets, community centers, and hospitals—a different picture emerges.

With these two often overlooked components of transformation in mind—compassionate persons and social conditions that pave the road to Jericho—we can better distinguish political compassion after Katrina from other less authentic expressions of Samaritanism. Compassion after Katrina attempts to transform our present-day equivalents of the three entities in Luke's parable: the traveler, or those who suffer unjustly at the hands of others; the Samaritan, or those who attempt to respond to these persons; and the road to Jericho itself, or the current sociohistorical conditions in which compassion after social disasters occurs.

Transforming Imperiled Travelers

Political compassion transforms suffering persons by bolstering what Nussbaum identifies as the two central human capabilities frequently thwarted by unjust suffering: practical reason and affiliation.

Practical reason pertains to our ability to determine our sense of self or personal identity, the direction we want our lives to take, and the means we will use to reach that destination. Political compassion empowers suffering persons to reclaim their identities, the orientation of their lives, and the tools they need to get back on their feet by privileging their memories and narratives. As a result, those struggling under the weight of social injustices can challenge powerful and externally imposed presuppositions, stereotypes, or labels such as *victim, refugee,* or even *sufferer.* These generic terms deny the distinctiveness of their voices, the multidimensional complexities of their experiences, the validity of their perspectives, and their personal agency and political rights to contribute to their own restoration. Political compassion places these persons in positions of influence and power in the process of recovery after social disasters not only because they have been long denied human dignity, but because they prophetically reveal what human dignity means and requires. And they do so through memory and narrative, which are often overlooked elements of human cognition and are capable of motivating action that seeks justice.

For example, many government officials were surprised by public resistance to demolishing nearly five thousand units of public housing in New Orleans, given the less than human conditions of many of the buildings prior to the storm. However, attention to the narratives of the protestors reveals that while far from ideal, the various buildings were "home" to many of the residents in ways that newer housing in different neighborhoods and among different people might not be. Even in their deteriorated condition, these public-housing complexes provided residents with a sense of familiarity, belonging, a network of relationships, and security, which are even more difficult to find in New Orleans after the storm. "We have mildew. We have mold, but we have been living with that for my whole, entire life," Stephanie Mingo, a resident of one of the largest housing projects in St. Bernard Parish told a reporter from "The NewsHour" in July 2006. "I've been here forty-four years. And why I want to stay here is because this is my neighborhood, and this is where I'm comfortable at. You want to tear this down because you want to get the poor, black people out. I mean, that's how I feel."[41]

Narratives like Mingo's call to our attention the distinction between being at home and being housed, and the priority that must be given to the former. Moreover, many resist the destruction of public housing based on the fact that many residents are still dispersed around the country and will be further deterred in returning if their homes are destroyed. This legitimate narrative reminds us of our failure to consider those receiving public assistance as full citizens of our local, state, and federal democracies. "Right now, we feel it's not the time to start huge building projects because there are lots of people who are displaced as we speak and need a place to stay," said Lynette Bickham, another St. Bernard project evacuee. "We're going to continue to fight for our homes."[42]

When suffering persons articulate their memories and flourishing persons deeply listen to them, a new potential for affiliation among all persons is created. Nussbaum identifies this central capability for relationships as essential for lifting persons out of conditions of dehumanizing suffering. It creates new opportunities for those on the margins of society to participate in rethinking how to shift and expand the values and practices that define life at the center of society. Compassion after Katrina, therefore, reconnects those isolated from civil society to life in community through a collaborative and relational process. It empowers them to determine their own plan for flourishing and to challenge notions of flourishing held by the wider community. As a result these folks can challenge the indicators used to measure the vitality of society and offer ways in which vitality might be more accurately understood and justly configured.

The Jeremiah Group, an ecumenical consortium of nearly forty faith communities in New Orleans, has worked for more than fifteen years across racial, economic and denominational lines to follow Jeremiah's command to the Israelites to "seek the welfare of the city" in order to determine personal welfare. However, the group insists on defining the welfare of the city from perspectives most often ignored by politicians and public policymakers. They canvass neighbors for input and participation. Their work in New Orleans before the hurricane included collaboration with foundations to create living-wage campaigns, to restore homes and schools, and partnering with police in dealing with public-safety concerns. Since Katrina, the Jeremiah Group has enabled citizens to bring their concerns about affordable housing to the attention of public officials in public action meetings where officials are asked to explain their plans and are held accountable. Moreover, they have developed a "soft second-mortgage" program that loans renters up to $50,000 for a mortgage and forgives it if they remain in the home for ten years.[43] This innovative initiative has been adopted by state and federal recovery programs and points to the empowering creativity of political compassion.

Transforming the Privileged Travelers

If our compassion is to be different after Katrina, then we must trigger our imaginative capabilities in order to create alternative understandings of and approaches to human flourishing. For example, the "long slow road home" for so many along the Gulf Coast who we "didn't know exist" reveals that compassion after social disasters must help privileged and comfortable persons to interrupt the logic that grows from the values that deny our inherent interdependence, vulnerability, and mutual responsibility to those beyond our immediate circles of concern. In addition, it must interrupt our skewed sense of what it means to live a fully human life. For example, we can no longer think that as long as persons have access to the appropriate "stuff"—newly constructed or renovated homes, electricity, food and water, medicine, cell phones, pets—they have all they need to flourish. We can no longer think that some persons' failure to thrive is a result of their individual poor choices. So long as survivors do not have access to social networks of neighbors or faith communities, meaningful employment, physical and mental health, personal safety, and natural beauty, they continue to face significant obstacles to living fully human lives. Perhaps more important, compassion after Katrina might help so-called thriving persons to realize that we too lack many of these intangibles social goods in our privileged lives.

Political compassion transforms the subjects of compassion, or those privileged enough to respond to social disasters—rather than to experience them firsthand—by restoring our capabilities for affiliation or authentic relationships with others. This rehabilitation occurs through the imaginative, liberating, and transformative process of narrative. Telling stories develops suffering persons' capacities for practical reason and affiliation. In the process of sharing their narrative, storytellers reclaim their history; take control over their present reality, if only by naming the injustices in it; and stake a claim in the future by articulating their dreams and visions. Through a narrative that articulates a memory of suffering, as well as a memory of a future that has yet to be obtained, they are able to relate more authentically to themselves, to others, and to the God of their understanding. But narrative also fosters relationality between those who tell stories and those who hear them. It can create connections or relationships among all people, if only through the invitation to share briefly imaginative space and time, and to view the world and their respective places in it from a different position.

Stories literally and figuratively turn our faces toward those who articulate them. They require that we assent to the storytellers' perspective on reality— that we see the world with their eyes, hear it with their ears, enter into it with their bodies, remember it with their memories, restore it through their visions of the future. Like any expression of art, narratives make visible to us the hidden things in our reality that we cannot see or refuse to see—in this case the debilitating effects of the cycle of charity or privileges that come with our skin color. Narrative incorporates intuition, emotion, imagination, and other under-used aspects of our cognitive abilities in order to open new ways of understanding and of responding to what is going on around us. Listening to narratives of suffering can transform privileged persons in three specific ways: through self-critical humility, asymmetrical relationality, and liberating imagination.

Self-critical Humility

Relationships created through narrative and the process of storytelling enable a self-critical humility within the listener that can trigger a liberating guilt and responsible engagement in the tragic circumstances of others' suffering. When we listen deeply to another's memories or stories we quickly realize that ours is not the only way to see the world, that others see us quite differently than we see ourselves, and that we are often more closely connected to others' afflictions than we think. When we listen deeply to narratives of suffering, we ingest the storyteller's wisdom and potentially question and reconstruct our own frameworks of meaning. This humility sparks a self-critical examination of conscience or a heightened awareness of the way that we "live, move, and have our being" in the world. Narratives of suffering prick our consciousness, particularly if the story reveals and condemns social values or beliefs that we hold or structures and institutions of which we are a part. This pinprick of discomfort or de-centering self-awareness interrupts our tendency to privatize our moral engagement in the world and further isolate ourselves from the fundamental goods of life in community. Through these interruptions we discover friendship that trumps fear, achievement of common goals that complements individual productivity, and mutual dependence that overpowers isolated individualism. Narratives can help us to resist what Hobgood names the "pathologies of privilege" that negatively influence so many of our moral decisions and actions, even those decisions and actions we take on behalf of others—whether "obsessiveness about work, restrictions on intimacy and emotional expression, limited capacity for friendship and community, or a highly regulated marriage ethic."[44]

For example, political compassion after Katrina reminds us that those of us not affected by the storm need to be liberated from our colorblindness or from the false claims that "in the post-civil rights era race no longer 'matters' in American society."[45] Ultimately, colorblindness conveniently denies the persistent problem of racism in American culture and leaves unchanged the values, behaviors, and systems of white privilege that made Katrina's winds and rains so destructive. Colorblindness further isolates privileged persons from life-sustaining relationships with others. Through the ability to see ourselves through others' eyes in their narratives of suffering, compassion deconstructs this denial and reveals it as the most dangerous expression of white privilege.

However, when we take the risk to see ourselves as others see us, the "invisible knapsack of white privilege" and its unevenly distributed contents become glaringly obvious. We also discover the weight that "unearned advantage and unshared power at others' expense"[46] place on our shoulders: fear that traps us in segregated communities so that we can protect ourselves and our assets, continuous dissatisfaction with our bodies, rejection of anything that might portray vulnerability or a wavering in our desire to achieve, idolatrous preoccupation with the markers of social pedigree, the crippling anxiety that we will never have or be enough, and the exhaustive measures we take to deny our vulnerability and mortality.

Listening to others' narratives of suffering, therefore, affords us the opportunity to remove the knapsack, critically examine its contents, and either more evenly distribute its resources and empowerments among our fellow travelers or use them to the benefit of all and not just a few. This struggle to acknowledge and dispense with our privilege, or to resist what Metz identified as our inherent desire to dominate others, is absolutely central to compassion after Katrina. It lifts the heavy burdens of beliefs, values, and practices that deny fully humanity to all persons, including ourselves, or that reject the inherent goodness of authentic relationships with others. It replaces these burdens with life-affirming and sustaining relationships of vulnerability, mutuality, shared burdens and joys, memories of the past, and visions of the future.

Moreover, political compassion offers those who do not live in pockets of concentrated poverty around the country a sense of liberating guilt that arises from these humble acknowledgments of the ways that we have failed others. In other words, this approach to suffering with others demands that we move beyond paralyzing emotions of fear and shame to acknowledge our complicity in the values and structures that create social disasters such as Katrina. It creates a desire to reach out to those who want to collaborate with us to create change and thus liberates us from the inertia of being overwhelmed by our seemingly inevitable and inescapable participation in structures of social sin. It frees us from a demoralizing sense that there is little that we as individuals or communities of individuals can do to reverse the devastating impact of social disasters with the confidence that a renewed commitment to live in right relationship with others is essential for any radical change. Wendy Farley captures this sense of freedom when she explains that a self-critical compassion provides a sense that "liberation from the tedious weight of one's own miserable little ego is not necessarily self-sacrificing but can be profoundly fulfilling."[47]

Asymmetrical Relationality

Metz reminds us that what he calls the "liberation of the haves" from our tendency to dominate others depends on the willingness on our part to enter into asymmetrical relationships with others. These persons, with their socially critical memories and their utter dependency on God's justice, become catalysts for our conversion away from values and practices rooted in privilege toward relationships of mutual responsibility. This call to and capacity for conversion offers a distinctive feature of political compassion that challenges less radically inclusive expressions of the virtue. In other words, the restoration of compassionate persons requires that we listen to stories of people who are quite different from us, whether in terms of gender, race, economic status, or religious affiliation.

A willingness to become vulnerable with a radically different "other" is no easy task in our contemporary culture with its focus on personal and national security. In our global age, impersonal and virtual relationships replace embodied human interactions, fear of others keeps us from engaging people different from ourselves, and over-stimulation distracts us from really seeing things going on around us. However, Traci West claims that relationships with very different persons makes possible "an ethical vision that recognizes multiple, dissimilar sources of valuable moral knowledge, especially from those unequal in social power and status."[48] Nussbaum calls this type of relationship "cosmopolitan citizenship," and Metz names it "solidarity." This relationality nurtures a part of first-world persons or privileged persons who are threatened by the "isolating individualism" of globalization.

These relationships of compassion offer constructive ways of taking responsibility for our complicity in others' suffering. For example, after Katrina we can listen to narratives of suffering people in other cities who grapple with the social disaster of concentrated poverty. We can identify organizations doing restorative work in these places and participate in their missions. We can speak publicly about these human tragedies in our respective faith communities and neighborhoods. All of these activities are expressions of compassion through which we suffer with others in truly transformative ways.

It is in the context of relationships of asymmetry that we are able to rise above what Metz calls the "logic of the marketplace" in order to explore new possibilities for human flourishing. Nussbaum suggests that this is possible through the dialogical process of "over-lapping consensus" that encourages relationality and mutual vulnerability through engagement of otherwise disparate persons in narratives of what people are actually able to do and become in the process of recovering from social disasters.

For example, in the case of Katrina, we might begin to recognize the collaborative work of organizations such as Common Ground, the Jeremiah Group, the People's Hurricane Relief Fund, and the Equity and Inclusion Campaign, all of which rely on the memories of those affected by the storm to shape creative and effective methods of responding to them—whether through soft second mortgages, health care clinics that employ internally displaced persons and offer long-term case management, or public meetings to share narratives and stories. Each unites diverse people in a common mission to restore the dignity of all persons, but particularly those affected by Katrina. The Equity and Inclusion Campaign, a consortium of more than one hundred grassroots community leaders, including religious leaders, from the three states affected by the storm, has made it a priority to hold federal, state, and local governments accountable for their promises to "confront poverty and injustice" faced by the most vulnerable persons in the process of Katrina recovery. On the third anniversary of the storm, the group drafted "One Nation, One Promise, One Gulf," a document that recalls these promises made at every level of government. The group then met with public officials, particularly those involved in the Republican and Democratic presidential campaigns, in order to remind them of just how much work needs to be done in order to honor these promises and of the importance of maintaining relationships of asymmetry to keep recovery initiatives on track.

Liberating Imagination

Ultimately, attending to narratives of suffering and entering into relationships with those who tell them unleashes the moral imagination. Narratives empower us to rethink things "as they are," using elements of our cognitive capacities that we often overlook, such as our emotions, senses, passions, intuitions, and nonverbal means of communication. Narratives create sympathetic understanding among otherwise disparate persons. They stir our emotions, help us to transcend the narrow confines of our privileged ways of knowing ourselves and the world, and stoke our sense of interdependence. Since political compassion relies on anamnestic reason that privileges the cognitive resources of memory and narrative in making sense of reality, it enables self-transcendence, attention to difference, awareness of relationality and vulnerability, and a more complete understanding of what it means to be human. This type of reasoning challenges our uncritical reliance on technical or strictly rational reason, on the prevailing logic of free-market capitalism, and the epistemologies of whiteness, all of which influence our understanding of what justice means and how we ought to go about creating it.

For example, since it insists on asking the tragic questions about others' suffering, political compassion incorporates our capability for imagination in the ways we think about justice, as well as in the ways we attempt to act justly. Artist and philosopher Maxine Greene explains: "Of all our cognitive capacities, imagination is the one that permits us to give credence to alternative realities. It allows us to break with the taken for granted, to set aside familiar distinctions and definitions."[49] When we ask ourselves the why questions about others' afflictions, we might also ask ourselves the why-not questions related to possibilities for their restoration: Why not more racially and economically integrated communities? Why not an unpacking of our knapsacks of white privilege? Why not more supermarkets to sustain healthy living in neighborhoods? Why not an overhaul of the public school system? Why not new approaches to retributive justice in our criminal justice system? Possibilities for practical answers to these questions present themselves in what Metz calls the "memories of the future" or a future of justice that takes seriously the injustices of the past. The combination of these prophetic perspectives, as well as relationships among storytellers and listeners, creates alternatives to the same old answers to the same old social problems. In Greene's estimation, "Imagination may be a new way of de-centering ourselves, of breaking out of the confinements of privatism and self-regard into a space where we can come face to face with others and call out, 'Here we are.'"[50]

Moreover, because it relies on memories and narratives as a source of moral authority, political compassion suggests that justice is not only something we know intellectually and articulate verbally, but also something that we know experientially and express sensually in the context of relationships with other people. When we engage in the narratives of suffering and enter into relationships with those who tell these tales, justice becomes a narrative image, a vision, a symbol, a dream that surfaces in our individual and collective consciousness as a result of encounters with a prophetic truth that we might not otherwise experience. When we suffer deeply with others, justice becomes a passionate vision that literally and figuratively compels us to create new ways of living well together so that this suffering can be eliminated. As a vision, justice is an endless cache of meanings that continue to be revealed as more and more people perceive these meanings in the midst of relationships with one another. But ultimately, justice is not merely something that has sound logic or is reasonable; rather, justice looks, sounds, feels, and tastes good.

Finally, by inviting people to imagine together new possibilities for the future, political compassion underscores important processes—and not simply social contracts or urban planning strategies or disaster recovery plans—that build a more complete justice and a thriving common good. These processes include storytelling, deep and humble listening, engaging all of our senses in understanding one another's situations, dialogues about common concerns, and brainstorming about ways to create alternatives to the way things are. This kind of activity thickens or enriches the common good to which all of us can contribute and from which all of us ought to benefit. "Community cannot be produced simply through rational formulation nor through edict," claims Greene. "Like freedom, it has to be achieved by persons offered the space in which to discover what they recognize together and appreciate in common; they have to find ways to make intersubjective sense."[51]

Transforming the Road to Jericho

Finally, political compassion transforms the road to Jericho or the wider social reality. It resists the structural and systemic causes of suffering by suggesting a series of values that counter those that currently dominate American culture. In many cases the causes of injustice stem from communally held values and beliefs that shape the perceptions, interpretations, and actions of those of us who flourish above the threshold and who have the power to spark wider social change if we so choose.

We have seen how values of individualism, self-sufficiency, consumerism, and bourgeois Christianity not only facilitate the dominating and dehumanizing treatment of others but also create unreflective and ineffective responses to others' afflictions. Political compassion, therefore, insists that first-world individualism needs to be tempered with an ever-widening sense of interdependence and social responsibility if we are to change the "threshold for flourishing" or the conditions necessary for authentic relationality. It replaces individualism with relationality, self-sufficient autonomy with vulnerability, and whiteness with humanness. While we will explore the transformative component of political compassion in much more global terms in the following chapter, there are at least three things that political compassion might do after Katrina to transform the Jericho road.

First, political compassion demands that we examine Hurricane Katrina as a racial event in order to debunk the prevailing colorblind ideology of many compassionate persons in this country. That 59 percent of Americans think that blacks are responsible for their poverty and that 69 percent of Americans believe that the conditions for African Americans continue to improve in this country, despite the staggering racial inequalities that Katrina revealed, speaks to just how much this ideology shapes our Jericho road.[52] Colorblindness suggests that situations of racial inequality are either rare or coincidental and therefore do not demand social analysis and resistance; it suggests that racial discrimination is the result of either individual perpetrators or individual plaintiffs and therefore does not demand social analysis or resistance; and it suggests that reverse discrimination occurs in situations where race is used as a factor in distributing social goods, in which case social analysis and resistance is called for.[53]

Political compassion interrupts this inaccurate and dehumanizing ideology and the cultural, social, and moral behavior it supports. It creates opportunities for disparate persons; in this case it allows those on different sides of the various racial divides in this country to enter into relationships through storytelling, active listening, and collaborative action on behalf of what is best for our neighbors. Stories of the past and narrative accounts of the present undermine the myths of race as a private and personal affair; relationships of storytelling and listening soften divisive emotions of distrust and fear and create new possibilities for mutual understanding; and active commitments to collaboration offer new alternatives for solving age-old problems. In many ways U.S. President Barack Obama in his now famous speech on racism in America, "A More Perfect Union," captured what political compassion can do: "I believe deeply that we cannot solve the challenges of our time unless we solve them together— unless we perfect our union by understanding that we may have different stories, but we hold common hopes; that we may not look the same and we may not have come from the same place, but we all want to move in the same direction—towards a better future for of children and our grandchildren."[54]

Moreover, political compassion after Katrina can help us to think critically about the American approach to charity and philanthropy. Certainly we can see that charitable organizations, particularly those affiliated with faith communities and traditions, are invaluable in assisting travelers left along the wayside of our Jericho road. However, despite their influence and ability to motivate and coordinate Americans' responses to others' suffering, many of these organizations employ a model of giving that traps donors and recipients in a less than desirable, and at times even dehumanizing, cycle of charity.

At the organizational level, political compassion encourages us to seek more collaboration and relationship-building among charitable organizations themselves. Katrina revealed that organizations with strong connections to a variety of other organizations on the national and local levels were more successful in delivering aid and jump-starting the long-term recovery process in ways that respected the dignity and agency of those affected by the storm.

Also, political compassion encourages Americans to increase our support of grassroots social-welfare agencies. There is a twofold reason for this. First, community-based organizations such as the Jeremiah Group have been what Ashley Tsongas of Oxfam America considers "the driving force of recovery," particularly in the marginalized communities. "If you go into communities of color, and you see any progress, nine times out of 10, it's grass-roots groups that have gotten things done."[55] We should increase our support of these groups so that they might have the resources not only to fill the safety net gaps effectively between the market and the government, but also to begin to do the advocacy work that would examine the causes of this gap in order to narrow or even eliminate it. If social-service agencies do not have resources to meet needs, they will not be freed to examine and resist the causes of need. In both cases Americans need to be encouraged to think about the value of the common good—the conditions that we collectively create that make communities of choice and connectivity possible. In other words, we need to incorporate a sense of humility into our charitable giving in order to avoid reinforcing the social fractures created by class, race, and religion that do not always directly correlate with the urgency of need when we self-consciously decide, based on our often limited and color-blind perspective, who is worthy of our generosity.

For example, if we choose to respond to social disasters with monetary donations, political compassion recommends that we inform ourselves in the process, perhaps taking time to come to know—virtually or even personally—an organization whose mission involves empowering those groups on the ground to do the long-term work. We can ask them what and how much they need, rather than dictating to them what we are willing to give.

Finally, political compassion can help Americans to rethink collectively our final destination on the Jericho road and the path we choose to get there. In other words, political compassion might offer alternative ideas about human flourishing by separating visions of the "good life" from the often harmful values of individualism, self-sufficiency, autonomy, and whiteness that deny the full flourishing of all persons. Political compassion might interrupt what Hobgood calls the "so-cially constructed identities [that] oblige most people in the society to act against their long-term interests so that elites can receive short-term benefits."[56] In addi-tion to calling attention to the harmful effects of these values in the lives of individuals above and below the threshold of flourishing, it might overcome the paralysis many good-intentioned and otherwise compassionate Americans con-tinue to experience after social disaster of Katrina. By endorsing social values of interdependence, voluntary vulnerability, connectivity, and cultural diversity, political compassion reminds us that flourishing is a collective enterprise rooted in a shared desire for what is best for the suffering neighbor.

With this in mind, political compassion can renew the broken and demoral-ized American spirit by reminding us that the process of working together to figure out what is best for our neighbors is in and of itself a restorative process. Moreover, this is a necessary component of human flourishing for all persons. Political compassion offers a blueprint for constructive action plans that effec-tively suffer with others. In concrete terms this might entail setting aside space in our churches, classrooms, public libraries, town halls, and other civic spaces to emotionally experience, feel, or participate in others' suffering in a way that interrupts voyeurism and ignorance; or engaging in individual or collective prac-tices of humility in order to think more critically about the divisive ideologies we use to rely on in order to interpret reality; or personally affiliating with or participating in a social-services organization or faith-based agency that works to restore both suffering and privileged persons; or supporting public-policy initiatives and tax reforms that support organizations that attempt to reconstruct a more just and safe road Jericho.

COMPASSION AFTER KATRINA

"It's not the act of God that we struggle with, the act of God is done," says Rev. Vien Nguyen of Mary Queen of Vietnam Catholic Church in a Versailles neigh-borhood of eastern New Orleans. Versailles is home to the densest community of Vietnamese Americans in the United States. "The problem is the human acts, that is what we struggle with."[57]

The more than one thousand members of his parish have worked together—often with little local, state, or federal assistance and frequently in spite of the American Red Cross—to restore their community with new homes, a revital-ized business district, a charter school, senior-citizen housing, and a new or-ganic garden. Nguyen suggests that part of the community's success after Katrina has been a commitment on the part of the church to provide space for collective decision making and a commitment to accompany its members as they advocate for themselves at different levels of government—whether with municipal lead-ers to delay demolition of homes, or with the federal government to reroute unsanitary runoff water away from the local water table.

"Foremost," reported columnist Lance Hill in *The Louisiana Weekly*, "[the community] possessed a group-oriented culture that emphasized community needs over individual rights and interests; each individual in the community was duty-bound to help everyone in their community make it home. From the outset, community members understood that the individual's survival depended on the community's survival."[58]

This community, and the values of interdependence and empowerment that bind it together, reflects many of the latent "political" characteristics of compassion that we identified. For example, if we wish to resist what Nussbaum and Metz identify as our tendency to think about the causes of and responses to human suffering in individual or private terms, or, more theologically, in terms of individual human sinfulness, then would-be good Samaritans have to turn and face the suffering people of the Gulf Coast and not simply the anonymous social problems of concentrated poverty or individual poor choices. When we face the people affected by the hurricane, we begin to ask the difficult questions about why Katrina was not a colorblind storm, why we perceived some of those it affected as resourceful survivors and others as thugs, why aid was so long in coming and so unevenly distributed, and why at least one-third of Katrina's diaspora, the largest in American history, remain far from their neighborhoods or housed in temporary trailers more three years after the storm. With our faces turned toward these persons, we see more clearly that "the problem is with human acts," as Rev. Nguyen so prophetically puts it.

These questions inevitably lead us to critical evaluations of the collective values that shape the way we see, interpret, and respond to others' suffering. When we dare to ask these questions, political compassion moves us beyond private charitable disaster relief, with its often dehumanizing and debilitating effects on suffering persons and its ineffectiveness in dismantling the values and practices that fuel social disasters. Our search to find the answers to these questions leads us instead toward more collaborative development aid that places the responsibility for change on all persons. Development aid empowers those laid low by the tragedy of poverty to take charge of their recovery, and it challenges the presumed innocence and self-exoneration of those of us not immediately affected by the storm.

Compassion after Katrina is necessarily political because it compels us to interrogate the collectively held values and beliefs that created and exacerbated these people's suffering long before the storm. In addition, compassion after Katrina must be "political" if we want to take seriously Nussbaum and Metz's claim that human flourishing depends on our commonly shared yet frequently stunted capability for relationships. Restoration that focuses on restoring desire and capability for relationships with others is undoubtedly political and not merely private or personal. It involves a transformation of social attitudes, structures, and systems that create and support relationships in civil society. In addition, when we focus on bolstering people's capacity for relationship—with self, God, and others—we interrupt traditional ways of evaluating and responding to humanly perpetrated assaults on human persons. It is no longer an issue of evaluating the poor choices of individuals and responding accordingly, but rather the responsibility of all to all, rooted in the inherent goodness of human relationships.

In the case of responding to those affected by Katrina, political compassion points to the dramatic difference between being housed in a FEMA trailer in an arbitrarily created "FEMAville" or being at home in a house and neighborhood of one's choosing and making. The former narrowly construes recovery in terms of material goods, while the latter understands that recovery requires access to the intangibles of the common good. In other words, political compassion highlights the difference between rebuilding neighborhoods that reinforce pre-storm social fault lines of segregation and entrenched poverty and creating neighborhoods of "choice and connectivity"[59] where the need for human relationality is visible, celebrated, and equally shared.

With its focus on relationships, political compassion reminds us that injustice has a negative impact on our—everyone's—capacity for affiliation or relationship as well as our capability for practical reason or meaning-making—whether we live in the disaster zone or far from it. This turns restoring human relationality into a political process. In the case of Katrina, political compassion requires that we support individuals' abilities to make meaning out of their experience of suffering in order to rebuild the civic life of a community or in order to create space for a national conversation that privileges the narratives of those most affected by the storm. It also entails encouraging critical reflection on our participation in distinctively American values that render certain types of suffering and our connections to them invisible. White privilege is one such value. Political compassion exposes the detrimental and demoralizing impact of the values of whiteness and unearned privilege, even for so-called privileged persons who, like Metz's fellow Germans, are aware of the social disaster of concentrated poverty and yet feel powerless to respond. Through its emphasis on emotion, imagination, and the rich resources of human relationships, political compassion can break through the matrix of justice issues connected to entrenched poverty in order to create change for all of us on the road to Jericho.

Clearly, in an age of social disasters such as Katrina, we have to be on guard that our compassion continues to evolve in order to meet the particular demands of social reality. Political compassion can help us to "go and do likewise" more effectively and authentically after Katrina.

7

Transforming the Jericho Road

Political Compassion and Global Ethics

On the one hand we are called to play the good Samaritan on life's road-side; but that will be only an initial act. One day we must come to see that the whole Jericho Road must be transformed so that men and women will not be constantly beaten and robbed as they make their journey on life's highway. True compassion is more than flinging a coin to a beggar; it is not haphazard and superficial. It comes to see that an edifice which produces beggars needs restructuring.

Martin Luther King, Jr., made this prophetic observation in a speech delivered at Riverside Church in New York City on 4 April 1967, exactly a year before he was killed. It reflects his awareness of the need for an evolving compassion in America that can respond to the changing circumstances of our social relationships. In the midst of the social unrest and inequalities of the 1960s, King felt that authentic compassion ought to transform both persons *and* social realities.

Up to this point we have primarily considered the transformative possibilities of political compassion for *individuals*—whether those who are afflicted by social injustices or those who attempt to respond to them. However, the fact that people around the world struggle every day in humanly exacerbated social disasters such as Hurricane Katrina directs us to a more challenging task. We need to identify ways in which political compassion might help us perceive, interpret, and transform *social structures, systems, and institutions* that create such life-threatening conditions for so many.

One way to do so is to incorporate political compassion into various approaches to global ethics, so that we might recognize that social systems are not natural or inevitable givens in our reality but rather humanly created webs of relationship sustained by communal beliefs, values, and practices. Moreover, when rooted in political compassion, global ethics enables us to examine the socially constructed values, self-understandings, and dispositions that shape and sustain structures often maintained by those in the First World. This suggests that global ethics ought to transform under-privileged *and* privileged persons. Political compassion, therefore, can assist global ethics in moving beyond the values of globalization and toward alternative visions and practices with the potential to transform any "edifice which produces beggars" in our global age.

GLOBAL ETHICS?
AN AGE-OLD QUESTION WITH NEW-AGE URGENCY

Questioning how to articulate Christian discipleship most appropriately and to live it most distinctively in the context of an ever-changing world is not a new phenomenon. These questions have been at the forefront of Christian witness since the first disciples ventured from the safety of the upper room into the chaotic streets of Jerusalem on Pentecost. From the letters of Paul to the fledgling Christian communities of the Mediterranean to the most recent papal encyclicals by Benedict XVI to a robust church with more than a billion members, Catholic Christianity boasts a long tradition of scholars, communities of disciples, and prophetic witnesses who have attempted to articulate the social responsibilities of Christian communities in continuously changing local, national, and world contexts.[1]

Particularly in the last century, when world wars, genocides, and the threat of atomic warfare challenged our collective confidence in the human capacity to know and do good, different groups within the world community attempted to articulate a set of globally shared values and principles to guide humanity away from catastrophe and toward more just social relationships. The Universal Declaration of Human Rights proclaimed by the then-fledgling United Nations in 1948, *Pacem in Terris* promulgated in 1963 by Pope John XXIII, and "Toward a Global Ethic" set forward by the World Parliament of Religions in 1993 reflect such efforts. Each articulation of global citizenship and discipleship has its own originating questions, motivating factors, framework of meaning, and vision of the human community.

However, as the dynamic processes of globalization continue to unfold, so too do the challenges of articulating a global approach to the good life, to justice, and to human flourishing. While the reality of human suffering may not have changed significantly through the course of human history, it is nevertheless an undeniable fact that globalization has significantly changed our awareness of and responses to human suffering. The socioeconomic and cultural processes of globalization increase our exposure to suffering people—if only one dimensionally through networks of communication and constant exposure to images. And certainly the financial institutions, technological infrastructure, and social networks of globalization make it possible for us to reach, almost immediately, historically unreachable persons with every imaginable material good.

However, these same processes, networks, and infrastructures also potentially anesthetize us to others' affliction. They generate a sense of resigned inevitability that simply accepts unjust suffering as an unavoidable way of the world. They cripple us with a paralyzing guilt that accompanies the daily onslaught of horrific pictures and stories of tragic suffering that come to us through global media outlets. They compel us toward a dismissive realism that denies our connection to or responsibility for the pain of others. And sometimes they simply numb us to the pain that grips the globe; we feel powerless as individuals before this complex matrix of socioeconomic institutions, structures, and systems.

As a result of these various aspects of globalization, it seems that at no point in human history have we had the resources that are available today to solve the world's most entrenched social problems. We have heard many times that this generation can make hunger, extreme poverty, inequalities between genders and among races, disease, violent ethnic tensions, or environmental degradation problems of the past. And yet, it seems that we have never been less collectively concerned, motivated, or committed to doing so. We have everything we need to climb up to King's mountaintop from where we can dream of a different future, but we can't seem to muster the collective moral will to start walking. So, stuck in a morass in the valley, we miss the inspiring view from the peak. Rather than create alternative visions of how things might be, we practice what King called a "haphazard and superficial" compassion that does little more than "fling a coin" in the direction of the people affected by these ever-present social problems.

With these urgent concerns in mind, the question in academic circles has increasingly shifted from *whether* a global ethics is possible toward a discussion of *what kind* of global ethics might be viable in our contemporary context.[2] However, scholars often start from different perspectives, operate with distinct visions of human flourishing, and employ varying methods for creating justice. These factors have contributed to a variety of articulations of the relationship between Christian discipleship and world citizenship, as well as several distinct strategies for articulating a global ethics in recent history. Let us consider four in particular.

The *universal approach* to global ethics articulates a set of moral norms built on visions of the good life that transcend cultural particularities, that can be collectively discerned and agreed to through appeals to common sources of moral wisdom, and that can be applied cross-culturally by focusing on and bolstering various common denominators in the human condition. This approach attempts to perceive, interpret, and transform situations of social injustice by creating a consensus among diverse persons about what it means to be human and what must be done to protect and support that humanness. It publicly articulates this consensus to a wide audience, often using appeals to the shared human capacity for reason, the inherently social nature of persons, and themes of humanism. Examples include the universalizing principle of the "veil of ignorance" in John Rawls's *A Theory of Justice*, David Hollenbach's insistence on the universal duties and obligations of human rights, the United Nation's Millennium Development Goals, and many of the statements of the conferences of Catholic bishops around the world regarding justice and human development.[3]

The *particularist approach* protects against potential Western cultural hegemony or global elitism in the universalist approach by highlighting the insights that contextuality, cultural particularity, and individual experience can offer to collective reflection on common or global morality. It privileges the specific perspectives, experiential wisdom and cultural traditions of concrete individuals and communities that are frequently overlooked by more dominant cultures and even by those in power within particular contexts or communities. Particularist approaches suggest that we cultivate our inherent relationality and interdependence as well as extra-rational ways of moral reasoning through embodied encounters with others, exposure to narrative, and aesthetic expressions of meaning. Practitioners seek to inspire a humble moral responsibility to others because of their concrete, contextual, embodied, and gendered "otherness" rather than despite these particular attributes. They suggest that the process of dialogical overlapping consensus and reflexive self-awareness in generating a global ethics embodies that ethics. Examples include the discourse ethics of Seyla Benhabib, the feminist ethics of Traci West, and Martha Nussbaum's capabilities approach, rooted in the universal "principle of each person as an end."[4]

The *discipleship/responsibility approach* finds its roots in the late-twentieth-century revival of virtue ethics in Christian and secular ethics, as well the return of a biblically rooted ethic in Catholic moral theology after Vatican II. This trajectory suggests that global ethics might overcome the fragmentation within contemporary moral discourse, and within the human community, by highlighting the social efficacy of individual and communal character. It incorporates ongoing communal contemplation of the narrative of Christ, as well as the pivotal virtue of practical reason, in order to orient the community's dispositions toward an active and yet appropriately Christian engagement in the increasingly public square. Examples include the prophetic/radical vision and virtues of discipleship prescribed by Stanley Hauerwas, James Keenan's Thomistic notion of how mercy and justice hone our abilities to respond to suffering others, feminist approaches to the practices of care as articulated by Virginia Held, and John Paul II's articulation of the virtue of solidarity in *Sollicitudo Rei Socialis*.[5] The discipleship approach also includes the lived witness of various transnational "intentional communities" that link discipleship with social action in order to create peace and justice, including Sant'Egidio, the Ignatian Solidarity Network, and Pax Christi.

The *love-command approach*, with roots in the ethical divine command theory of Karl Barth, the moral theology of Gérard Gilleman, and the reflections of Anders Nygren, has also experienced a recent resurgence in theological circles.[6] It views obedience to the life-giving invitation of the covenant of the Hebrew Bible and New Testament to love God in one's neighbor as the heart of global justice. Right relationships with others in an increasingly global community begin with an individual and collective spirituality rooted in love of the neighbor. This deep-seated emotion gives rise to practical action that challenges the prevailing logic, power dynamics, social relationships, and patterns of behavior encouraged by globalization, all of which deny our responsibility to others and the social effectiveness of love. It incorporates ongoing reflections about the radical nature of God's love, a deepening of the efficacy of the emotions, and a closer connection between religious piety or personal mysticism and civic engagement or public justice. Contemporary examples include the 1993 statement by the Parliament of the World Religions, "Declaration toward a Global Ethic," rooted in the "Golden Rule of Humanity"; the claims of Edward C. Vacek, S.J., regarding the centrality of our response to God's invitation in Christian ethics; and Pope Benedict XVI's commitment to social charity as the appropriate guide to just living in *Deus Caritas Est*.[7]

Each of these approaches offers its own viable contribution to the ongoing debate, whether in terms of method, sources of wisdom, or vision of interdependence and flourishing. However, two relatively unexplored facets of our global reality present new challenges to travelers on the Jericho road. They also challenge previously articulated approaches to global ethics: first, the emotional costs of globalization for first-world persons—those who do not immediately identify with the Jew in the ditch in Christ's parable; and second, the unfolding impact of 9/11. These circumstances increasingly dictate what kind of global ethics we will need to navigate the unfolding reality of globalization.

Interrupting the Effects and Affects of Globalization

As we saw in Chapter 1, globalization involves the interconnected processes of increased interaction among peoples. For some, globalization creates unprecedented opportunities for increased economic, political, and cultural participation in an exponentially expanding public square. It creates new channels of communication, cultivates the political activity of a multiplicity of NGOs, makes the increased movement of peoples and resources possible, and fosters a "flat" world that facilitates human interdependence. For others, globalization denies participation in that same public square. It consolidates the power of communication, politics, and material resources in the hands of a few, it creates sharp divides between economic and cultural winners and losers within and between nations, and it undercuts the efficacy of national and international governing bodies in meeting the needs of the disadvantaged. As Rebecca Todd Peters succinctly puts it, "Globalization represents different realities to different people."[8] Therefore, since not all of those realities are equally life sustaining, we need to evaluate critically the various outcomes of the processes of globalization from perspectives that receive little if any credence in discussions controlled by global elites.

While it is certainly too late in the game to question *whether* globalization should exert the influence that it does in our reality, dialogue regarding what *kind* of globalization we want to shape our reality and our social relationships remains particularly urgent. We need a global approach to ethics that helps us evaluate more critically the external outcomes of globalization from a variety of perspectives. For example, we need to incorporate global memories, narratives, and biographies of globalization into our ethical evaluation of the processes of globalization, so that these alternative sources of wisdom might interrogate the insights of the cultural, economic, and intellectual elite, who frequently monopolize evaluative conversations.

Furthermore, as we saw in the post-Katrina recovery process, we need to make space for storytelling and deep listening if we want to restore and cultivate the kind of relationality that prevents the social disasters of poverty, racial conflict, and the pandemics of curable diseases. The transformative power of narrative—for storyteller and listener alike—is a relatively unexplored possibility in global ethics.

In addition, we need an approach to global ethics that can assist us in understanding globalization as a humanly created system of relationships that we can shape and control. This might interrupt prevailing notions that globalization is a natural, inevitable, or larger-than-life phenomenon that shapes and controls us. For example, J. Bryan Hehir suggests that while we can acknowledge that the processes of globalization have their own internal logic, their own motivating forces, and their own cultural, social, and economic drivers, globalization is not a self-conscious entity that seeks its own ends. Rather, the objectives of globalization are determined by the vision of those who create and sustain it through knowing and unknowing participation in its various systems and structures that touch every sphere of life.[9] And Peters recommends that we resist the temptation to view globalization as either "the way things are" or as an "inevitable part of an evolutionary process that we can't do much about."[10] She invites us to acknowledge our human agency in the face of this complex and overwhelming phenomenon in order to accept that globalization is a humanly created process that, as such, can be shaped and directed according to a variety of visions of what it means to be human and to live in community.

Many previously articulated approaches to global ethics have attempted to react to the rapid changes that globalization generates in just about every sphere of life. We need to move beyond these reactive stances with a global ethics that promotes *active* approaches to globalization that attempt to proceed with an eye to the future. We need to take a long view that reflects on the impact of these processes on aspects of creation that have yet to unfold—whether human or natural. We need to ask ourselves whether our actions in the present reflect the hopes we have for the human community and the earth in a future that we may not live to experience.

Moreover, in addition to our need for a global ethics that can facilitate critical analysis about the *external outcomes* of globalization and our shared vision for the future, we need to articulate a set of globally shared dispositions and practices that might resist the damaging, anesthetizing, and dehumanizing *internal or emotional experiences* of globalization that many persons around the world currently experience. The psychological impact of globalization weighs heavily on most of us who live in the epicenter of its matrix of economic, political, and cultural structures. Consider the following examples:

- William Schweiker suggests that "overhumanization" drives globalization and the self-understanding of first-world persons. By this he means the human power to "intervene to change and direct the dynamics of life on the planet" through a "free reign to conquer and control life."[11] Overhumanization ultimately suggests that maximizing human power ought to be the ultimate goal of existence. This creates a paralyzing awareness of the "titanic power of human beings" as well as a sense of helplessness and hopelessness, even among the winners of globalization, given our inability to control fully our realities.[12]

- Anthony Elliot and Charles Lemert identify a "new individualism" characterized by "individual self-aggrandizement, desire for unrestrained individualism, instant gratification and insulated hedonism." This self-understanding leads us to consider our vision of the world and responsibilities to it "less as interwoven with cultural relations and social problems, and more as shaped by individual decisions, capacities and incapacities, personal achievements and failures." As a result we are less willing to make long-standing commitments to projects, missions, or others; we lack a desire to search for meaning and value; we are increasingly unable to articulate personal or communal narratives; we experience increased levels of depression and a general "hallowing out of [our] emotional intimacies," all of which leave us "living without any other emotional ties, pursuing only short-term interests, completely alone and lonely."[13]
- Rabbi Jonathan Sacks detects a debilitating anxiety that we experience in the midst of the rapid and dramatic change that defines our times. We feel a destabilizing insecurity in the collapse of some of the basic institutions that structure our lives (marriage and family, neighborhood and civic associations, employment) and a demoralizing awareness that our individual choices are at once significant in the lives of others and at the same time rendered insignificant by the actions of large and anonymous economic and political institutions.[14]
- Peter Berger describes the experience of "individuation" in which individuals come to understand themselves as independent from and in some cases over and against "tradition and collectivity."[15]
- Roland Robertson identifies a variety of stressful "contractions" in our daily lives that arise as a result of the processes of globalization that "compress" the world: the simultaneous integration and fragmentation of communities, mediated and immediate encounters with persons of different cultures, the proximity and distance of others in relation to ourselves, or invitations to transcend traditional boundaries and threats against doing so.[16]

Many of these affective experiences of globalization underscore the need for a global ethics that can break through these disenfranchising, disempowering, disengaging, and demoralizing dispositions that prevent us from seeing and addressing the pain that globalization creates for us, and for our fellow travelers on the road to Jericho. Where many existing expressions of global ethics focus primarily on changing conditions of politically and socioeconomically threatened persons—whether through economic rights, political and religious freedoms, access to the common good, or participation in decision-making process—the affective costs of globalization on privileged persons suggest that contemporary approaches must also address their suffering and incapacities. We need a global ethics that can restore our sense of moral agency, our capability for authentic relationships with self and others, the values of participation and vulnerability in our daily engagement in the world, and a desire for empowerment with others, rather than power over others, in our various social relationships.

These sensibilities make it possible collectively to change the dehumanizing systems and structures that perpetuate injustice along the Jericho road.

Interrupting the Interruption of 9/11

The terrorist attacks of 9/11 provocatively revealed the "underside" or "shadow side" of globalization. A variety of factors related to the external and internal implications of globalization motivated those involved in the attacks and facilitated the execution of their plans. Globalization fueled a tribalism that reacted to the destabilizing compression of the world, a strong religion that reacted to the deterioration of traditional institutions, an actively offensive posture that attempted to assert control over others, and a violent expression of identity in the midst of a monolithic sociopolitical culture dominated by American self-interest. It facilitated a network of communications that enabled virtual planning sessions, porous national borders that permitted travel under false identities, and multicultural and religiously plural communities that camouflaged "sleeper cells." Globalization contributed to the declining power of nation-states in domestic and international affairs and to the increased efficacy of terrorist NGOs, as well as the formal and informal global monetary systems that facilitated financial transactions.

The events of 9/11 have altered the parameters of the discussion of global ethics by reinforcing a latent suspicion of religious contributions to global ethics programs. The fact that a small group of non-state actors committed violence in the name of religion reminds the international community, particularly its religious leaders and members, of the real potential in all religious traditions in our global age toward what sociologists of religion call a "resurgence" of "strong" religious identity and expression. The desacralizing processes of globalization fuels "true believers' attempt to arrest the erosion of religious identity, fortify the borders of the religious community, and create viable alternatives to secular institutions and behaviors."[17] Strong religion loses sight of the neighbor in a narrow focus on truth, individual purity, salvation, or scriptural literalism. As a result, we end up with an increasingly fragmented society—with significant divisions within religious traditions, as well as between religious and secularists.

Therefore, the attacks of 9/11 placed all religious traditions under the microscope of public scrutiny and caused many to question the ability of religion to foster global unity and provide universal guidelines for ethical action. Strong religion, a seemingly unavoidable consequence of globalization, obviously presents significant obstacles to articulating a global ethics. It makes it more difficult to identify with those beyond our immediate enclaves and precludes the possibility of religiously rooted moral values and ethical guidelines with wide cross-cultural appeal.

Moreover, 9/11 has changed the contours of global ethics discussions because it narrowly proposes security or impenetrability or self-defense as a primary individual and social value that shapes all relationships from the local to global level. Since the terrorist attacks, citizens of the United States—the political, economic, and cultural drivers of globalization—have become increasingly preoccupied with eliminating potential threats to our personal and national security both within our national borders and local communities and in various countries that are somehow connected to our national interests. The prevailing sense that we need to protect American "values" or the American "way of life" from a pending dramatic "clash of civilizations" between Western democratic capitalism and Islamic jihadist terrorism only heightens our wariness of cultural differences among persons, communities, nations, and regions of the globe. This wariness reinforces cultural differences and also fosters a defensive stance in our encounters with the "other." We quickly distance ourselves from others with dehumanizing labels such alien, illegal, undocumented, collateral damage, or enemy noncombatant. Moreover, our obsession with security cultivates an uncritical nationalism that places the security or impenetrability of one country above the peace and harmony of the wider international community. All of these factors present significant obstacles to any attempt to articulate a global approach to justice.

In addition, our reallocation of financial and social capital toward personal and national security undermines the dispositions, values, and governance structures from which any authentic ethic in this age will need to come. For example, protection from our neighbors rather than love for them shapes many personal interactions, and the security needs of the United States trump the needs for global security as assessed by the United Nations Security Council. When we place absolute value on security, we run the risk of destroying existing and potential relationships among individuals and communities with an irrational fear of people who are somehow different from us. This fear fuels divisiveness and aggravates tensions along existing fault lines. Those committed to a global ethics must attempt to bridge this gap.

Global ethics after 9/11, therefore, must cultivate an appreciation for mutually informative and critical engagement within and across religious traditions. It must place the religiously motivated violence of 9/11 at the heart of deliberations about what it means to be human, what it means to believe in God, and what it means to live a righteous life in communion with others. Global ethics after 9/11 must challenge religious believers not to distance ourselves and our respective faith traditions from the violent actions of the 9/11 hijackers and their associates, or from other terrorists who kill in the name of their God. Rather, the tragedy of this event should invite us to examine the tendencies toward fundamentalism in every religious tradition and to recommit ourselves to a collaborative effort toward peace in the name of the God of multiple global understandings. Such a global ethics will need to facilitate a humble, mutually informative, and collectively motivating interreligious dialogue about (1) the role of faith in human development strategies, (2) global structures that seek social justice, and (3) initiatives for international peace.

New Directions in Global Ethics

With these conditions in mind, contemporary articulations of global ethics in a new millennium will have to differ from the "classics" that were put forward in the latter half of the last century. For example, the power and influence of a variety of non-state actors in creating and destroying authentic human relationality challenge the basic assumptions in the Universal Declaration of Human Rights concerning the international commitment by states never to revisit the horrors of two world wars and the Holocaust. Today, NGOs and other grassroots groups, and not just nation-states or even international governing bodies such as the United Nations,will need to articulate and practice a global ethics.

Furthermore, since the logic of many responses to globalization is often influenced by what Berger calls "ideas and behaviors invented by Western intellectuals," the new global ethics will need to diverge from previous statements about global justice, such as *Pacem in Terris* in 1963, that are rooted in natural law, a particularly Eurocentric approach to ethics that relies on the human capacity for reason to ascertain and practice principles that can guide human behavior. We need to interrupt the predominantly white and masculine logic of globalization that often stems from a false sense that its processes simply reflect the natural and therefore unavoidable order of things, and our assumptions that its processes are reasonable to those with a rational world view. We need a new global ethics that can move beyond the natural-law framework toward emotive, embodied, and imaginative approaches to ethics. We also need to incorporate culturally embedded practices and narratives that can more critically orient our ethical evaluations of globalization, cultivate a sense of human interdependence and shared vulnerability, and give rise to a vision of human relationality and flourishing for all. Although natural law seeks these practices, it might not necessarily be able to deliver them in the current circumstances.

A global ethics after 9/11 will also need to encourage religious traditions to think critically, humbly, and collaboratively about the ways in which certain fundamental values, standards, and attitudes can drift toward fundamentalism. Contemporary articulations of a global ethics will differ from previous religiously motivated statements in a critical awareness of the dangers of religions in the global public square. For example, where the statement put forward by the Parliament of the World's Religions in 1993 was motivated by a sense of responsibility on the part of religious believers through their confidence in a "fundamental consensus" when it comes to "binding values, irrevocable standards, and fundamental moral attitudes," new statements will need to be rooted in shared humility among religious believers that acknowledges and atones for the violence inherent in the fundamentalist strains in every religious tradition.

In addition, contemporary global ethics will need to fill in the gaps in the four prevailing approaches to global ethics—universal, particular, discipleship/responsibility, and love-command—created by the impact of globalization on first-world individuals, as well as the continuing effects of 9/11. For example, those who pursue the *universal approach* must be even more aware of the ways in which universal approaches are frequently articulated from the perspective of those who already enjoy the benefits of the norms they wish to see universally applied—whether rights, or the common good, or relationships rooted in care. In his compelling analysis of the connection between structural poverty and disease, Paul Farmer notes that "those who formulate health policy in Geneva,

Washington, New York or Paris do not really labor to transform the social conditions of the wretched of the earth. Instead, the actions of technocrats . . . are most often tantamount to *managing* social inequality, to keeping the problem under control."[18]

Those who engage in the *particularist approach* must take seriously Max Stackhouse's concern about the caustic language and inflexible ideologies that often arise out of a particular way of seeing the world. The particularist approach also faces the challenge of moving beyond enclaves of similar circumstances—whether cultural, economic, geographical, or political—in order not to amplify experiences of fragmentation, compression, and isolation already inherent in the processes of globalization.

And the *responsibility* and *love-command approaches* both must remain aware of the tendency toward a bourgeois Christianity that individualizes and privatizes notions of discipleship or responses to God's invitation to love our neighbor. In other words, we must vigilantly resist instances where "Samaritans" are encouraged to use our privilege to the benefit of others but not necessarily to examine critically the impact of our privilege on us and on others in our global reality.

In short, uncritical confidence in our capacities for practical reason or authentic relationality, in our ability to cultivate intentional dispositions and habituated action, or in our commitments to loving the neighbor leads us to focus on the condition of suffering persons on the road to Jericho rather than on our contributions to the causes of that suffering. For example, do any of these approaches to global ethics challenge unearned privilege by pointing out that the excessive rights of some contribute to the lack of rights of others, or that the common good understood from the perspective of unearned privilege might not be as comprehensive as it could be? In other words, as Nussbaum puts it, do any of these approaches sufficiently disturb those who enjoy human rights as they are currently understood with "what that this conception requires *us* to do with and for the rest of the world?"[19]

Simply put, we need to encourage a moral agency on the part of contemporary Samaritans that can shape the processes of globalization, address its emotional costs, and create an awareness of the ways that privilege precludes many of us from fully understanding the ways in which the road to Jericho must be overhauled.

POLITICAL COMPASSION:
LOVING OUR NEIGHBOR IN AN AGE OF GLOBALIZATION

As the drivers of the processes of globalization it would seem that Americans in general, and American Christians in particular, are in an optimal position to contemplate and create the kind of globalization that makes it possible for all travelers on the road to Jericho to reach their respective destinations. However, as we have just discussed, these same processes of globalization, increasingly shaped by the American desire for personal and national security, often leave us feeling demoralized, disengaged, isolated, and powerless to create any real change beyond the ineffective scope of private charity or bourgeois compassion. For many of us, any attempt to control globalization, rather than to be controlled by it, can seem like an exercise in futility.

In order to break open this impasse, we need to devise ethical strategies that seek to change not only the circumstances faced by the vast majority of humanity, but also the oppressive circumstances in which the privileged minority find ourselves, since we knowingly and unknowingly control the dehumanizing systems and structures of globalization. Paradoxically, we too are controlled, oppressed, and dehumanized by these same systems and structures.

Political compassion targets that minority, and not simply because these individuals can most readily identify with the travelers on the road to Jericho in Jesus' parable—whether priest, Levite, or Samaritan. Rather, the interruptive and socially critical praxis of political compassion deconstructs the first-world perceptions, evaluations, and practices that have gradually undermined other approaches to global ethics. Political compassion sparks the corporate moral imagination in order to construct practical alternatives to the way things are. As such, it navigates the increasingly global terrain in the field of ethics, critically evaluates the values that support existing frameworks for a global ethics, complements existing approaches to ethics, and articulates new ideas about living well together in a global age.

While this is certainly a tall order, it is feasible in light of the reconstructed definition that we have culled from the Christian tradition, as well as from Martha Nussbaum and Johann Baptist Metz: loving our suffering neighbor in an age of globalization entails the *ability to perceive self-critically* both ourselves and our connections to the causes of others' suffering, the *humble willingness to interpret* situations of suffering with often overlooked aspects of human reason and in the context of larger social relationships, and an *active commitment to transform* these situations through authentic relationships of participation and empowerment. We will unpack this three-part praxis in order to identify the contributions that political compassion might make to loving our neighbor in a global age.

Compassionate Perception in Global Ethics

Political compassion pops the safe, comfortable, and potentially ideological bubbles of global elitism from within which many of even the best-intentioned persons attempt to articulate and practice strategies for human development. It does this by turning to face actual persons struggling with injustice, and by paying attention to the tragic circumstances of their situations or the causes for their suffering that lie beyond their personal control.

From this perspective, political compassion exposes the flaws in our self-understanding and the world views that shape our approach to global ethics. This self-awareness or self-observation creates what Schweiker calls "reflexivity" or "the wondrous capacity to be aware of oneself in the midst of acting and to be able to make adjustments, to learn in that very process."[20] Facing others and seeing them in the context of wider social injustices reveals white privilege as an egregious epistemological and practical blind spot in the four prevailing approaches to global justice we just discussed.

White Privilege

If Peter Berger is correct in suggesting that the emerging global culture is "heavily American in origin and content,"[21] then we need to be critical of the values, beliefs, and mores that shape our perception and interpretation of others' suffering. We have already discussed several of the values that wreak emotional havoc on first-world persons and hinder us in responding to others in need. For example, individualism isolates us from others, self-sufficiency rejects vulnerability, consumerism creates an anxious insatiability, competitiveness pits social "winners" against "losers," and fear perpetuates a defensive posture toward the world.

All of these values find their roots in the historic American ideal of whiteness and in the attitudes, systems, and structures that privilege whiteness. Laurie M. Cassidy and Alex Mikulich define white privilege as the "benefits that come simply from the fact that one is born with white skin." These benefits condition practically every aspect of the ordinary lives of all persons—from self-understanding and cultural identity to social interactions and investments in the common good.[22] The unearned advantage and conferred dominance of whiteness perpetuates the privileges and penalties that reinforce systems, structures, attitudes, and practices of racism. For example, Traci West notes that white privilege allows the privileged to deny the reality of racism or to exculpate ourselves from responsibility for it by claiming that only intentionally racist individuals are guilty of racism.[23]

Simply put, those who benefit from whiteness have a difficult time perceiving it. Recall Peggy McIntosh's analogy of white privilege as a knapsack filled with resources needed for a successful journey through life. These packs are conveniently invisible to those of us who carry them. For example, many of us are unaware of the entitlements we receive and penalties we do not face by virtue of our skin color. However, our packs of privilege are glaringly obvious to those who do not carry them. In fact, we must often rely on those without privilege to point out how the privileges that we enjoy negatively affect others.

The reflexivity of political compassion gives privileged persons the courage to turn and face those who are less privileged in order to perceive the unearned or unfairly distributed resources we have at our disposal. With their help we become aware of the damaging impact of the value of whiteness on our sense of self and the way that we relate to others, particularly in our good-intentioned attempts to love our neighbors. For example, with our faces turned to those who suffer, we discover that whiteness precludes deep relationality, makes us fearful of being vulnerable, views others as potential threats or competitors for limited resources, and compels us to reject being comfortable with our own bodies or dependency of any kind on others. When seen through the eyes of the suffering, the ways in which we integrate these aversions into our responses become more obvious: we avoid tactile contact, we steer clear of emotional drama, we force charities to compete with one another for our donations using quantifiable and faceless statistics, we equate exercising consumerist choice with living the "American dream."

By sparking this critical self-awareness, political compassion empowers us to interrogate the dangerous values that stem from and reinforce the oppressive power dynamics of privilege. But it also offers counter values that reinforce a more authentic self-understanding and animate a more socially responsible engagement in the world. These values can be of real use in strategies that continue to be articulated by those with knapsacks of privilege. For example, suffering with persons with this kind of reflexivity gives us the courage to embrace the inherent vulnerability that all human beings share, and it awakens a deeper concern for those who experience it more acutely than others. It cultivates the value of deep relationality with others that motivates us to embrace rather than avoid the dangers and mysteries of difference. It values the messiness and beauty of human embodiment so that we risk asking people how they actually experience different strategies of development—physically and emotionally—and not just safely seek the perspectives of other privileged persons.

The point here is that political compassion "interrogate[s] and resist[s] whiteness as a social location of unjust structured advantage"[24] by enabling us to see ourselves more critically in the eyes of others. With our faces turned toward suffering others, global elites are better able to see how whiteness influences so many of our social interactions, even those in which we attempt to suffer with the neighbor. Informed by this perspective of ourselves, we take what Peters identifies as "the first step toward responsible action" by identifying "the relationships of accountability that are so artfully hidden by the global economy."[25] In addition, we begin to realize that one of our primary responsibilities is to liberate ourselves from the dehumanizing demands of a culture of whiteness, and that in so doing, we are better able to liberate those with whom we are connected in the tangled web of globalization.

Political compassion privileges the perspective of suffering persons or the moral authority of their experiences. Therefore, it empowers those who travel down to Jericho without excessive privileges to identify the causal relationship between the ease of our passage and the difficulties in their journey. This kind of compassion gives unjustly waylaid travelers the ability to name their experiences of exclusion, or of living as persons of color in a world controlled by a colorblind elite, or of acquiescing power and authority to white outsiders, or of being dissatisfied with white persons' notions of what it means to flourish. The ability to name the cause or source of their suffering is an important step in resisting it.

Compassionate Interpretation in Global Ethics

Political compassion relies on emotion and memory as constructive and evocative sources of knowledge and wisdom. These relatively untapped sources of wisdom in global ethics break through the debilitating logic and demoralizing emotional effects of globalization that perpetuate a sense of futility. For instance, theodicy and anthropodicy questions that examine divine and human connections to social injustice do not avoid the pain and paralysis of doubt and guilt, but rather wrestle with them. These emotional bouts with the God of our understandings and with ourselves incorporate feelings, longings, fears, hopes, stories, images, laments, disappointments, and excitement into the economic and moral calculus of global ethics. Moreover, since the people we face do not merely articulate emotions and memories but physically embody them, our emotive and intellectual encounters with them not only move our minds in new directions, but they also move our bodies into dialogical and imaginative contact with one another.

Emotions and memory bring what Hobgood calls a much-needed tactile "emotional intelligence" to our reflections on global ethics. This kind of intelligence puts us "more fully in touch physically and emotionally with ourselves and others" and reminds us that "moral wisdom and insight emanate primarily from sensuous relationships not precepts."[26] Emotional intelligence not only informs the types of judgments necessary for global ethics, but it also incorporates new ways of reasoning that can unleash our moral imaginations.

Emotional, Embodied, and Relational Judgments

By stirring our emotions and pricking our historical consciousness, political compassion resists the detrimental impact of whiteness and privilege on the judgments we make about suffering and human development. White privilege individualizes our judgments regarding the suffering of others and cultivates a reward-and-punishment approach to human development. Said differently, privileged persons tend to evaluate whether or not individuals deserve the suffering or flourishing they experience based on their individual choices. However, through an emphasis on vulnerability and the socioeconomic context of individual suffering, political compassion corrects the individualistic, disembodied, and defensive logic of white privilege that negatively influences compassion's three judgments of seriousness, desert, and similar possibility.

For example, emotional cognition lifts up the inherent vulnerability that we all experience by virtue of our shared human nature—whether in terms of our attachments to things and people we cannot control, our concerns about threats to our dignity, or our basic dependency on others for our emotional well-being. Rather than reject this vulnerability or relational intimacy as an indicator of weakness or poor character, and therefore of little importance when evaluating the seriousness of suffering, political compassion suggests that inordinate vulnerability and the inability to sustain meaningful relationships are in fact markers of the most radical kind of suffering. Global ethics strategies need to respond to these expressions of suffering and not simply the kind of suffering that stems from a lack of material goods. Political compassion suggests that global ethics must also deliver relational goods—intangible things such as emotional connections with others, the ability to participate with others in something bigger than self, the chance to dream with neighbors about new directions for a community.

In addition, whereas whiteness values self-sufficiency and leads us to judge others as responsible for their own suffering, political compassion refuses to separate individuals from the social circumstances in which they find themselves. Through the historical consciousness of memory we move from an evaluation of another's suffering in terms of personal choices toward an analysis of the social relationships that contribute to these decisions. For example, we cannot evaluate individual choices regarding sexual activity, substance abuse, reproductive health, violence, employment, or housing without also evaluating the collective choices that perpetuate a hyper-sexualized, consumerist, and violent culture, or collective choices that sustain oppressive poverty, that undermine social support for families, or that fuel a racially unjust prison-industrial complex. By incorporating memory into our evaluation of another's suffering, political compassion reminds those involved in global ethics that broken individuals or even communities cannot flourish in a society crippled by broken social structures.

Finally, memories of things that tend to be forgotten by the privileged minority offer a nonverbal wisdom that can transcend cultural differences and assist us in judging similar possibilities or even in assessing whether another's fate might befall us. A more inclusive future—one that envisions full flourishing for all and not just for some—depends on a more inclusive memory of the past. This kind of inclusive memory can surface only in the context of what Metz calls "asymmetrical relationality" or relationships among individuals who might otherwise choose not to associate with one another. Remembering events or histories from asymmetrical places not only gives us a more complete understanding of that history, and likewise of the present, but also illuminates the desire to become a relational subject in the future. This shared desire, laid bare by collectively probing the past, can "re-member" fragmented communities that would otherwise deny their inherent similarities through a shared commitment to creating that future.

Humility and Moral Evaluation

Political compassion is rooted in a reflexivity that arises from the self-critical examination of our connection to others' suffering, from the emotional encounters we have with suffering others, and from the moral authority of their memories. This reflexivity brings a much-needed sense of humility to the global elites or the often-good-intentioned persons who dominate much of the conversation about global ethics, as well as to the four approaches we discussed earlier.

For example, with our faces turned to the faces of those who suffer, we discover that our ability to articulate universal truths about human nature and life in community is constantly evolving and dependent on the wisdom that we gain through relationships with people quite different from ourselves. When we pay attention to the memories of suffering, we realize that unjust human suffering is a common denominator that transcends cultural difference and particularity. And we remember that even religious institutions, traditions, and believers have contributed to a history of suffering and continue to perpetuate situations of injustice. Political compassion forbids those who seek a global approach to ethics to glaze over these shortcomings but rather compels them to examine them for the insights they hold.

In addition, humility breaks through the social paralysis that globalization creates among the global elite. Humility allows us to acknowledge and embrace our individual and collective brokenness in light of our shared human history of suffering. This acceptance of our failures, brokenness, vulnerabilities, weaknesses, and mistakes interrupts the power dynamics of globalization rooted in competitive capitalism. This dynamic sets up a false dichotomy between winners and losers, those who have and those who do not, those who are privileged and those who are not, those who set policy agendas and those whose lives are affected by them. Humility, however, reveals the inherent flaw in this dualism by reminding us of the unity among people that stems from our commonly shared limitations and vulnerability. Humility liberates global "winners" from the defensive postures we use to hold power over others—whether in distributing resources or in articulating strategies for human development—and frees us to experience the power of socially responsible relationships with others.

Imagination and Global Ethics

Given the role that telling and hearing stories plays in bolstering the human capability of affiliation or relationality, political compassion brings the human capability of imagination to global ethics debates. Maxine Greene notes that "the role of the imagination is not to resolve, not to point the way, not to improve," but rather "to awaken, to disclose the ordinarily unseen, unheard and unexpected."[27] In the case of global ethics, imagination helps first-world individuals to understand that social injustices are not anonymous, disembodied intellectual problems to be grappled with from a distance. Rather, they are human realities with very real sensations and physical urgencies that are experienced by actual persons. It also suggests that global ethics is not merely an intellectual discipline but a way of living creatively with others in the world.

Imagination "de-centers" and "de-privatizes" our self-understanding as well as our approaches to global ethics. For example, Jonathan Glover observes that when the moral imagination is stimulated "there is a break through in human responses otherwise deadened by things such as distance, tribalism or ideology."[28] Imagination interrupts our self-referential myopia by exposing us to an endless stream of unfamiliar images, sounds, tastes, textures, and feelings, all of which call into question the seemingly predetermined givens of our global reality and the various ideologies that dictate our understanding of them. Moreover, it transports us to different "epistemological standpoints"[29] from which we see ourselves, our reality, our notions of God, and our commitments to others in a dramatically different way. When these are called into question, our moral imaginations are unleashed and we are free to conjure, envision, craft, hone, and express alternative visions, strategies, and practices that can support our creative capacities. The imagination awakens the senses, often dulled by the processes of globalization, and refuses to limit human capabilities for change.

In addition, the human imagination re-creates, re-invents, and re-members the broken aspects of our human condition. With these active verbs in mind, the imagination reminds us that narrative and memory are participatory acts and, in fact, a way of participating in the creative act of an incarnational God, whose own narrative reveals a desire to heal, liberate, re-member, and create justice. This kind of imaginative engagement with others "rests on the assumption that people create through the act of perceiving and imagining, thereby becoming co-creators with God."[30] Moreover, the imagination enables us sensually to experience justice as something beautiful, something to which we are irresistibly

200 Transforming the Jericho Road

attracted in a "deeply beneficent momentum," and something that we wish to replicate or reproduce so that it might remain "sensorily present" to us.[31] This suggests that we think of global ethics as an imaginative attempt to chase after and replicate the beauty of human relationality.

Imagination also knits people together by making it possible to enter into other people's reality in a way that mere intellectual engagement cannot. We attempt to share or even enter into their consciousness, into the physicality of their bodies, into the intensity of their emotions, into the deep longing of their desires, into the visceral details of their dreams for the future. Through imagination we literally "become the friend of someone else's mind";[32] in the context of imagining another's suffering and recovery this friendship helps to reconstitute that person as well as our own sense of brokenness. This companionship bridges the distance between us and them, between those that merely think about injustices and those who experience them, between communities that flourish and those that do not.

Through the imaginative capacity to tell and deeply listen to stories, political compassion brings to global ethics a whole series of activities that in and of themselves serve as important ways of experiencing and sustaining justice: dreaming, conjuring, making, creating, crafting, designing. These active ways of being in the world move global ethics beyond various expressions of the social contract that focus on how we ought to better organize ourselves and toward an active commitment to envision collectively who we want to become in the future. Greene observes: "Community cannot be produced simply through rational formulation nor through edict. Like freedom, it has to be achieved by persons offered the space in which to discover what they recognize together and appreciate in common; they have to find ways to make intersubjective sense."[33] Political compassion brings this intersubjective sense to global ethics and suggests that the very attempt at this kind of relational subjectivity itself is an experience and expression of living in right relationship.

Compassionate Transformation and Global Ethics

Global ethics in the Christian tradition has been largely a reactionary enterprise. We have developed a variety of theories and strategies that either attempt to evaluate or respond to the givens of globalization or attempt to integrate the givens of Christian discipleship into the changing dynamics of our global age. Both approaches come at the expense of developing a more active approach that interrogates these givens and attempts to shape the processes of globalization and Christian discipleship according to a vibrantly colorful vision of the future. Said differently, we have not done enough to determine what kind of globalization we want and how to channel its processes accordingly.

Political compassion, however, can contribute the missing pieces—the subjective, emotional, embodied, and organic qualities of social relationships and the good life—that cultivate an active approach to global ethics. These elements can create affective, moral, and cognitive conversions within so-called flourishing persons and communities. Political compassion does so by fostering an authentic relationship with God, self, and others, and by proposing that justice is best understood as a collective and sensory vision that animates and sustains ethical living rather than as an intellectual precept that supports abstract theories or paradigms.

Authentic Relationality

So many aspects of our global age underscore first-world persons' inherent connections with and impact on people beyond our immediate circles of concern. This is the great promise of globalization. And, yet, this global relationality is not always intentional, authentic, life-sustaining, or liberating. In fact, our increased relationality frequently comes in the form of self-selected, disembodied, and virtual connectivity; or it presents itself in the context of involuntarily chosen ties to people we don't know; or it unfolds in the context of the power dynamics of privilege, which denies intimacy.

These relationships threaten our capacity for real relationships with ourselves and others and therefore deny full humanity to us and them. They also trap the privileged in desensitizing and demoralizing cycles of consumption that erroneously equate "having" with "being." They fuel a "new individualism" that is emotionally isolating and psychologically destructive. They individualize many of our social concerns and then privatize our responses to them, trapping us and others in endlessly ineffective cycles of charity. Instrumentalized relationality ultimately denies the privileged the much-needed opportunity to consider the ways in which our lifestyles contribute to the causes of others' suffering, and it denies the underprivileged the much-needed agency that comes with participation in social change.

Political compassion interrupts with intentionality. Recall, for example, the intentional relationality that motivated the good Samaritan in his care for the Jew in the ditch—he refused to submit to the prevailing sensibilities that outlawed tactile encounters with certain others, or that endorsed relationality only under certain conditions of religious purity or personal safety, or that justified turning one's back on another in need in the name of personal security. He interrupted what might have otherwise been an uneventful journey to risk taking a very different path with another because of a deep sense of shared humanity and an equally sensory vision of what the road to Jericho ought to be. Bryan Massingale observes that this kind of compassion "propels one to act beyond the limits of what is considered reasonable" and "arises not through an avoidance of suffering but from a deeper entering into it."[34]

Jesus commands his disciples to live with the same deep intentionality and desire for intimacy when it comes to our relationships with others. If we are to "go, and do likewise," then we must not simply behave according to a set of social or religious mores, or the guidelines of an abstract social contract. Blind obedience or contractual legalism can instrumentalize our relationship with our neighbors, who become little more than pawns in our personal quest for righteousness, or salvation, or even relationship with God. Rather, we must act intentionally, imaginatively, and collaboratively to deepen our relationships with others through participation in their memories, narratives, and visions. Here, as we are forced from the familiarity of our lives into the foreign struggle of others' lives, the grace of the struggle for justice is revealed and realized. For when the struggle of others becomes so familiar that it is indistinguishable from our own, we interrupt the prevailing logic of instrumentalized relationality with an experiential understanding of what it means to have one's flourishing inextricably tied to another. Mary Hobgood observes that only this kind of intentional relationality resists the logic of "ignorance, arrogance, and isolation" that keeps us trapped in lifeless and meaningless cycles of apathy at worst and charity at best.[35]

In addition, political compassion encourages those engaged in global ethics debates or strategizing to *reflect with the faces* of social injustice or suffering, and *not simply reflect on the facts* of injustice. In other words, suffering with others enables any approach to global ethics to be vigilant not only about *what* is said or what is decided about the good life, but also about *who* articulates these ideas and *how* they express them. The ways in which people engage one another in these exchanges is just as important as what is exchanged. Political compassion ensures a diversity in the "whos" and the "hows" of global ethics, given Metz's insistence that genuine compassion occurs in the context of asymmetry, in the context of unequal relationships. Again, with our faces turned toward the faces of others who exist beyond our various enclaves, we begin to pay more attention to *who* articulates these strategies as well as *how* we arrive at conclusions or *how* we implement strategies. Relationships of asymmetry interrupt the dictatorship of similar minds, frameworks of meanings, and experiences.

In the context of embodied, emotive, and historically conscious collective expression we discover that justice is in fact a commitment to this kind of vigilance and sensitivity, as well as a commitment to acting with others toward a commonly shared end, and not simply on their behalf toward an end in which they have little stake. We move beyond *thinking about* justice in terms of its classic definition of "giving others their due," which sustains a competitive relationality among persons, and toward *being about* justice, which sustains an empowering and corporate resolve to "do what is ours to do."[36]

The point here is that when rooted in political compassion, justice becomes a way of being in the world—whether in the context of local, national, or global relationships. Political compassion cultivates a thick and textured relationality that scholars in the various camps of global ethics have begun to identify as an important corrective to purely intellectual, rational, or like-minded approaches to justice. For example, this kind of capacity to suffer with others facilitates Kwame Anthony Appiah's notion of a "rooted cosmopolitanism" that makes it possible to claim unapologetically our own position, while remaining humble enough to evaluate it in light of radically different ideas offered by people radically different from us.[37] It would also offer the kind of emotive and imaginative reason that Lisa Sowle Cahill identifies as necessary for "transversalism," which she defines as "mutually empathetic and cultural communication in which participants cross imaginatively into one another's territories and express their own values."[38]

JUSTICE AS EXPERIENTIAL VISION

Political compassion ultimately seeks to reconstitute, revitalize, renew, and re-member individuals and communities through collective and intentional action. Unlike compassion by proxy, political compassion brings people together in order to dream collectively a vision of what might be in such a way that the very process of dreaming begins to create that which is envisioned. Political compassion enables us to know justice as more than a cognitive category or an abstract concept, which is an epistemological privilege for those who do not regularly experience injustice. Nor is justice simply a useful building block of social relationships that we rationally work out, diplomatically deliberate, or strategically apply, a practical privilege for those whose time and emotional energy are not consumed with survival. Rather, through the mystical and political elements of compassion, we come to know justice experientially and viscerally as a collaborative and creative process that incorporates a multiplicity of ways of knowing.

Mystically, compassion reminds us that justice is a vision that arises out of embodied, emotive, imaginative, and relational encounters with self, God, and others in the context of suffering. Just as the mystical vision of the promised land from the metaphorical mountaintop shaped King's civil disobedience throughout the civil rights movement, the vision that we create with others in the context of compassion animates our engagement in the world. Because it is emotional, imaginative, and visceral, it can redirect us around the various intellectual and psychological impasses of our global reality, whether demoralizing apathy or paralyzing guilt. Also, because it is nourished by human relationality that rejects competitive individualism and impenetrable isolationism, this vision can rejuvenate us when our commitment to a shared vision understandably wanes. We become capable of leaning on others or comfortable with others leaning on us as we journey together toward that shared vision.

Politically, compassion also reminds first-world persons that our vision of the future needs to include a sense of collective accountability for our contributions to the socioeconomic contexts of suffering in the past and in the present. Recall, for example, Metz's confidence in the freedom that comes with "memories of the future." This seemingly paradoxical idea suggests that any vision of future that does not wrestle with the social sins of the past will never break through the impasses of the present. Simply put, we cannot expect to heal a broken world without taking responsibility for the havoc we have wrecked. To do so, we must enter into social relationships with those who cannot only forgive us for these social sins but also awaken within us a desire to join them on the shared journey to recovery.

Concluding Remarks

Through this mystical and political praxis, political compassion complements each of the approaches to global ethics we discussed at the beginning of the chapter. It also fills in the respective gaps. It affirms *universal* claims regarding the commonalities that bind all persons, particularly our shared desires for authentic relationality that can resist the dehumanizing characteristics of human suffering. However, political compassion brings to universal approaches the experiential and tactile wisdom of encounters with actual suffering persons. Their experiences can humanize and concretize the abstract principles and precepts of justice and the demands these principles make on those who already benefit from them.

With our faces turned toward suffering persons we are compelled to move from a relatively comfortable intellectual solidarity toward a more difficult embodied solidarity. By integrating the emotions and imagination into reflections on living in just relationships, political compassion also corrects an over-reliance on rational and intellectual approaches. Guided by the wisdom of those who are suffering, we are better able to understand what justice might look like, or how it might sound or feel. It is no longer something that we think about but something that we deeply desire for ourselves and for others.

Political compassion can overcome the dynamics of privilege, especially white privilege, that *particular* approaches often bring to global ethics. However, political compassion also insists that the experiences of unjust and dehumanizing suffering serve as an unfortunate common denominator that unites the majority of the world's population. After all, most of the world's population lives without privilege. Today, citizens of the United States are beginning to experience this sense of commonality as the financial crisis continues to increase the vulnerability of Americans, regardless of economic and cultural boundaries. Moreover, political compassion reminds us that particular approaches can rightly rely on the universally shared desire to be a human subject and to maintain healthy relationships with self, God, and others. This is necessary in order to turn particular cultural practices toward strategies for justice that transcend cultural differences.

As a paradigmatic characteristic of Christian discipleship, political compassion affirms the *discipleship* model. It insists on the practical and constructive role of religion in global ethics, particularly when it comes to care of the suffering neighbor—whether in telling stories of healing and forgiveness, fostering imaginative visions, cultivating intentional relationality, or supporting grassroots activism. However, political compassion also reminds disciples of the need for humility, particularly in our contemporary context of religious pluralism, and the need to take responsibility for violence against a neighbor committed in the name of religion. It also encourages the more difficult and transformative task of engaging the *people* of other religious and secular traditions, and not just the traditions themselves. This is how we can discover the sacramental wisdom of their memories and narratives. It reminds us that in order to "go, and do likewise," we must constantly reinterpret biblical mandates of discipleship in light of our changing context.

And, finally, political compassion affirms the deep relationality with God and others of the *love-command* approach. However, political compassion provides a much-needed critical self-awareness that reminds us of the ways that white privilege can dangerously privatize and individualize our expressions of love of neighbor. It also calls to mind the liberating characteristics of God's love—which refuse to heal oppressed persons without also condemning the causes of their oppression whether they are denied community due to illness or disability, or marginalized because of gender or ethnicity, or enslaved by the progress of empire.

Political compassion insists that the human face be the touchstone for global ethics. Suffering with others begins with our choice to turn and face those who have been assaulted and then abandoned in the ditch on the road down to Jericho. Compassion invites us to look into the faces of other people, to be present with them where they are, and to create fellowship in the midst of their pain. With our faces turned toward theirs, we realize that human development is not an intellectual exercise or a field for economic experimentation. When we stop long enough to gaze into the eyes of our suffering neighbors, we begin to see human development as a collective venture of groups of people rather than as an economic project or social program that targets a few. When we force ourselves to listen deeply to the narratives of others, we gain knowledge that is often overlooked or ignored by the usual benchmarks of human flourishing. And when we conjure their memories in our own imaginations, we begin to envision human development as a way of living in an intentional relationship with others rather than as a topic of political debate about how to distribute limited resources, protect basic rights, or transcend cultural moralities.

A REPRISE OF THE GOOD SAMARITAN

To some extent, my reconstruction of compassion interrupts the traditional interpretations of the parable of the good Samaritan. After all, the story is the paradigmatic narrative of neighbor love in the Christian tradition. Political compassion also drastically changes the nature of our discipleship.

When we turn to face suffering persons, we realize that it is no longer enough for individual travelers to step into the ditch and offer emergency aid to the victims of humanly perpetrated violence. Samaritanism calls for a collective response to whole groups of people. Our contemporary reality is defined by dehumanizing suffering and increasingly gross inequality. Because it is driven by an expanding global market economy, it is no longer sufficient simply to give of our surplus and continue on our way. Those incapacitated along the roadside far out-number those able to travel safely. And the same persons who pave the road with their unjust labor and deprivation are all too often excluded from their destination.

Samaritanism today must move beyond charitable aid. Charity merely perpetuates cycles of structural violence. We can no longer leave suffering persons in the care of someone else or assume that material resources will provide the needed healing. Rather, Samaritanism requires a willingness to offer intangible goods—ourselves, our willingness to listen deeply, and our commitment to figuring out a new way forward together. It is no longer possible to absolve ourselves of the sinful conditions of the passage down to Jericho. Globalization has blurred the distinction between those who innocently travel and those who rob others of their dignity along the way. Today, the road grows more and more treacherous for more and more people. Consequently, Samaritanism means we must integrate loving our suffering neighbors with seeking their forgiveness for our participation in the sins of individualism, consumerism, and privilege.

The three tasks of political compassion offer a new way to respond to Jesus' mandate to "go, and do likewise." *First, we must perceive our connections to the causes of others' suffering.* If we turn to face those who are suffering, we will see ourselves through their eyes and become self-critical, identifying the values, attitudes, and practices that deny others, and even ourselves, the capability for authentic relationships. Perhaps we will become aware for the first time of the dehumanizing values of whiteness and privilege, the emotional effects of globalization, and our own desire for personal security. We may also confront our tendencies to individualize the causes of others' suffering, our blindness to the social causes of natural disasters, our obsessions with personal sinfulness, and the paralyzing effect of fear in our post-9/11 world. Political compassion can free us to see ourselves and our social reality in a different light.

Second, we must learn to interpret the social contexts of suffering by listening to the memories and narratives of those who suffer. Too often we ignore perspectives and overlook facets of moral reasoning. We should seek out innovative ways of responding to entrenched social problems and take responsibility for our direct and indirect connections to them. To make sense of what is going on around us, we no longer have to rely exclusively on the logic of the marketplace, rationality, or even the natural-law reasoning of Catholic social thought. Instead, political compassion offers alternative sources of practical reason, including emotion, memory, narrative, and imagination. Memories and narratives shared by suffering neighbors can give us not only information but also moral courage. When we unleash these embodied and creative aspects of our capability to reason, we push ourselves beyond worries about what might be feasible to more exciting speculation on the feasibility of the impossible. We move from just questioning why things work the way they do to a more arresting notion: Why can't we arrange things differently?

Third, Samaritans must understand human flourishing in terms of our shared capabilities for relationships. Political compassion can give us a resolve to break through the emotional ennui of globalization and to harness the energy and passion that arise from relationships with real people who seek a common goal. To flourish means to be able to claim our past, to participate in constructing meaningful lives in the present, and to dream of a different future—and to do all of these things in collaboration with others. Eventually we may realize that our liberation as privileged Samaritans is indeed caught up in the liberation of others. None of us will reach our destination if others are left behind.

When traveling down to Jericho equipped with political compassion, today's Good Samaritans are not just individuals willing to interrupt their journeys for someone they recognize as a neighbor in need. While individuals still can accomplish great good, in our globalized world the Good Samaritans are more than likely to be bands of socially conscious and self-aware people who accept the challenge to free their neighbors from the oppressive processes of globalization *and* to free themselves from its dehumanizing values and practices. Through relationships, Samaritans will work to understand the socially disastrous conditions of Jericho road while they accompany waylaid travelers, engaging the travelers' memories and narratives and sharing their own. Their journey together will deepen their connection and their sense of mutual responsibility for the other. To follow the example of the Good Samaritan in an age of globalization demands as much; it is only through such reflection and action that we can truly begin to "go, and do likewise."

Notes

Introduction

1. Kristin A. Bates and Richelle M. Swan, *Through the Eye of Katrina*: *Social Justice in the United States* (Durham, NC: Carolina Academic Press, 2007), 5.

2. See Kevin Burke's interpretation in Ignacio Ellacuría's 1975 essay "Toward a Philosophical Foundation for Latin American Theological Method," in Kevin F. Burke, S.J., *The Ground beneath the Cross: The Theology of Ignacio Ellacuría* (Washington DC: Georgetown University Press, 2000), 100–108; and Michael E. Lee's *Bearing the Weight of Salvation: The Soteriology of Ignacio Ellacuría* (New York: Crossroad, 2008).

3. For her outline of this understanding of theology and vocation in light of the reality of racism, see M. Shawn Copeland, "Racism and the Vocation of the Christian Theologian," *Spiritus: A Journal of Christian Spirituality* 2, no. 1 (2002): 15–29.

1. American Compassion in a Global Age

1. Presidents Bill Clinton and George H. W. Bush, "In Katrina, Compassion Met Adversity," *USA Today*, 22 August 2006.

2. Greg Warner and Ken Camp, "Will Katrina-inspired Compassion Change Long-term Poverty Fight?" *American Baptist Press*, 20 December 2005, quoting Jimmy Dorrell, director of Christian Community Ministry, Waco, Texas.

3. See Ada María Isasi-Díaz, *Mujerista Theology* (Maryknoll, NY: Orbis Books, 1996), 83.

4. William C. Spohn, *Go and Do Likewise: Jesus and Ethics* (New York: Continuum, 2000).

5. Clifford Orwin, "Compassion," *American Scholar* (Summer 1980): 316.

6. Ibid., 313.

7. Wendy Farley, *Tragic Vision and Divine Compassion: A Contemporary Theodicy* (Louisville, KY: Westminster/John Knox Press, 1990) 53–54.

8. Retrieved from http://www.care.org/campaigns/world-hunger/facts.asp?source =170740250000&channel=default on 8 July 2008.

9. Retrieved from http://www.care.org/campaigns/hiv.asp?source=170740250000 &channel=default on 8 July 2008.

10. Retrieved from the World Bank: http://web.worldbank.org/WBSITE/EXTERNAL/ TOPICS/EXTPOVERTY/EXTPA/0,,contentMDK:20153855~menuPK:435040 ~pagePK:148956~piPK:216618~theSitePK:430367,00.html#trends on 8 July 2008.

11. Retrieved from http://www.one.org/node/275.html on 8 July 2008.

12. Retrieved from the World Bank: http://web.worldbank.org/WBSITE/EXTERNAL/ TOPICS/EXTPOVERTY/EXTPA/0,,contentMDK:20207590~isCURL:Y ~menuPK:435735~pagePK:148956~piPK:216618~theSitePK:430367,00.html on 8 July 2008.

13. In addition to those offered in the bulleted list, see also George Ritzer, ed., *The Blackwell Companion to Globalization* (Boston: Blackwell Publishing, 2007); William

Sullivan, *The Globalization of Ethics* (Cambridge: Cambridge University Press, 2007); Pamela Brubaker, ed., *Justice in a Global Economy: Strategies for Home, Community, and World* (Louisville, KY: Westminster John Knox Press, 2006); and Paul Knitter and Chandra Muzaffar, eds., *Subverting Greed: Religious Perspectives on the Global Economy* (Maryknoll, NY: Orbis Books, 2002).

14. Max Stackhouse, *God and Globalization: Religion and the Powers of the Common Life*, vol. 1 in the Theology for the Twenty-first Century series, ed. Max Stackhouse and Peter Paris (Harrisburg, PA: Trinity Press International, 2000), 8.

15. Anthony Giddens, *Runaway World: How Globalization Is Reshaping Our Lives* (New York: Routledge, 2003), 6–19.

16. Rebecca Todd Peters, *In Search of the Good Life: The Ethics of Globalization* (New York: Continuum, 2006).

17. Cynthia D. Moe-Loebeda, *Healing a Broken World: Globalization and God* (Minneapolis: Fortress Press, 2002), 22.

18. Richard Gillet, *The New Globalization: Reclaiming the Lost Ground of Our Christian Tradition* (Cleveland, OH: Pilgrim Press, 2005).

19. William Schweiker, *Theological Ethics and Global Dynamics: In a Time of Many Worlds* (Boston: Wiley-Blackwell, 2004), xv.

20. John A. Coleman, "Making the Connections: Globalization and Catholic Social Thought," in *Globalization and Catholic Social Thought: Current Crisis, Future Hope*, ed. John A. Coleman, S.J., and William F. Ryan, S.J. (Maryknoll, NY: Orbis Books, 2005), 13–15.

21. Jon Sobrino, S.J., and Felix Wilfred, "Introduction: The Reasons for Returning to This Theme," in *Globalization and Its Victims*, ed. Jon Sobrino, S.J., and Felix Wilfred, *Concilium* 5 (2001): 11–12.

22. Peters, *In Search of the Good Life*, 206.

23. Anthony Elliot and Charles Lemert, *The New Individualism: The Emotional Costs of Globalization* (New York: Routledge, 2006), 5.

24. Moe-Loebeda, *Healing a Broken World*, 3.

25. David Hollenbach, S.J., *The Common Good and Christian Ethics*, New Studies in Christian Ethics (New York: Cambridge University Press, 2002), 219.

26. Hille Haker, "Compassion as a Global Programme for Christianity," in *In Search of Universal Values*, ed. Karl-Josef Kuschel and Dietman Mieth, *Concilium* 4 (2001): 55–70.

27. Retrieved from http://www.one.org/trade_justice/ on 8 July 2008.

28. Retrieved from http://www.one.org/debt_cancellation/ on 8 July 2008.

29. Douglas Hicks, *Inequality and Christian Ethics* (New York: Cambridge University Press, 2000), 65.

30. Holly Hall, "A Charitable Divide," *The Chronicle of Philanthropy* (10 January 2008), 15.

31. Donald McNeill, Douglas Morrison, and Henri J. M. Nouwen, *Compassion: A Reflection on the Christian Life* (Garden City, NY: Doubleday, 1982), 125.

32. Mary Elizabeth Hobgood, *Dismantling Privilege: An Ethics of Accountability* (Cleveland, OH: Pilgrim Press, 2000), 37–39; see also "White Economic and Erotic Disempowerment: A Theological Exploration in the Struggle against Racism," in *Interrupting White Privilege: Catholic Theologians Break the Silence*, ed. Laurie M. Cassidy and Alex Mikulich, 40–55 (Maryknoll, NY: Orbis Books, 2007).

33. Ruth Frankenberg, "The Mirage of an Unmarked Whiteness," in *The Making and Unmaking of Whiteness*, ed. Birgit Brander Rasmussen, Irene J. Nexica, Eric Klinenberg, and Matt Wray (Durham, NC: Duke University Press, 2001), 76.

34. Peggy McIntosh, "White Privilege: Unpacking the Invisible Knapsack," available from several websites.

35. Traci C. West, *Disruptive Christian Ethics: When Racism and Women's Lives Matter* (Louisville, KY: Westminster John Knox Press, 2006), 116–40.

36. Miguel A. De La Torre, *Doing Christian Ethics from the Margins* (Maryknoll, NY: Orbis Books, 2007), 5.

37. Martin Luther King, Jr., "I've Been on the Mountaintop." Retrieved from http://www.stanford.edu/group/King/publications/speeches/I've_been_to_the_mountaintop.pdf on 24 March 2008.

38. Jeannie Haubert Weil, "Discrimination, Segregation, and the Racialized Search for Housing Post-Katrina," in *Through the Eye of Katrina: Social Justice in the United States*, ed. Kristin A. Bates and Richelle Swan (Durham, NC: Carolina Academic Press, 2007), 221–37.

39. Ashley Doane, "New Song, Same Old Tune: Racial Discourse in the Aftermath of Hurricane Katrina," in Bates and Swan, *Through the Eye of Katrina*, 111.

40. Shana Agid, "Locked and Loaded: The Prison Industrial Complex and the Response to Hurricane Katrina," in Bates and Swan, *Through the Eye of Katrina*, 57.

41. West, *Disruptive Christian Ethics*, 107.

42. Ibid., 119.

43. Ibid., 17.

44. Oliver Davies, *A Theology of Compassion: The Metaphysics of Difference and Renewal of Tradition* (Grand Rapids, MI: Eerdmans, 2001).

45. See Steven Tudor, *Compassion and Remorse: Acknowleding the Suffering Other*, vol. 11 in the Morality and the Meaning of Life series, ed. Albert W. Musschenga and Paul J. M. van Tongeran (Leuven: Peeters, 2001).

46. Ibid., 80, emphasis added.

47. Diana Fritz Cates, *Choosing to Feel: Virtue, Friendship and Compassion for Friends* (Notre Dame, IN: University of Notre Dame Press, 1997).

48. McNeill et al., *Compassion*, 124.

49. Orwin, "Compassion," 323.

50. *Chronicle of Philanthropy*, Annual Report (2006).

51. See the Substance Abuse and Mental Health Services Administration, "2007 National Survey on Drug Use and Health." Available on the www.oas.samhsa.gov website.

52. Paul Farmer, *Pathologies of Power: Health, Human Rights, and the New War on the Poor* (Berkeley and Los Angeles: University of California Press, 2004).

53. See Madonna Meyer, ed., *Care Work: Gender, Love and the Welfare State* (New York: Routledge, 2000); and Virginia Held, *The Ethics of Care: Personal, Political, and Global* (New York: Oxford University Press, 2006).

54. Johann Baptist Metz, *The Emergent Church* (New York: Crossroad, 1981), 2.

55. Ibid., 3.

56. James D. Davidson, "Generations of American Catholics," plenary address to the Catholic Theological Society of America, Miami, 6 June 2008.

57. Gloria Albrecht, "A Marriage Proposal: The Union of Human Rights with Policies That Value Families," paper presented at Pulpit Politics: Gender, Religion, and Justice in 2008, sponsored by the Center for Ethics Education at Fordham University, New York City, 22 April 2008.

58. Alan Wolfe, *One Nation after All: What Middle-Class Americans Really Think about God, Country, Family, Racism, Welfare, Immigration, Homosexuality, Work, The Right, The Left, and Each Other* (New York: Viking, 1998), 5. Wolfe interviewed two hundred Americans in eight national suburbs in an attempt to discern whether

middle-class Americans share a common world view or are divided along stereotypical lines of conservative or liberal, red state or blue state, and so on.

59. Ibid., 54. See also David Hollenbach's discussion of the impact of tolerance on urban poverty in *The Common Good and Christian Ethics* (Cambridge: Cambridge University Press, 2002), 34–42.

60. Pew Forum on Religion and Public Life, "U.S. Religious Landscape Survey," released 23 June 2008. Retrieved from http://religions.pewforum.org/reports on 8 July 2008.

61. Wolfe, *One Nation after All,* 43.

62. According to a survey of the 2004 election, "Voters Like Campaign 2004, But Too Much 'Mud-Slinging,'" conducted by the Pew Forum for People and The Press, among voters who chose moral values as most important from the list of seven issues, about half gave a response that mentioned a specific issue. Forty-four percent defined the phrase specifically in terms of social issues, including abortion (28 percent), homosexuality and gay marriage (29 percent), and stem cell research (4 percent). A few other issues were mentioned, including poverty, economic inequality, and the like. But the definition of moral values is not limited to policy references. Nearly a quarter of respondents (23 percent) who cited moral values as important explained their thinking in terms of the personal characteristics of the candidates, including honesty and integrity (cited by 9 percent); 18 percent explicitly mentioned religion, Christianity, God, or the Bible. Another 17 percent answered in terms of traditional values, using such language as "family values," "right and wrong," and "the way people live their lives." For a summary of the findings, see http://people-press.org. Preliminary analysis of religious voters in the 2008 election suggests that while Obama made inroads in all faith traditions, a significant gap persisted between white Protestants (34 percent), evangelical Protestants (26 percent), and unaffiliated voters (75 percent). See Pew Forum on Religion and Public Life, "How the Faithful Voted." Available at http://pewforum.org/docs/?DocID=367.

63. Christian Smith and Melinda Lundquist Denton, *Soul Searching: The Religious and Spiritual Lives of American Teenagers* (New York: Oxford University Press, 2005), 162–63.

64. See Robert Bellah, et al., *Habits of the Heart: Individualism and Commitment in American Life*, 3rd ed. (Berkeley and Los Angeles: University of California Press, 2007); Reid Locklin, *Spiritual But Not Religious? An Oar Closer to the Farther Shore* (Collegeville, MN: The Order of Saint Benedict, 2005); and Robert Wuthnow, *After the Baby Boomers: How Twenty- and Thirty-Somethings Are Shaping the Future of American Religion* (Princeton, NJ: Princeton University Press, 2007).

65. Johann Baptist Metz, "Passion for God: Religious Orders Today," in *Passion for God: The Mystical-Political Dimension of Christianity*, trans. J. Matthew Ashley (New York: Paulist Press, 1998), 159.

66. Martha C. Nussbaum, *Upheavals of Thought: The Intelligence of Emotions* (New York: Cambridge University Press, 2003), 403.

67. For a basic outline of Nussbaum's arguments against theocentric ethics, see Martha C. Nussbaum, "Religion and Women's Human Rights," in *Sex and Social Justice* (New York: Oxford University Press, 1999), 81–117. She justifies her rejection by insisting that "it is right for human beings to think as human beings, not as something other than human," because doing otherwise relegates the "good" and the "perfect" to a separate, external realm. See Martha C. Nussbaum, "Transcendence and Human Values," *Philosophy and Phenomenological Research* 64, no. 2 (2002): 445–52; and *Upheavals of Thought,* 551–56. In her opinion a preference for the transcendent cultivates destructive

emotions of shame and disgust, reinforces what humans are not able to accomplish on their own, and makes compassion an almost impossible ideal only feasible for the divine.

68. Martha C. Nussbaum, "Judaism and the Love of Reason," in *Philosophy, Feminism and Faith*, ed., Ruth Groenhout and Marya Bower, 9–39 (Bloomington: Indiana University Press, 2003), 13.

69. Ibid., 14.

70. Nussbaum acknowledges central themes of Reform Judaism to which she is drawn and which complement her own work: the primacy of the moral, the priority of conscience, core moral tenets such as love of humanity, social justice, peace and mercy, emphasis upon cosmopolitan religion, historical understanding of tradition, the role of ritual in moral formation and expression, and sex equality. See Nussbaum, "Judaism and the Love of Reason."

71. Ibid., 28.

72. In addition, several scholars argue that this presentation of Christianity is oversimplified and set in a false dichotomy when compared with Judaism. See Diana Fritz Cates, "Conceiving Emotions: Martha Nussbaum's Upheavals of Thought," *Journal of Religious Ethics* 31 (2003): 325–41; and Martin Kavka, "Judaism and Theology in Martha Nussbaum's Ethics," *Journal of Religious Ethics* 31 (2003): 343–59.

73. Martha C. Nussbaum, "Religion and Women's Human Rights," in Nussbaum, *Sex and Social Justice*, 88–102.

74. Nussbaum, "Judaism and the Love of Reason," 28.

75. Johann Baptist Metz, quoted in Kevin Burke, S.J., and Robert Lassalle-Klein, *Love That Produces Hope: The Thought of Ignacio Ellacuría* (Collegeville, MN: Liturgical Press, 2006), 251.

76. Johann B. Metz, *The Emergent Church: The Future of Christianity in a Post-Bourgeois World*, trans. Peter Mann (New York: Crossroad, 1981), 2.

77. Johann B. Metz, "On the Biographical Itinerary of My Theology," in *A Passion for God*, 1–2. For other bibliographical analysis, see James Matthew Ashley, *Interruptions: Mysticism, Politics, and Theology in the Work of Johann Baptist Metz* (Notre Dame, IN: University of Notre Dame Press, 1998), 27–58; and Gaspar Martinez, *Confronting the Mystery of God: Political, Liberation, and Public Theologies* (New York: Continuum, 2001), 25–38.

78. Johann Baptist Metz, "Political Theology," in *Sacramentum Mundi: An Encyclopedia of Theology*, vol. 5, ed. Karl Rahner (New York: Herder and Herder, 1970), 1239.

79. Ibid., 1241.

80. Ibid., 1239.

2. What Are They Saying about Compassion in Philosophical Ethics?

1. See Laurence Blum, "Compassion," in *The Westminster Dictionary of Christian Ethics*, ed. James F. Childress and John Macquarrie (Philadelphia: Westminster Press, 1986), 109.

2. Ibid., 612.

3. Ibid., 84.

4. Plato, *The Republic*, §519a, trans. Robin Waterfield (New York: Oxford University Press, 1993), 247.

5. Ibid., §577e, 322.

6. Ibid., §604c, 357–58.

7. Clifford Orwin, "Compassion," *American Scholar* (Summer 1980): 325.

8. Ibid.

9. For a more descriptive explanation, see Tad Brennan, "Stoic Moral Psychology," in *The Cambridge Companion to the Stoics*, ed. Brad Inwood (New York: Cambridge University Press, 2003), 269–70.

10. Nancy Sherman, *Making a Necessity of Virtue: Aristotle and Kant on Virtue* (New York: Cambridge University Press, 1997), 101–3.

11. Ibid., 103.

12. Cicero, "Discussions at Tusculum," Book V, in *Readings from Cicero*, trans. Michael Gant (New York: Penguin Books, 1917), 74.

13. For a brief historical overview of compassion in political philosophy, see Nussbaum's discussion in *Upheavals of Thought*, 297–326; and Davies's review in *A Theology of Compassion*, 232–40.

14. See Troel Engberg-Pedersen, *Paul and the Stoics* (Louisville, KY: Westminster John Knox Press, 2000), 35–47, 301–4.

15. See Nussbaum, *Upheavals of Thought*, 528.

16. Christopher Gill, "The School in the Roman Imperial Period," in *The Cambridge Companion to the Stoics*, ed. Brad Inwood (New York: Cambridge University Press, 2003), 42.

17. Cheryl Hall, *The Trouble with Passion: Political Theory beyond the Reign of Reason* (New York: Routledge, 2005), 5.

18. Aristotle, *Nichomachean Ethics*, trans. Terence Irwin (Indianapolis, IN: Hackett Publishing, 1985), §1149.b, 187.

19. Ibid.

20. Martha Nussbaum, "Morality and Emotions," in *Routledge Encyclopedia of Philosophy*, ed. E. Craig (London: Routledge, 1998).

21. Aristotle, *On Rhetoric*, trans. W. Rhys Roberts (New York: The Modern Library, 1954), §1385b, 113.

22. See Aristotle, *Nicomachean Ethics*, 178.

23. Davies, *A Theology of Compassion*, 217.

24. Nancy Sherman's evaluation of Kant and the emotions is quite informative here (see *Making a Necessity of Virtue*, 146–48).

25. Immanuel Kant, *The Metaphysical Principles of Virtue*, trans. James Ellington (Indianapolis: Bobbs-Merrill Company, 1964), 122.

26. See Dana Radcliff, "Compassion and Commanded Love," *Faith and Philosophy* 11, no. 1 (January 1994): 53.

27. For an overview of the role of virtue theory in Christian moral theology, see John Mahoney, *The Making of Moral Theology: A Study of Roman Catholic Moral Theology* (New York: Oxford University Press, 1989). For a similar overview of its development in Christian social ethics, see Alasdair MacIntyre, *A Short History of Ethics* (New York: Routledge, 1990) and Joseph J. Kotva, Jr., *The Christian Case for Virtue Ethics* (Washington DC: Georgetown University Press, 1997).

28. For contemporary scholarship on the contribution of virtue ethics in various aspects of social ethics, see Stanley Hauerwas, *A Community of Character: Toward a Constructive Christian Social Ethic* (Notre Dame, IN: University of Notre Dame Press, 1981); Spohn, *Go and Do Likewise*; James F. Keenan, *Virtues for Ordinary Christians* (Kansas City, MO: Sheed and Ward, 1996); Daniel J. Harrington and James F. Keenan, *Jesus and Virtue Ethics: Building Bridges between New Testament Studies and Moral Theology* (Kansas City, MO: Sheed and Ward, 2002); and Darlene Weaver, *Self-Love and Christian Ethics* (Cambridge, MA: Cambridge University Press, 2002).

29. For scholarship on Aristotelian virtue, see Alasdair MacIntrye, *After Virtue: A Study in Moral Theory*, 2nd ed. (Notre Dame, IN: University of Notre Dame Press, 1984); and Martha Nussbaum, *The Fragility of Goodness: Luck and Ethics in Greek Tragedy and Philosophy*, 2nd ed. (Cambridge, MA: Cambridge University Press, 2001). For the heritage and contribution of Aquinas, see Jean Porter, *The Recovery of Virtue: The Relevance of Aquinas for Christian Ethics* (Louisville, KY: Westminster John Knox Press, 1990); James F. Keenan, "Proposing Cardinal Virtues," *Theological Studies* 56 (1995); and Stephen Pope, *The Ethics of Thomas Aquinas* (Washington DC: Georgetown University Press, 2002).

30. Kotva, *The Christian Case for Virtue Ethics,* 8.

31. Plato, *The Republic*, §517c, 244.

32. Spohn, *Go and Do Likewise*, 87.

33. Aristotle, *Nichomachean Ethics*, §1130a.

34. Ibid.

35. Kotva, *The Christian Case for Virtue Ethics*, 16–47.

36. Aquinas, *Summa Theologica*, trans. Fathers of the English Dominican Province, 2 vols. (New York: Benziger Brothers, 1947), II.II.30.4 sed contra and ad. 2, 1320.

37. Ibid., II.II.31.3 sed contra, 1322.

38. Ibid., I.II.56.1 sed contra, 823.

39. See Cates, *Choosing to Feel,* 5–15.

40. Edward Schillebeeckx, "Church, Sacrament of Dialogue," in *God the Future of Man*, trans. N. D. Smith (New York: Sheed and Ward, 1968), 136.

41. James F. Keenan, *Moral Wisdom: Lessons and Texts from the Catholic Tradition* (New York: Sheed and Ward, 2004), 139–57.

42. Aquinas, *Summa Theologica*, II.II.30.2 sed contra, 1318.

43. MacIntyre, *After Virtue*, 127.

44. Kotva, *The Christian Case for Virtue Ethics*, 108.

45. Hauerwas, *A Community of Character*, 37.

46. Ibid., 18.

47. Kotva, *The Christian Case for the Virtue Ethics*, 144–47.

48. For an overview of the Enlightenment orientation to the fundamental ethical questions, see James Delaney, *Rousseau and the Ethics of Virtue* (New York: Continuum, 2006), 40–42.

49. See Charles Griswold, *Adam Smith and the Virtues of the Enlightenment* (Cambridge: Cambridge University Press, 1999), 15.

50. Adam Smith, *The Theory of Moral Sentiments* (Amherst, NY: Prometheus Books, 2000), 3.

51. Alexander Broade, "Sympathy and the Impartial Spectator," in *The Cambridge Companion to Adam Smith*, ed. Knud Haakonssen (Cambridge: Cambridge University Press, 2006), 177.

52. Smith, *The Theory of Moral Sentiments*, 4.

53. Ibid.

54. Knud Haakonssen, "Introduction," in Haakonssen, *The Cambridge Companion to Adam Smith*, 10.

55. Broade, "Sympathy and the Impartial Spectator," 163.

56. Smith, *The Theory of Moral Sentiments*, 22.

57. Ibid., 7.

58. Ibid., 24.

59. Haakonssen, "Introduction," 13.

60. Smith, *The Theory of Moral Sentiments*, 10.

61. Jean-Jacques Rousseau, *Émile, or Treatise on Education* <1762>, trans. William H. Payne (Amherst, NY: Prometheus Books, 2003; New York: D. Appleton, 1896), 42.

62. Delaney, *Rousseau and the Ethics of Virtue*, 49.

63. Ibid.

64. Ibid., 223.

65. Ibid., 210.

66. Rousseau, *Émile*, 203.

67. Arthur Schopenhauer, *On the Basis of Morality*, trans. E. F. J. Payne (Indianapolis, IN: Hackett, 1995), 172.

68. Arthur Schopenhauer, *The World as Will and Representation*, trans. E. F. J. Payne (New York: Dover Publications, 1966), 1:315.

69. Schopenhauer, *On the Basis of Morality*, 147.

3. What Are They Saying about Compassion in Theological Ethics?

1. Dianne Bergant, "Compassion in the Bible," in *Compassionate Ministry*, ed. Gary L. Sapp (Birmingham, AL: Religious Education Press, 1993), 12.

2. Ibid., 24–25.

3. John Donahue, "Biblical Perspectives on Justice," in *The Faith That Does Justice*, ed. John C. Haughey, S.J., 68–112 (New York: Paulist Press, 1977), 69.

4. Bergant, "Compassion in the Bible," 27.

5. Wayne Whitson Floyd, Jr., "Compassion in Theology," in Sapp, *Compassionate Ministry*, 40.

6. Bergant, "Compassion in the Bible," 28.

7. Ibid., 30.

8. John R. Donahue, S.J., *The Gospel in Parable: Metaphor, Narrative, and Theology in the Synoptic Gospels* (Minneapolis: Augsburg Fortress, 1990), 126.

9. Ibid., 127.

10. Ibid., 131.

11. "Luke," in *The Oxford Bible Dictionary*, ed. John Barton and John Muddiman (Oxford: Oxford University Press, 2001), 924.

12. Pheme Perkins, *Love Commandments in the New Testament* (New York: Paulist Press, 1982), 43.

13. Ibid., 64.

14. Edward Collins Vacek, S.J., "A Catholic Theology of Philanthropy," paper presented at Fordham University, 3 December 2007.

15. Cates, *Choosing to Feel*, 203.

16. Tsvi Blanchard, "Life outside the Ark: Jewish Reflections on American Politics and Public Duties," paper presented at Pulpit Politics: Gender, Religion and Social Justice in 2008, Fordham University Center for Ethics Education, New York City, 22 April 2008.

17. Jim Wallis, *God's Politics: Why the Right Gets It Wrong and the Left Doesn't Get It* (San Francisco: HarperOne, 2006), 20–30.

18. Martinez, *Confronting the Mystery of God*, 81.

19. Norbert F. Lohfink, S.J., *Option for the Poor: The Basic Principle of Liberation Theology in Light of the Bible* (N. Richland Hills, TX: BIBAL Press, 1987).

20. Daniel J. Harrington, S.J., and James F. Keenan, S.J., *Jesus and Virtue Ethics: Building Bridges between New Testament Studies and Moral Theology* (Lanham, MD: Sheed and Ward, 2002), 58.

21. Augustine, "The Moral Behavior of the Catholic Church," in *The Essential Augustine*, ed. Vernon J. Bourke (Indianapolis: Hackett, 1974), 165.

22. Augustine, *The Confessions* III/2, trans. Maria Boulding, series ed. John E. Rotelle (Hyde Park, NY: New City Press, 1997), 76.

23. Ibid., 77.

24. Augustine, *On Christian Doctrine Book II*, "On the Steps to Wisdom," §11.

25. Augustine's Sermon #259, quoted in John Burnaby, *Amor Dei: A Study of the Religion of St. Augustine* (Norwich, England: Canterbury Press, 1991), 5.

26. Daniel H. Williams, "Augustine Says We Must Love the Very Best the Most," *Christianity Today* (September 2007): 55.

27. Augustine, "The Moral Behavior of the Catholic Church," in Bourke, *The Essential Augustine*, 165.

28. Augustine, *Exposition on Psalm 46*.

29. Susan R. Holman, *The Hungry Are Dying: Beggars and Bishops in Roman Cappadocia* (Oxford: Oxford University Press, 2001).

30. Basil, "In a Time of Famine and Drought §2," trans. Susan R. Holman, in ibid., 185.

31. Gregory of Nanzianzus, Oration 14:39–40, trans. M. F. Toal, *The Sunday Sermons of the Great Fathers* (Chicago: Henry Regnery, 1963), 43–64, quoted in Holman, *The Hungry Are Dying*, 142.

32. Gregory of Nyssa, "On the Love of the Poor: 2 On the Saying 'Whoever Has Done It to One of These Has Done It to Me' §477," trans. Susan R. Holman, in Holman, *The Hungry Are Dying*, 199.

33. Basil, "Homily 7.8: Patrologiae Cursus," series Graeca, trans. J. Migne, quoted by Holman in *The Hungry Are Dying*, 107.

34. Gregory of Nyssa, "On the Love of the Poor: 2 On the Saying 'Whoever Has Done It to One of These Has Done It to Me,'" in Holman, *The Hungry Are Dying,* 205.

35. Gregory of Nyssa, "On the Love of the Poor: 1 'On Good Works'" §453, in ibid., 195.

36. Holman, *The Hungry Are Dying*, 105.

37. Basil, Homily 6.2, quoted in Brian Daly, S.J., "Building a New City: The Cappadocian Fathers and the Rhetoric of Philanthropy," *Journal of Early Christian Studies* 7, no. 3 (1999): 444.

38. Basil, "Homily 6," in Toal (trans.), *The Sunday Sermons of the Great Fathers*, 43–64, quoted in Holman, *The Hungry Are Dying*, 55.

39. Holman, *The Hungry Are Dying*, 98.

40. Aquinas, *Summa contra Gentiles*, trans. Vernon J. Bourke (Garden City, NY: Hanover House, 1956), III 17.6.

41. Ibid., III.25.8.

42. Aquinas, *Summa Theologica*, II.II.30.4 sed contra, 1320.

43. Hollenbach, *The Common Good and Christian Ethics,* 9.

44. Ibid., 82.

45. Aquinas, *Summa Theologica*, I.II.76.3 sed contra, 932.

46. Gregory Baum, *Compassion and Solidarity: The Church for Others* (Toronto: House of Anansi Press, 1992), 84.

47. Wendy Farley, *Tragic Vision and Divine Compassion,* 87.

48. Ibid., 89.

49. Ibid., 79.

50. Margaret Farley, *Compassionate Respect: A Feminist Approach to Medical Ethics and Other Questions* (New York: Paulist Press, 2002).

51. Chung Hyun Kyung, *Struggle to Be the Sun Again: Introducing Asian Women's Theology* (Maryknoll, NY: Orbis Books, 1993), 36–52.

52. M. Shawn Copeland, "To Live at the Disposal of the Cross: Mystical-political Discipleship as Christological Locus," in *Christology: Memory, Inquiry, Practice*, College Theology Society 48, ed. Anne M. Clifford and Anthony J. Godzieba (Maryknoll, NY: Orbis Books, 2002), 177–98.

53. Lisa Sowle Cahill, "Christology, Ethics and Spirituality," in *Re-Thinking Christ: Proclamation, Explanation, and Meaning*, ed. Tatha Wiley (New York: Continuum, 2003), 206.

54. Gustavo Gutiérrez, *A Theology of Liberation*, 15th anniv. ed. (Maryknoll, NY: Orbis Books, 1988), xxi.

55. Ibid., 115.

56. Jon Sobrino, S.J., *The Principle of Mercy: Taking the Crucified People from the Cross* (Maryknoll, NY: Orbis Books, 1992), 2.

57. Ibid., 1–11.

58. Ibid., 24.

59. See Anne E. Patrick, "Toward Renewing the 'Life and Culture of the Fallen Man': *Gaudium et Spes* as Catalyst for Catholic Feminist Theology," in *Feminist Ethics and the Catholic Moral Tradition*, Readings in Moral Theology 9, ed. Charles E. Curran, Margaret A. Farley, and Richard A. McCormick, S.J. (New York: Paulist Press, 1996); Mary Elizabeth Hobgood, "Poor Women, Work, and US Catholic Bishops: Discerning Myth from Reality in Welfare Reform," *Journal of Religious Ethics* 25, no. 2 (Fall 1997).

60. For example, Charles Curran argues that "precisely because Catholic social teaching is authoritative and binding on Catholics to some degree, it remains somewhat general and avoids specifics." See Charles Curran, *Catholic Social Teaching: A Historical, Theological and Ethical Analysis* (Washington DC: Georgetown University Press, 2002), 109.

4. Compassion as "Upheaval" in the Political Philosophy of Martha C. Nussbaum

1. Martha C. Nussbaum, "Narratives of Inequality," commencement address to the Odyssey Project, Chicago, 31 May 2003.

2. The following offer evidence of the various trajectories of Nussbaum's thought: *Liberty of Conscience: In Defense of America's Tradition of Religious Equality* (New York: Basic Books, 2008) evaluates the vibrancy of American democracy in light of contemporary challenges to religious tolerance and equality; *The Clash Within: Democracy, Religious Violence and India's Future* (Cambridge, MA: Harvard University/Belknap Press, 2007) challenges the famous "clash of civilizations" theory through an examination of the evolution of democracy in the world's largest democratic society; *The Frontiers of Justice: Disability, Nationality and Species Membership* (Cambridge, MA: Harvard University/Belknap Press, 2007) expands traditional theories of justice by exploring three groups that are not normally included in justice debates (the disabled, transnational organizations, and nonrational animals); *Upheavals of Thought: The Intelligence of Emotions* (Cambridge: Cambridge University Press, 2001) provides a literary analysis of compassion in a variety of sources; *The Fragility of Goodness: Luck and Ethics in*

Greek Tragedy and Philosophy (Cambridge: Cambridge University Press, 2001) explores themes of vulnerability in the Greek poets and philosophers; *Hiding from Humanity: Disgust, Shame, and the Law* (Princeton, NJ: Princeton University Press, 2004) considers the impact of the emotions of shame and disgust on conceptions of law; *Women and Human Development: The Capabilities Approach* (Cambridge: Cambridge University Press, 2001) debates theories of global human development using the personal narratives of two poor Indian women; and *Cultivating Humanity: A Classical Defense of Reform in Liberal Education* (Cambridge: Harvard University Press, 1997) considers the role of liberal arts education in creating more international citizenship.

3. For an example of her scholarship in this area, see Martha C. Nussbaum, "The Enduring Significance of John Rawls," *Chronicle of Higher Education*, 20 July 2001.

4. Martha C. Nussbaum, "Aristotle, Politics, and Human Capabilities," *Ethics* 111 (October 2000): 2.

5. Nussbaum, *The Fragility of Goodness*, xxx.

6. Martha C. Nussbaum, "Aristotelian Social Democracy," in *Liberalism and the Good*, ed. Bruce Douglas, Gerald Mara, and Henry Richardson (New York: Routledge, 2000), 217.

7. See Nussbaum, *Cultivating Humanity*, 9–11.

8. Nussbaum, "Aristotle, Politics, and Human Capabilities," 132.

9. Martha C. Nussbaum, "Patriotism and Cosmopolitanism," in *For Love of Country: Debating the Limits of Patriotism*, ed. Joshua Cohen (Boston: Beacon Press, 1996), 5.

10. Nussbaum, *Upheavals of Thought*, 301–2.

11. Nussbaum, *Women and Human Development*, 33, emphasis added.

12. Nussbaum, "Aristotle, Politics, and Capabilities," 103.

13. Nussbaum, *Cultivating Humanity*, 98–99.

14. In the preface of the revised edition of *The Fragility of Goodness*, Nussbaum asserts that her orientation to Aristotle distinguishes her from other neo-Aristotelians whose agenda in returning to the ancient philosopher involves "discrediting" the Enlightenment project for its overemphasis on the role of reason in the moral life, or in creating what she considers to be a false dichotomy between utilitarian/Kantian theories of ethics and virtue theory (see xxv–xxvi).

15. See Nussbaum, *Frontiers of Justice*, 159–60.

16. Nussbaum, *Sex and Social Justice,* 57.

17. Nussbaum notes a dichotomy in contemporary eudaimonistic theories between the "good-condition approach" and the "activity-condition approach." The former is easily recognizable as Platonic and proposes that human flourishing "exists in a stable condition of the self which is impervious to external conditions." Human dignity is not in any way contingent upon goods, and the human need for them is an embarrassing feature of human existence. The more Aristotelian activity-condition approach, on the other hand, claims that good action creates flourishing, but that such action depends upon access to a variety of material resources (*The Fragility of Goodness*, 322).

18. Nussbaum, *Frontiers of Justice*, 74.

19. Nussbaum, "Aristotelian Social Democracy," 243. See also "The Future of Feminist Liberalism," *Proceedings and Addresses of the American Philosophical Association* 74, no. 2 (November 2000): 49.

20. Nussbaum, *The Fragility of Goodness*, xxii.

21. Nussbaum, *Women and Human Development*, 79.

22. Nussbaum, "The Feminist Critique of Liberalism," in *Sex and Social Justice*, 55–80. She asserts that while the individual's free choice of religion ought to be protected

by the political sphere, a stance she claims to share with Catholic philosophical theologian Jacques Maritain, societies invariably construct religions and religious values, which in turn affect capabilities for flourishing.

23. Nussbaum, *Frontiers of Justice*, 96–154.

24. Ibid, 160.

25. Ibid., 168–69.

26. Nussbaum, "Aristotelian Social Democracy," 217.

27. Nussbaum, *Women and Human Development*, 78–80. The preliminary list of these goods, which she ultimately develops into a list of human capabilities, includes morality, the human body, capacity for pleasure and pain, cognitive capability, early infant development, practical reason, affiliation with others, relatedness to other species and nature, recreation, and individuality.

28. Nussbaum, "Patriotism and Cosmopolitanism," 2–20.

29. See Nussbaum's full argument in "Aristotelian Social Democracy," 228–40. She suggests that one approach to liberalism assesses flourishing according to one's accumulation of wealth and is clearly evident in policies directing economic development in the developing world. She faults this approach for violating the Kantian practical imperative of treating persons as ends. A second expression of liberalism recognizes wealth as a good but focuses on distributing it equally and fairly. The Rawlsian theory of justice falls into this category. She argues that this approach also misses the mark because it uncritically ties human flourishing to material goods, rather than questioning if people are actually able to use these goods to flourish. The third expression emphasizes the centrality of choice as the source of human dignity and therefore shapes public policy in a way that protects preferences and desires. Nussbaum criticizes this approach for failing to recognize that desires and preferences are culturally constructed and therefore not necessarily indicative of actual choice.

30. Nussbaum, "Aristotelian Social Democracy," 211.

31. Ibid., 209.

32. Nussbaum, *Upheavals of Thought*, 1.

33. Nussbaum situates herself in the same trajectory as Carol Gilligan in *In a Different Voice: Psychological Theory and Women's Development* (Cambridge, MA: Harvard University Press, 1982), Nel Noddings in *Caring: A Feminine Approach to Ethics and Moral Education* (Berkeley and Los Angeles: University of California Press, 1984); and Susan Okin, "Reason and Feeling in Thinking about Justice," *Ethics* 99, no. 2 (January 1989): 229–49.

34. Nussbaum, *Upheavals of Thought*, 2.

35. Ibid., 3.

36. Ibid., 43.

37. Ibid., 22.

38. Nussbaum, *Women and Human Development*, 79.

39. Ibid., 60–64.

40. Nussbaum, *Upheavals of Thought*, 38.

41. Ibid., 33.

42. Nussbaum notes the way in which the capabilities in this light echo Aristotle's own list of serious suffering, including death, bodily assault or ill-treatment, old age, weakness, disfigurement, immobility, reversals of expectations, absence of good prospects (see *Upheavals of Thought*, 307).

43. Cates, "Conceiving Compassion," 328.

44. Nussbaum, *Upheavals of Thought*, 319.

45. Ibid., 319.

46. Nussbaum claims that the "non-eudaimonistic emotion" of wonder helps moral agents tighten their circles of concern but wonder does not necessarily tie others' ends into our own (*Upheavals of Thought*, 55, 321).

47. Charles E. Curran, *Directions in Fundamental Moral Theology* (Notre Dame, IN: University of Notre Dame Press, 1985), 138–55.

48. Martha C. Nussbaum, "Compassion and Terror," *Daedalus* 132 (Winter 2003): 25.

49. Nussbaum initially devised the capabilities approach to human development with economist Amartya Sen in the mid-1980s when collaborating with him on the World Institute for Development Economics Research in Finland. Together, they asserted that U.N. models for development ought to shift their focus from the distribution of material goods to an assessment of people's actual conditions of flourishing. See *The Quality of Life*, ed. Martha C. Nussbaum and Amartya Sen (Oxford: Oxford University Press, 1993). Nearly two decades later Nussbaum articulated a distinct methodology for the approach in her book *Women and Human Development: The Capabilities Approach to Justice*.

50. Nussbaum, *Women and Human Development*, 105.

51. For the full description of the ten central capabilities, see ibid., 78–80.

52. Nussbaum provides helpful parameters for defining what she means by choice. It involves functioning well in a variety of spheres, creating a plan for one's life to avoid feeling like a herd animal, actual options made possible by a vague notion of the good, and a strong sense of separateness or idea that each person is his or her own end (see "Aristotelian Social Democracy," 238).

53. Nussbaum, *Women and Human Development*, 71.

54. Martha C. Nussbaum, "Tragedy and Human Capabilities: A Response to Vivian Walsh," *Review of Political Economy* 15, no. 3 (2003): 415, emphasis added.

55. Sen's approach is explained in *Development as Freedom* (New York: Knopf, 1999). For several differences between them, see Nussbaum's discussions in *Women and Human Development*, 11–15, and "Tragedy and Human Capability," 417. For example, Sen envisions the capabilities approach as a comparison among quality of life standards with the intention of achieving equality of capability, while Nussbaum argues for a "threshold" of capabilities that provides a basis for constitutional principles citizens can demand of their governments. Although Sen never actually devised a list of capabilities, he prioritizes them; Nussbaum's list of ten all are of equal importance, and therefore one cannot be suppressed in the hopes of advancing another. Sen does not emphasize the political importance of imagination and emotion both in devising the capabilities and as actual capabilities themselves.

56. Nussbaum, "Aristotelian Social Democracy," 216.

57. Nussbaum, "Patriotism and Cosmopolitanism," 13.

58. Mary Elizabeth Hobgood, *Dismantling Privilege: An Ethics of Accountability* (Cleveland: Pilgrim Press, 2000), 7.

59. Nussbaum, *Women and Human Development*, 77.

60. Lisa Cahill notes the connections between Nussbaum and the feminist natural law tradition: there are certain things that we can recognize as necessary for human flourishing, there are certain things we can hold to be true about human persons, and there are certain obligations we can derive from these common observations. See Lisa Cahill, "Embodiment and Justice for Women: Martha Nussbaum and Catholic Social Teaching," presented at the Transforming Unjust Structures: Capability and Justice conference, Von Hügel Institute, University of Cambridge, June 2003. Suzanne DeCrane suggests that other approaches to justice would do well to start with Nussbaum's comprehensive anthropology. She notes that embodiment, appreciation of culture, the

importance of critical reflection, and the possibility for revision have been missing in much Christian anthropology. She argues that not having an anthropology that makes minimal claims about what it means to be a human person "is to trust that unconstrained social forces will eventually produce an appropriate set of circumstances for human living." See Susanne M. DeCrane, *Aquinas, Feminism, and the Common Good* (Washington DC: Georgetown University Press, 2004), 38.

61. Nussbaum, *Upheavals of Thought*, 45.
62. Ibid., 187–88.
63. Cates, "Conceiving Emotions," 330.

5. Compassion as "Interruption" in the Political Theology of Johann Baptist Metz

1. Johann B. Metz, "Toward a Christianity of Political Compassion," in *Love That Produces Hope: The Thought of Ignacio Ellacuría*, ed. Kevin Burke, S.J., and Robert Lassalle-Klein (Collegeville, MN: Liturgical Press, 2006), 251.

2. Metz, "Political Theology," in Rahner, *Sacramentum Mundi*, 1239.

3. Metz, "The Church's Social Function in the Light of a 'Political Theology,'" in *Love's Strategy: The Political Theology of Johann Baptist Metz*, ed. John K. Downey (Harrisburg, PA: Trinity Press International, 1999), 26, 31.

4. Metz, "The Church and the World," in *Love's Strategy: The Political Theology of Johann Baptist Metz*, ed. John K. Downey (Harrisburg, PA: Trinity Press International, 1999), 23, 24.

5. Metz, "The Church's Social Function in the Light of a 'Political Theology,'" 27.

6. M. Shawn Copeland unpacked this latent theme in Metz's theology in her presidential address to the Catholic Theological Society of America in 2002. She contended that political theology might interrupt American theologians and practicing Christians who prefer to examine intellectually (and therefore safely) "contexts and questions at a distance," rather than to resist the sociopolitical conditions of our times that cause unjust suffering. See "Political Theology as Interruptive," *CTSA Proceedings* 59 (2004): 71–82. See also a roundtable discussion, "The Future of Political Theology," *Horizons* 32, no. 2 (Fall 2007): 306–28.

7. Johann Baptist Metz, in *Hope against Hope: Johann Baptist Metz and Elie Wiesel Speak Out on the Holocaust*, ed. Ekkehard Schuster et al. (New York: Paulist Press, 1999), 14.

8. Metz, *A Passion for God*, 54.

9. Metz, *Hope against Hope*, 19.

10. This is Jim Wallis's main argument in *God's Politics*.

11. Although this orientation is implicit in many of the documents of modern Catholic social teaching, it is explicitly stated in *Gaudium et Spes*.

12. Metz, *A Passion for God*, 56.

13. Metz, *Hope against Hope*, 44, 45.

14. For Metz's argument for the development of a moral awareness of tradition in Jewish-Christian ecumenism, see "Christians and Jews after Auschwitz," in *The Emergent Church*, 17–33.

15. Johann Baptist Metz, "On the Biographical Itinerary of My Theology," in *A Passion for God*, 3.

16. James Forbes, "A Letter of Reference from the Poor," paper presented at Celebrating Faith in Action: The Faith Community's Response to the Challenge of Poverty,

sponsored by the Bertram A. Beck Institute on Religion and Poverty, Fordham University, New York City, 16 April 2007.

17. See Bruce Morrill's assessment in *Anamnesis as Dangerous Memory: Political and Liturgical Theology in Dialogue* (Collegeville, MN: Liturgical Press, 2000), 44.

18. Metz, "The Church's Social Function," 38.

19. Metz, *The Emergent Church*, 20.

20. Metz, *A Passion for God*, 27.

21. Metz, *The Emergent Church*, 21.

22. Metz, *A Passion for God*, 27.

23. Johann Baptist Metz, "Theology in the Struggle," in Johann Baptist Metz and Jürgen Moltmann, *Faith and the Future: Essays on Theology, Solidarity, and Modernity* (Maryknoll, NY: Orbis Books, 1995), 50.

24. Metz, *A Passion for God*, 134.

25. Metz, "Suffering from God: Theology as Theoldicy," *Pacifica* 5 (October 1992): 274–87.

26. Johann Baptist Metz, "1492—Through the Eyes of a European Theologian," in Metz and Moltmann, *Faith and the Future*, 67.

27. Johann Baptist Metz, "Between Evolution and Dialetics," in Downey, *Love's Strategy*, 84.

28. For Metz's discussion, see "The Future of Faith in a Hominized World," in *Theology of the World* (New York: Herder and Herder, 1969), 57–77. For Taylor's thorough treatment of secularism, see *A Secular Age* (Cambridge, MA: Belknap Press, 2007).

29. Metz, "The Future of Faith in a Hominized World," 6.

30. Johann Baptist Metz, "Theology Today: New Crises and New Visions," *Proceedings of the Catholic Theology Society of America* 40 (1985), 2.

31. Metz, "The Future of Faith in a Hominized World," 63.

32. Johann Baptist Metz, "Bread of Survival," in Downey, *Love's Strategy*, 55.

33. Johann Baptist Metz, "Unity and Diversity: Problems and Prospects for Inculturation," in Metz and Moltmann, *Faith and the Future*, 63.

34. Metz, in Schuster et al., *Hope against Hope*, 49–50.

35. Metz, *A Passion for God*, 37–39.

36. Metz, "Christians and Jews after Auschwitz," in Downey, *Love's Strategy*, 50.

37. Ibid., 44.

38. Metz, "The Church's Social Function," 29.

39. J. Matthew Ashley, "Johann Baptist Metz," in *The Blackwell Companion to Political Theology*, ed. Peter Scott and William T. Cavanaugh (Malden, MA: Blackwell Publishing, 2007), 241.

40. For example, see Arne Rasmusson, *The Church as Polis: From Political Theology to Theological Politics as Exemplified by Jürgen Moltmann and Stanley Hauerwas* (Notre Dame, IN: University of Notre Dame Press, 1995), 12–13; and Martinez, *Confronting the Mystery of God*, 52.

41. Metz, *Hope against Hope*, 12.

42. See Metz, "Political Theology," in Rahner, *Sacramentum Mundi*, 1238–43.

43. John K. Downey, "Risking Memory," in Downey, *Love's Strategy*, 4.

44. Metz, "The Church and the World," 24.

45. Metz, "The Church's Social Function," 30–31.

46. Metz, "The Church and the World," 25, 24.

47. Ashley, *Interruptions*, 146.

48. Metz, "The Church's Social Function," 31.

49. Metz, *A Passion for God*, 38. For liberation theologians' perspectives, see Gustavo Gutiérrez, *A Theology of Liberation*, 15th anniv. ed. (Maryknoll, NY: Orbis Books, 1988), 83–140; and Ignacio Ellacuría, S.J., "The Historicity of Christian Salvation," in *Mysterium Liberationis: Fundamental Concepts of Liberation Theology*, ed. Ignacio Ellacuría, S.J., and John Sobrino, S.J. (Maryknoll, NY: Orbis Books, 1990), 251–88.

50. Metz, "The Future Church," 18.

51. Metz, "The Church's Social Function," 32, 34.

52. Metz, "Bread of Survival," 54.

53. Ibid., 54.

54. Metz, "Christians and Jews after Auschwitz," in Downey, *Love's Strategy,* 47–48.

55. Metz, *The Emergent Church*, 17–18.

56. Ibid., 163.

57. Metz, "Bread of Survival," 57.

58. Heribert Fischer, "Mysticism," in Rahner, *Sacramentum Mundi*, 4:137.

59. John Welch, "Mysticism," in *The New Dictionary of Theology,* ed. Joseph A. Komonchak, Mary Collins, and Dermot Lane (Collegeville, MN: Liturgical Press, 1987), 694.

60. For Ashley's evaluations of Metz's foundations in Rahner's theology, see *Interruptions*, 59–95.

61. Metz, *A Passion for God,* 56.

62. Eli Wiesel, quoted in Metz, "The Church after Auschwitz," in *A Passion for God,* 121. Metz echoes this sentiment in "Disciples in the Emerging Church," National Sisters Vocation Conference, Chicago, 17–21 March 1982: "For the holocaust is not just a German catastrophe but, on closer inspection, a Christian catastrophe."

63. Johann Baptist Metz, "Communicating a Dangerous Memory," in Downey, *Love's Strategy*, 137, emphasis added.

64. Rebecca Chopp, *The Praxis of Suffering: An Interpretation of Liberation and Political Theologies* (Maryknoll, NY: Orbis Books, 1986), 44.

65. Metz, in Schuster et al., *Hope against Hope*, 17, emphasis added.

66. Metz, "The Courage to Pray," in Downey, *Love's Strategy*, 165–68.

67. Metz, in Schuster et al., *Hope against Hope*, 49.

68. Johann Baptist Metz, *Poverty of Spirit,* trans. John Drury (New York: Paulist Press, 1968), 21.

69. Ibid., 63.

70. Metz, "The Church and the World," 23.

71. Metz, "Theology Today," 69.

72. Johann Baptist Metz, *Faith in History and Society: Toward a Practical Fundamental Theology*, trans. J. Matthew Ashley (New York: Crossroad, 2007), 182.

73. Ibid.

74. Metz, "The Future in the Memory of Suffering," 8.

75. Metz, *Faith in History and Society*, 182.

76. Ashley translates the German *Eingedenken* as "remembrance," given the usage of the German adverb *eingedenk* in the Order of the Mass. See Metz, *Passion for God*, 181n10.

77. Metz, *Faith in History and Society*, 210, 222.

78. Metz, *Faith in History and Society*, 62.

79. Ibid., 194.

80. Metz, in Schuster et al., *Hope against Hope*, 30.

81. Metz, *Faith in History and Society*, 194.

82. Ibid., 196.

83. Ibid., 208.

84. Metz, "Christians and Jews after Auschwitz," in Downey, *Love's Strategy,* 47.

6. Christian Ethics after Katrina

1. Kristin A. Bates and Richelle M. Swan, *Through the Eye of Katrina*: *Social Justice in the United States* (Durham, NC: Carolina Academic Press, 2007), 5.

2. For examples of socioeconomic analysis, see ibid.; Chester Hartman and Gregory D. Squires, *There Is No Such Thing as a Natural Disaster: Race, Class, and Hurricane Katrina* (New York: Routledge, 2006); David Dante Troutt, Charles Ogletree, and Derrick Bell, eds., *After the Storm: Black Intellectuals Explore the Meaning of Hurricane Katrina* (New York: The New Press, 2006); Hillary Potter, ed., *Racing the Storm: Racial Implications and Lessons Learned from Hurricane Katrina* (Lanham, MD: Lexington Books, 2007); The South End Press Collective, *What Lies Beneath: Katrina, Race and the State of the Union* (Cambridge, MA: South End Press, 2007); Marvin Olasky, *The Politics of Disaster: Katrina, Big Government, and a New Strategy for the Future* (Nashville, TN: Thomas Nelson, 2006); Eric Mann, *Katrina's Legacy: White Racism and Black Reconstruction in New Orleans and the Gulf Coast* (Charleston, SC: Frontlines Press, 2007); Michael Eric Dyson, *Come Hell or High Water: Hurricane Katrina and the Color of Disaster* (New York: Basic Books, 2006); Manning Marable and Kristen Clarke, *Seeking Higher Ground: The Hurricane Katrina Crisis, Race and Public Policy Reader* (New York: Palgrave MacMillan, 2007).

3. For a theological analysis, see Michael Eric Dyson's analysis of the relationship between Katrina and Christianity in *Come Hell or High Water,* chap. 10; Barbara Hilkert Andolsen examines Christian colorblind perceptions of the storm in "Social Justice, the Common Good, and New Signs of Racism," in Cassidy and Mikulich, *Interrupting White Privilege,* 56–75; Rabbi Michael Lerner, "Hurricane Katrina: God and Social Morality," in *Hurricane Katrina: Response and Responsibilities*, ed. John Brown Childs (Nampa, ID: New Pacific Press, 2007); Jacob Hee Cheol Lee, "A Lesson from Katrina: Pastoral Care from an Asian Theological Perspective," *The Journal of Pastoral Care and Counseling* 61, nos. 1–2 (Spring-Summer 2007): 113–18.

4. Metz, "Christians and Jews after Auschwitz," in Downey, *Love's Strategy,* 48.

5. Thomas Gabe, Gene Falk, and Maggie McCarty, "Hurricane Katrina: Socio-Demographic Characteristics of Impacted Areas" (Washington DC: Congressional Research Service, 4 November 2005).

6. Troutt, *After the Storm,* 5.

7. Brookings Institution, "New Orleans after the Storm: Lessons from the Past, a Plan for the Future"; Alan Berube and Bruce Katz, "Katrina's Window: Confronting Concentrated Poverty across America," Brookings Institution (October 2005), available at www.brookings.edu; Arloc Sherman and Isaac Shapiro, "Essential Facts about the Victims of Hurricane Katrina," The Center on Budget and Political Priorities, 19 September 2005; and "Katrina: The Demographics of Disaster," The Urban Institute, 9 September 2005.

8. Gabe, Falk, and McCarty, "Hurricane Katrina: Socio-Demographic Characteristics of Impacted Areas." By "acute" impact this Congressional Research Service report refers to flooding and "catastrophic, significant or moderate structural damage."

9. Haeyoun Park, Kassie Bracken, and Erin Aiger, "The Patchy Return of New Orleans," *The New York Times*, 31 August 2008.

10. Metropolitan Policy Program at Brookings, "The New Orleans Index," anniv. ed. (August 2008). Available online.

11. Park, Bracken, and Aiger, "The Patchy Return of New Orleans."

12. Oxfam America, "Mirror on America: How the State of Gulf Coast Recovery Reflects on Us All" (Washington DC: Oxfam America, August 2008), 11.

13. Heather Joslyn, "Struggling toward Recovery," *The Chronicle of Philanthropy* 19, no. 21 (August 23, 2007): 32.

14. Elizabeth T. Boris and C. Eugene Steuerle, eds., "After Katrina: Public Expectation and Charities' Response," Policy Brief. Emerging Issues in Philanthropy Series (Washington DC: The Urban Institute, 2006), 7.

15. Charity Navigator's transcript of a round table discussion with representatives of leading charities a year after Katrina. Available at www.charitynavigator.org.

16. Ashley Tsongas, quoted in Joslyn, "Struggling toward Recovery," 32.

17. Pablo Eisenberg, "Americans Generous? Not Really," *The Chronicle of Philanthropy* 20, no. 5 (January 24, 2008): 64.

18. Boris and Steuerle, "After Katrina," 6.

19. Hall, "A Charitable Divide," 15.

20. Ibid.

21. The Red Cross has since received an "A-" from the American Institute of Philanthropy, an independent watch-dog organization that offered a progress report on the work of charities in the Gulf Region to Congress in December 2005. The report is available at www.charitywatch.org.

22. Dyson, *Come Hell or High Water*, 207.

23. Benjamin R. Bates and Rukhsana Ahmed, "Disaster Pornography: Hurricane Katrina, Voyeurism, and the Television Viewer," in Bates and Swan, *Through the Eye of Katrina*, 191.

24. Ibid.

25. Metz, *The Emergent Church*, 27.

26. Dyson, *Come Hell or High Water*, 13.

27. Virginia R. Dominguez, "Seeing and Not Seeing: Complicity in Surprise," Understanding Katrina: Perspectives from the Social Sciences, 11 September 2005, posted 11 June 2006 on the Social Sciences Review Council website.

28. Ibid.

29. Mukoma Wa Ngugi, "New Orleans the Third World," *Znet*, 8 September 2005.

30. Sheryll Cashin, "Katrina: The American Dilemma Redux," in Troutt, *After the Storm*, 30.

31. The Pew Research Center for the People and the Press, "The Black and White of Public Opinion: Did the Racial Divide in Attitudes about Katrina Mislead Us?" 31 October 2005. Available at people-press.org.

32. See Doane, "New Song, Same Old Tune, 108–10.

33. Sherman and Shapiro, "Essential Facts about the Victims of Hurricane Katrina," Center on Budget and Policy Priorities, 19 September 2005.

34. David Bentley Hart, *The Doors of the Sea: Where Was God in the Tsunami?* (Grand Rapids, MI: Eerdmans, 2005), 37.

35. Bates and Ahmed, *Through the Eye of Katrina*, 189.

36. Terrence Check, "The Voices of Katrina: Ethos, Race, and Congressional Testimonials," in Bates and Swan, *Through the Eye of Katrina*, 241.

37. Dyson, *Come Hell or High Water*, 212.

38. Janet Densmore, speaking in Patrick Lewis, "The Katrina Canvass," a video piece that accompanied Carmen Sisson's "One Town Uses the Arts to Revive after Hurricane Katrina," *The Christian Science Monitor* (14 May 2008).

39. For first-person narrative accounts of the storm and its aftermath, see Rebecca Antoine, ed., *Voices Rising: Stories from the Katrina Narrative Project* (New Orleans: University of New Orleans Press, 2008); Lolla Vollen and Chris Ying, eds., *Voices from the Storm: Stories of Hurricane Katrina and Its Aftermath* (New York: McSweeney's, 2006); Spike Lee and Sam Pollard, *When the Levees Broke—A Requiem in Four Parts* (HBO Home Studio, 2006); "Healthcare in the Aftermath of Katrina," a documentary created by the Henry J. Kaiser Foundation, clips and information available at www.kff.org/uninsured/voices.cfm.

40. Rick Burton, quoted in Susan Larson, "Homegrown Effort of UNO Keeps Katrina Stories Alive," in *The Times-Picayune*, 26 March 2008.

41. Stephanie Mingo, quoted in "Housing Woes in New Orleans Continue Nearly a Year after Katrina," *The News Hour with Jim Lehrer*, 27 July 2006.

42. Susan Saulny, "5,000 Public Housing Units in New Orleans Are to Be Razed," *The New York Times*, 15 June 2006.

43. "Religious Leaders Help Renters Buy in New Orleans," National Public Radio, 14 March 2008.

44. Hobgood, *Dismantling Privilege*, 7.

45. Doane, "New Song, Same Old Tune," 107.

46. Hobgood, *Dismantling Privilege*, 31.

47. Wendy Farley, *Tragic Vision and Divine Compassion*, 76.

48. West, *Disruptive Christian Ethics*, 9.

49. Maxine Greene, *Releasing the Imagination* (San Francisco: Jossey-Bass Publishers, 1995), 3.

50. Ibid., 33.

51. Ibid., 39.

52. The Pew Research Center for the People and the Press, "The Black and White of Public Opinion."

53. Doane, "New Song, Same Old Tune," 110–17.

54. Barack Obama, "A More Perfect Union," United States Constitution Center, Philadelphia, 17 March 2008. Available at http://my.barackobama.com/page/content/hisownwords.

55. Ashley Tsongas, quoted in Joslyn, "Struggling toward Recovery."

56. Hobgood, *Dismantling Privilege*, 5.

57. Rev. Vien Nguyen, quoted in Patrick Strange, "Strength to Lead the Charge," *The Times-Picayune*, 29 August 2006.

58. Lance Hill, "The Miracle of Versailles: New Orleans Vietnamese Community Rebuilds," *The Louisiana Weekly*, 23 January 2006.

59. "Choice and connectivity" is a phrase used frequently by the Brookings Institution in its recommendations for rebuilding the Gulf Coast (see, for example, "New Orleans after the Storm"). By this the authors mean creating racially, ethnically, and economically integrated neighborhoods where inhabitants are empowered to participate in life in community.

7. Transforming the Jericho Road

1. For an overview of the historical development of the Christian community's engagement in social questions, see Roger Haight, *Christian Community in History*, 2 vols. (New York: Continuum, 2004).

2. For a historical overview of this debate and more recent trajectories, see Jean Porter, "The Search for a Global Ethic," *Theological Studies* 62 (2001): 105–21; Lisa

Sowle Cahill, "Toward Global Ethics," *Theological Studies* 63 (2002): 324–44; and Mary Elsbernd, O.S.F., "Social Ethics," *Theological Studies* 66 (2005): 137–58.

3. John Rawls, *A Theory of Justice*, rev. ed. (Cambridge, MA: The Belknap Press of Harvard University, 1999); David Hollenbach, *Refugee Rights: Ethics, Advocacy, and Africa* (Washington DC: Georgetown University Press, 2008), and *The Global Face of Public Faith: Politics, Human Rights, and Christian Ethics* (Washington DC: Georgetown University Press, 2003). For a list and explanation of the eight UN MDGs, see www.undp.org/mdg/basics.shtml. Examples of bishops' statements include the Synod of Bishops, *Justice in the World* (1971) and the U.S. Conference of Catholic Bishops, *Economic Justice for All* (1986). For an overview of statements put forward by Catholic bishops conferences around the world, see Terrence McGoldrick, "Episcopal Conferences Worldwide on Catholic Social Teaching," *Theological Studies* 59 (1998): 22–50.

4. Seyla Benhabib, *Situating the Self: Gender, Community, and Postmodernism in Contemporary Ethics* (New York: Routledge, 1992). She argues that her goal "is to situate reason and the moral self more decisively in contexts of gender and community, while insisting upon the discursive power of individuals to challenge such situatedness in the name of universal principles, future identities and as yet undiscovered communities" (8). West notes that "any attempt to sever universal concerns from particular ones will most often create an ethical analysis that ignores or disadvantages women by minimizing the significance of moral issues tied to concrete circumstances in their daily lives or related to their bodily integrity" (see *Disruptive Christian Ethics*, 43). Martha Nussbaum notes that while it is important to "preserve types of diversity that are compatible with human dignity and other basic values" through a wariness of the ways in which universal claims can overpower cultural particularities, at the same time "getting beaten up and being malnourished have depressing similarities everywhere," a reality that bolsters the need for an approach that can respond to the common denominator of dehumanizing suffering (see *Women and Human Development*, 51).

5. See Stanley Hauerwas, who provocatively claims that "Jesus did not have a social ethic, but that his story is a social ethic." Therefore, the central task of Christianity when it comes to engaging the world is to "recapture the social significance" of the many behaviors that constitute Jesus' ethic, including "kindness, friendship, and the formation of families," which do not reform the world but create a new one (see *A Community of Character: Toward a Constructive Christian Social Ethic* [Notre Dame, IN: University of Notre Dame Press, 1981], 11). James F. Keenan proposes that the virtue of justice can guide our more "universal relationships" with those in our wider circles of concern particularly when informed by mercy, which empowers us to "enter into the chaos of another" (see "Proposing Cardinal Virtues," 709–29). Virginia Held notes that where the previously mentioned strategies do not take historical embeddedness or the complexity of human relationality sufficiently into consideration, an ethic of care "focuses on attentiveness to context, trust, responding to needs, and offers narrative nuance; it cultivates caring relations in both personal, political, and global contexts" (see *The Ethics of Care*, 157). John Paul II notes that the virtue of solidarity ought to shape the relationships between developed and undeveloped persons and nations through a "firm and preserving determination to commit oneself to good of all and to each individual because we are all really are responsible for all" (*Sollicitudo Rei Socialis*, no. 38).

6. Foundational texts in this trajectory include Karl Barth's discussion of the ethical implications of the love command in *The Christian Life: Church Dogmatics*, Book 4 (Grand Rapids, MI: Eerdmans, 1981); Gérard Gilleman, *The Primacy of Charity in Moral Theology* (Westminster, MD: Newman Press, 1959); Gene Outka, *Agape: An Ethical*

Analysis (New Haven, CT: Yale University Press, 1972); and Anders Nygren, *Agape and Eros* (Chicago: University of Chicago Press, 1982).

7. The World Parliament of Religions suggests four basic global commitments for religious believers based on the notion of love of neighbor as self, commonly shared by many religious traditions: a commitment to a culture of nonviolence, a culture of solidarity and just economic order, a culture of tolerance and life of truthfulness, and a culture of human rights and equal partnership between men and women. Edwark C. Vacek, S.J., argues for the centrality of love of God in Christian ethics in *Love, Human and Divine: The Heart of Christian Ethics* (Washington DC: Georgetown University Press, 1994). In his first social encyclical Pope Benedict XVI suggests that encounters with God's love animate Christian political engagement in the world in the form of "social charity" that can guide the mission of the "lay faithful" "to configure social life correctly, respecting its legitimate autonomy and cooperating with other citizens according to their respective competences and fulfilling their own responsibility (*Deus Caritas Est,* no. 29). In addition, he recommends that "ecclesial charity" guide the church, particularly its charitable organizations. This love mirrors that of the Good Samaritan and therefore "is first of all the simple response to immediate needs and specific situations: feeding the hungry, clothing the naked, caring for and healing the sick, visiting those in prison" (§31). For a global perspective on the viability of the love command in global ethics, see Enrico Chiavacci, "Globalization and Justice: New Horizons for Moral Theology," in *Catholic Theological Ethics in the World Church*, ed. James F. Keenan, 239–44 (New York: Continuum, 2007), as well as a collection of essays in *A Just and True Love: Feminism at the Frontiers of Theological Ethics*, ed. Francine Cardman, Maura A. Ryan, and Brian F. Linnane (Notre Dame, IN: University of Notre Dame Press, 2008).

8. Peters, *In Search of the Good Life,* 9.

9. J. Bryan Hehir, "Making Globalisation Work for the World's Poor," in *Ethical Globalisation*, ed. Lorna Gold, J. Bryan Hehir, and Enda McDonagh (Maynooth, Ireland: Trocaire, 2005), 28–29.

10. Peters, *In Search of the Good Life*, 4.

11. Schweiker, *Theological Ethics and Global Dynamics*, xv.

12. Ibid., xx.

13. Elliot and Lemert, *The New Individualism*, 5–7.

14. Jonathan Sacks, *The Dignity of Difference: How to Avoid the Clash of Civilizations* (New York: Continuum, 2003), 67–81.

15. Peter L. Berger and Samuel P. Huntington, *Many Globalizations: Cultural Diversity in the Contemporary World* (New York: Oxford University Press, 2002), 9.

16. Roland Robertson, *Globalization: Social Theory and Global Culture* (New York: Sage Publications, 1992).

17. See Peter Berger, ed., *The Desacralization of the World: Resurgent Religion and World Politics* (Grand Rapids, MI: Eerdmans, 1999); and Gabriel A. Almond, R. Scott Appleby, and Emmanuel Sivan, *Strong Religion: The Rise of Fundamentalisms around the World* (Chicago: University of Chicago Press, 2003), 86.

18. Farmer, *Pathologies of Power*, 140, emphasis added.

19. Nussbaum, "Patriotism and Cosmopolitanism," 13, emphasis added.

20. Schweiker, *Theological Ethics and Global Dynamics*, 158.

21. Berger and Huntington, *Many Globalizations*, 3.

22. Cassidy and Mikulich, *Interrupting White Privilege*, 2.

23. West, *Disruptive Christian Ethics*.

24. Hobgood, "White Economic and Erotic Disempowerment," 40.

25. Peters, *In Search of the Good Life*, 195.

26. Hobgood, "White Economic and Erotic Disempowerment," 51.

27. Greene, *Releasing the Imagination*, 28.

28. Jonathan Glover, *Humanity: A Moral History* (New Haven, CT: Yale University Press, 2001), 408–9.

29. Margie Pfeil, "The Transformative Power of the Periphery," in Cassidy and Mikulich, *Interrupting White Privilege*, 130.

30. Robert Wuthnow, *All in Sync: How Music and Art Are Revitalizing American Religion* (Berkeley and Los Angeles: University of California Press, 2006), 240.

31. Elaine Scary, *On Beauty and Being Just* (Princeton, NJ: Princeton University Press, 1999), 6.

32. Wuthnow, *All in Sync*, 241.

33. Greene, *Releasing the Imagination*, 39.

34. Bryan Massingale, "Healing a Divided World," *Origins* 37, no. 11 (16 August 2007).

35. Hobgood, *Dismantling Privilege*, 10.

36. Denise Breton and Stephen Lehman, *The Mystic Heart of Justice: Restoring Wholeness in a Broken World* (West Chester, PA: Chrysalis Books, 2001), xv.

37. Kwame Anthony Appiah, *The Ethics of Identity* (Princeton, NJ: Princeton University Press, 2004).

38. Lisa Sowle Cahill, "Moral Theology: From Evolutionary to Revolutionary Change," in Keenan, *Catholic Theological Ethics in a World Church*, 221–27.

Selected Bibliography

Agid, Shana. "Locked and Loaded: The Prison Industrial Complex and the Response to Hurricane Katrina." In Bates and Swan, *Through the Eye of Katrina*, 55–76.

Almond, Gabriel A., R. Scott Appleby, and Emmanuel Sivan. *Strong Religion: The Rise of Fundamentalisms Around the World*. Chicago: University of Chicago Press, 2003.

Aquinas, Thomas. *Summa Theologica*. Translated by Fathers of the English Dominican Province. New York: Benziger Brothers, 1947.

Aristotle. *Nichomachean Ethics*. Translated by Terence Irwin. Indianapolis, IN: Hacket Publishing, 1985.

Ashley, James Matthew. *Interruptions: Mysticism, Politics, and Theology in the Work of Johann Baptist Metz*. Notre Dame, IN: University of Notre Dame Press, 1998.

———. "Johann Baptist Metz." In *The Blackwell Companion to Political Theology*, ed. Peter Scott and William T. Cavanaugh, 241–55. Malden, MA: Blackwell Publishing, 2004.

Bates, Kristin, and Richelle Swan. *Through the Eye of Katrina: Social Justice in the United States*. Durham, NC: Carolina Academic Press, 2007.

Benhabib, Seyla, ed. *Situating the Self: Gender, Community, and Postmodernism in Contemporary Ethics*. New York: Routledge, 1992.

Bergant, Dianne. "Compassion in the Bible." In *Compassionate Ministry,* ed. Gary L. Sapp, 9–34. Birmingham, AL: Religious Education Press, 1993.

Berger, Peter L., and Samuel P. Huntington, eds. *Many Globalizations: Cultural Diversity in the Contemporary World*. New York: Oxford University Press, 2002.

Breton, Denise, and Stephen Lehman. *The Mystic Heart of Justice: Restoring Wholeness in a Broken World*. West Chester, PA: Chrysalis Books, 2001.

Brookings Institution. "New Orleans after the Storm: Lessons from the Past, a Plan for the Future." October 2005. Available at www.brookings.edu.

Brubaker, Pamela, ed. *Justice in a Global Economy: Strategies for Home, Community, and World*. Louisville, KY: Westminster John Knox Press, 2006.

Burke, Kevin F., and Robert Lassalle-Klein, eds. *Love That Produces Hope: The Thought of Ignacio Ellacuría*. Collegeville, MN: Liturgical Press, 2006.

Burnaby, John. *Amor Dei: A Study of the Religion of St. Augustine*. Norwich, England: Canterbury Press, 1991.

Cahill, Lisa Sowle. "Embodiment and Justice for Women: Martha Nussbaum and Catholic Social Teaching." Presented at the Transforming Unjust Structures: Capability and Justice conference, Von Hügel Institute, University of Cambridge, June 2003.

———. "Toward Global Ethics." *Theological Studies* 63 (2002): 324–44.

Cassidy, Laurie M., and Alex Mikulich, eds. *Interrupting White Privilege: Catholic Theologians Break the Silence*. Maryknoll, NY: Orbis Books, 2007.

Cates, Diana Fritz. *Choosing to Feel: Virtue, Friendship, and Compassion for Friends*. Notre Dame, IN: University of Notre Dame Press, 1997.

———. "Conceiving Emotions: Martha Nussbaum's Upheavals of Thought." *Journal of Religious Ethics* 31 (2003): 325–41.

Childress, James F., and John Macquarrie, eds. *The Westminster Dictionary of Christian Ethics*. Philadelphia: Westminster Press, 1986.

Chopp, Rebecca. *The Praxis of Suffering: An Interpretation of Liberation and Political Theologies*. Maryknoll, NY: Orbis Books, 1986.

Chung Hyun Kyung. *Struggle to be the Sun Again: Introducing Asian Women's Theology*. Maryknoll, NY: Orbis Books, 1993.

Coleman, John A. "Making the Connections: Globalization and Catholic Social Thought." In *Globalization and Catholic Social Thought: Current Crisis, Future Hope*, ed. John A. Coleman, S.J., and William F. Ryan, S.J., 9–27 (Maryknoll, NY: Orbis Books, 2005; Toronto: Novalis, 2005).

Copeland, M. Shawn. "To Live at the Disposal of the Cross: Mystical-Political Discipleship as Christological Locus." In *Christology: Memory, Inquiry, Practice*, College Theology Society 48, ed. Anne M. Clifford and Anthony J. Godzieba, 177–98. Maryknoll, NY: Orbis Books, 2002.

Curran, Charles E. *Directions in Fundamental Moral Theology*. Notre Dame, IN: University of Notre Dame Press, 1985.

Curran, Charles E., Margaret A. Farley, and Richard A. McCormick, S.J., eds. *Feminist Ethics and the Catholic Moral Tradition*. Readings in Moral Theology 9. New York: Paulist Press, 1996.

Davies, Oliver. *A Theology of Compassion: Metaphysics of Difference and the Renewal of Tradition*. Grand Rapids, MI: Eerdmans, 2001.

DeCrane, Susanne M. *Aquinas, Feminism, and the Common Good*. Washington, DC: Georgetown University Press, 2004.

Delaney, James. *Rousseau and the Ethics of Virtue*. New York: Continuum, 2006.

De La Torre, Miguel. *Doing Christian Ethics from the Margins*. Maryknoll, NY: Orbis Books, 2007.

Downey, John K., ed. *Love's Strategy: The Political Theology of Johann Baptist Metz*. Harrisburg, PA: Trinity Press, 1999.

Dwyer, Judith, ed. *The New Dictionary of Catholic Social Thought*. Collegeville, MN: Liturgical Press, 1994.

Dyson, Michael Eric. *Come Hell or High Water: Hurricane Katrina and the Color of Disaster*. New York: Basic Books, 2006.

Elliot, Anthony, and Charles Lemert. *The New Individualism: The Emotional Costs of Globalization*. New York: Routledge, 2006.

Farley, Margaret A. *Compassionate Respect: A Feminist Approach to Medical Ethics and Other Questions*. New York: Paulist Press, 2002.

Farley, Wendy. *Tragic Vision and Divine Compassion: A Contemporary Theodicy*. Louisville, KY: Westminster John Knox Press, 1990.

Farmer, Paul. *Pathologies of Power: Health, Human Rights, and the New War on the Poor*. Berkeley and Los Angeles: University of California Press, 2005.

Floyd, Wayne Whitson, Jr. "Compassion in Theology." In *Compassionate Ministry*, ed. Gary L. Sapp, 35–63. Birmingham, AL: Religious Education Press, 1993.

Frankenberg, Ruth. "The Mirage of an Unmarked Whiteness." In Rasmussen et al., *The Making and Unmaking of Whiteness*, 72–96.

Giddens, Anthony. *Runaway World: How Globalization Is Reshaping Our Lives*. New York: Routledge, 2003.

Gillet, Richard. *The New Globalization: Reclaiming the Lost Ground of Our Christian Tradition*. Cleveland, OH: Pilgrim Press, 2005.

Glover, Jonathan. *Humanity: A Moral History*. New Haven, CT: Yale University Press, 2001.

Gold, Lorna, J. Bryan Hehir, and Enda McDonagh, eds. *Ethical Globalisation.* Maynooth, Ireland: Trocaire, 2005.

Greene, Maxine. *Releasing the Imagination.* San Francisco: Jossey-Bass Publishers, 1995.

Griswold, Charles. *Adam Smith and the Virtues of the Enlightenment.* Cambridge: Cambridge University Press, 1999.

Haakonssen, Knud, ed. *The Cambridge Companion to Adam Smith.* Cambridge: Cambridge University Press, 2006.

Haight, Roger. *Christian Community in History.* 2 vols. New York: Continuum, 2004.

Haker, Hille. "Compassion as a Global Programme for Christianity." In *In Search of Universal Values,* ed. Karl-Josep Kuschel and Dietman Mieth, 55–70. *Concilium* 4 (2001).

Hall, Holly. "A Charitable Divide." *Chronicle of Philanthropy* 20, no. 6 (10 January 2008).

Hart, David Bentley. *The Doors of the Sea: Where Was God in the Tsunami?* Grand Rapids, MI: Eerdmans, 2005.

Hartman, Chester, and Gregory D. Squires. *There Is No Such Thing as a Natural Disaster: Race, Class, and Hurricane Katrina.* New York: Routledge, 2006.

Held, Virginia. *The Ethics of Care: Personal, Political, and Global.* New York: Oxford University Press, 2006.

Hicks, Douglas. *Inequality and Christian Ethics.* New York: Cambridge University Press, 2000.

Hobgood, Mary Elizabeth. *Dismantling Privilege: An Ethics of Accountability.* Cleveland, OH: Pilgrim Press, 2000.

———. "White Economic and Erotic Disempowerment: A Theological Exploration in the Struggle against Racism." In Cassidy and Mikulich, *Interrupting White Privilege,* 40–55.

Hollenbach, David, S.J. *The Common Good and Christian Ethics.* New Studies in Christian Ethics. New York: Cambridge University Press, 2002.

Holman, Susan R. *The Hungry Are Dying: Beggars and Bishops in Roman Cappadocia.* Oxford: Oxford University Press, 2001.

Isasi-Díaz, Ada María, ed. *Mujerista Theology: A Challenge to Traditional Theology.* Maryknoll, NY: Orbis Books, 1996.

Kant, Immanuel. *The Metaphysical Principles of Virtue.* Translated by James Ellington. Indianapolis, IN: Bobbs-Merrill Co., 1964.

Kavka, Martin. "Judaism and Theology in Martha Nussbaum's Ethics." *Journal of Religious Ethics* 31 (2003): 343–59.

Keenan, James F. *Catholic Theological Ethics in the World Church.* New York: Continuum, 2007.

———. "Proposing Cardinal Virtues." *Theological Studies* 56 (1995).

———. *Virtues for Ordinary Christians.* Kansas City, MO: Sheed & Ward, 1996.

Knitter, Paul, and Chandra Muzaffar, eds. *Subverting Greed: Religious Perspectives on the Global Economy.* Maryknoll, NY: Orbis Books, 2002.

Komonchak, Joseph, Mary Collins, and Dermot Lane, eds. *The New Dictionary of Theology.* Collegeville, MN: Liturgical Press, 1987.

Kotva, Joseph J. *The Christian Case for Virtue Ethics: Moral Traditions and Moral Arguments.* Washington, DC: Georgetown University Press, 1996.

Lohfink, Norbert, S.J. *Option for the Pool: The Basic Principle of Liberation Theology in Light of the Bible.* N. Richland Hills, TX: Bibal Press, 1987.

MacIntyre, Alasdair C. *After Virtue: A Study in Moral Theory.* 2nd ed. Notre Dame, IN: University of Notre Dame Press, 1984.

Martinez, Gaspar. *Confronting the Mystery of God: Political, Liberation, and Public Theologies*. New York: Continuum, 2001.

Massingale, Bryan. "Healing a Divided World." *Origins* 37, no. 11 (16 August 2007).

McIntosh, Peggy. "White Privilege: Unpacking the Invisible Knapsack." Available on a number of websites.

McNeill, Donald P., Douglas A. Morrison, and Henri J. M. Nouwen. *Compassion: A Reflection on the Christian Life*. Garden City, NY: Doubleday, 1982.

Metz, Johann Baptist. "Bread of Survival." In Downey, *Love's Strategy*, 53–63.

———. "The Church after Auschwitz." In *A Passion for God*, 121–32.

———. "The Church and the World." In Downey, *Love's Strategy*, 13–25.

———. "The Church's Social Function." In Downey, *Love's Strategy*, 26–38.

———. "Communicating a Dangerous Memory." In Downey, *Love's Strategy*, 135–49.

———. "Disciples in the Emerging Church." Three seminars presented to the National Sisters Vocation Conference, Chicago, 17–21 March 1982.

———. *The Emergent Church: The Future of Christianity in a Post-Bourgeois World*. New York: Crossroad, 1981.

———. *Faith in History and Society: Toward a Practical Fundamental Theology*. Translated by J. Matthew Ashley. New York: Crossroad, 2007.

———. *A Passion for God: The Mystical-Political Dimension of Christianity*. Translated by J. Matthew Ashley. New York: Paulist Press, 1998.

———. "Political Theology." In *Sacramentum Mundi: An Encyclopedia of Theology*, vol. 5, ed. Karl Rahner. New York: Herder and Herder, 1970, 1238–43.

———. *Poverty of Spirit*. Translated by John Drury. New York: Paulist Press, 1968.

———. "Suffering from God: Theology as Theodicy." *Pacifica* 5 (1992): 274–87.

———. *Theology of the World*. Translated by William Glen-Doepel. New York: Herder and Herder, 1969.

———. "Theology Today: New Crises and New Visions." *Proceedings of the Catholic Theology Society of America* 40 (1985): 1–15.

———. "Toward a Christianity of Political Compassion." In *Love That Produces Hope: The Thought of Ignacio Ellacuría*, ed. Kevin Burke, S.J., and Robert Lassalle-Klein, 250–53. Collegeville, MN: Liturgical Press, 2006.

Metz, Johann Baptist, and Jürgen Moltmann. *Faith and the Future: Essays on Theology, Solidarity, and Modernity*. Maryknoll, NY: Orbis Books, 1995.

Moe-Loebeda, Cynthia. *Healing a Broken World: Globalization and God*. Minneapolis: Fortress Press, 2002.

Morrill, Bruce, S.J. *Anamnesis as Dangerous Memory: Political and Liturgical Theology in Dialogue*. Collegeville, MN: Liturgical Press, 2000.

Noddings, Nel. *Caring: A Feminine Approach to Ethics and Moral Education*. Berkeley and Los Angeles: University of California Press, 1984.

Nussbaum, Martha Craven. "Aristotelian Social Democracy." In *Liberalism and the Good*, ed. Bruce Douglas, Gerald Mara, and Henry Richardson, 203–52. New York: Routledge, 2000.

———. "Aristotle, Politics, and Human Capabilities." *Ethics* 111 (October 2000): 1–140.

———. "Compassion and Terror." *Daedalus* 132 (Winter 2003): 10–26.

———. *Cultivating Humanity: A Classical Defense of Reform in Liberal Education*. Cambridge: Harvard University Press, 1997.

———. *The Fragility of Goodness: Luck and Ethics in Greek Tragedy and Philosophy*. Cambridge: Cambridge University Press, 2001.

———. *Frontiers of Justice: Disability, Nationality, and Species Membership*. Cambridge, MA: Belknap Press, 2007.

———. "The Future of Feminist Liberalism." *Proceedings and Addresses of the American Philosophical Association* 74, no. 2 (November 2000): 47–79.

———. *Hiding from Humanity: Disgust, Shame, and the Law.* Princeton, NJ: Princeton University Press, 2004.

———. "Judaism and the Love of Reason." In *Philosophy, Feminism, and Faith*, ed. Ruth E. Groenhout and Marya Bower, 9–39. Bloomington: Indiana University Press, 2003.

———. "Patriotism and Cosmopolitanism" and "Reply." In *For Love of Country: Debating the Limits of Patriotism*, ed. Joshua Cohen, 2–20, 131–40. Boston: Beacon Press, 1996.

———. *Sex and Social Justice.* New York: Oxford University Press, 1999.

———. "Tragedy and Human Capabilities: A Response to Vivian Walsh." *Review of Political Economy* 15, no. 3 (2003): 413–418.

———. "Transcendence and Human Values." *Philosophy and Phenomenological Research* 64, no. 2 (2002): 445–52.

———. *Upheavals of Thought: The Intelligence of Emotions.* New York: Cambridge University Press, 2003.

———. *Women and Human Development: The Capabilities Approach.* Cambridge: Cambridge University Press, 2001.

Nussbaum, Martha C., and Amartya Sen, eds. *The Quality of Life.* Oxford: Oxford University Press, 1993.

Okin, Susan Moller. "Reason and Feeling in Thinking about Justice." *Ethics* 99 (January 1989): 229–49.

Olasky, Marvin. *The Politics of Disaster: Katrina, Big Government, and a New Strategy for the Future.* Nashville, TN: Thomas Nelson, 2006.

Orwin, Clifford. "Compassion." *American Scholar* (Summer 1980): 309–33.

Outka, Gene. *Agape: An Ethical Analysis.* New Haven, CT: Yale University Press, 1972,

Perkins, Pheme. *Love Commandments in the New Testament.* New York: Paulist Press, 1982.

Peters, Rebecca Todd. *In Search of the Good Life: The Ethics of Globalization.* New York: Continuum, 2006.

Porter, Jean. "The Search for a Global Ethic." *Theological Studies* 62 (2001): 105–21.

Potter, Hillary, ed. *Racing the Storm: Racial Implications and Lessons Learned from Hurricane Katrina.* Lanham, MD: Lexington Books, 2007.

Radcliff, Dana. "Compassion and Commanded Love." *Faith and Philosophy* 11, no. 1 (1994): 50–71.

Rasmussen, Birgit Brander, Irene J. Nexica, Eric Klinenberg, and Matt Wray, eds. *The Making and Unmaking of Whiteness.* Durham, NC: Duke University Press, 2001.

Rasmusson, Arne. *The Church as Polis: From Political Theology to Theological Politics as Exemplified by Jürgen Moltmann and Stanley Hauerwas.* Notre Dame, IN: University of Notre Dame Press, 1995.

Ritzer, George, ed. *The Blackwell Companion to Globalization.* Boston: Blackwell Publishing, 2007.

Robertson, Roland. *Globalization: Social Theory and Global Culture.* New York: Sage Publications, 1992.

Rousseau, Jean Jacques. *Émile, or Treatise on Education.* Translated by William H. Payne. Amherst, NY: Prometheus Books, 2003; New York: D. Appleton, 1909.

Sacks, Jonathan. *The Dignity of Difference: How to Avoid the Clash of Civilization.* New York: Continuum, 2003.

Scary, Elaine. *On Beauty and Being Just.* Princeton, NJ: Princeton University Press, 1999.

Schopenhauer, Arthur. *On the Basis of Morality*. Translated by E. F. J. Payne. Indianapolis: Hackett, 1995.

Schuster, Ekkehard, Johannes Baptist Metz, Elie Wiesel, and Reinhold Boschert-Kimmig, eds. *Hope against Hope: Johann Baptist Metz and Elie Wiesel Speak Out on the Holocaust Studies in Judaism and Christianity*. New York: Paulist Press, 1999.

Schweiker, William. *Theological Ethics and Global Dynamics: In a Time of Many Worlds*. Boston: Wiley-Blackwell, 2004.

Sen, Amartya. *Development as Freedom*. New York: Knopf, 1999.

Smith, Adam. *The Theory of Moral Sentiments* (1759). Amherst, NY: Prometheus Books, 2000.

Smith, Christian, and Melinda Lundquist Denton. *Soul Searching: The Religious and Spiritual Lives of American Teenagers*. New York: Oxford University Press, 2005.

Sobrino, Jon, S.J. *The Principle of Mercy: Taking the Crucified People from the Cross*. Maryknoll, NY: Orbis Books, 1994.

Sobrino, Jon, S.J., and Felix Wilfred, eds. *Globalization and Its Victims*. Concilium 5 (2001).

Spohn, William. *Go and Do Likewise: Jesus and Ethics*. New York: Continuum, 2000.

Stackhouse, Max. *God and Globalization: God and the Powers of Common Life*. Vol. 1 in Theology for the Twenty-first Century series, ed. Peter Stackhouse and Peter Paris. Harrisburg, PA: Trinity Press International, 2008.

Sullivan, William. *The Globalization of Ethics*. Cambridge: Cambridge University Press, 2007.

Taylor, Charles. *A Secular Age*. Cambridge, MA: Belknap Press, 2007.

Troutt, David Dante, Charles Ogletree, and Derrick Bell, eds. *After the Storm: Black Intellectuals Explore the Meaning of Hurricane Katrina*. New York: New Press, 2006.

Tudor, Steven. *Compassion and Remorse: Acknowledging the Suffering Other*. Morality and the Meaning of Life 11, ed. Albert W. Musschenga and Paul J. M. van Tongeran. Leuven, France: Peeters, 2001.

Vacek, Edward, S.J. *Love, Human and Divine: The Heart of Christian Ethics*. Washington DC: Georgetown University Press, 1994.

Wallis, Jim. *God's Politics: Why the Right Gets It Wrong and the Left Doesn't Get It*. San Francisco: HarperOne, 2006.

Weil, Jeannie Haubert. "Discrimination, Segregation, and the Racialized Search for Housing Post-Katrina." In Bates and Swan, *Through the Eye of Katrina*, 221–37.

West, Traci C. *Disruptive Christian Ethics: When Racism and Women's Lives Matter*. Louisville, KY: Westminster John Knox Press, 2006.

Wolfe, Alan. *One Nation after All: What Middle-Class Americans Really Think about God, Country, Family, Racism, Welfare, Immigration, Homosexuality, Work, The Right, The Left, and Each Other*. New York: Viking, 1998.

Wuthnow, Robert. *All in Sync: How Music and Art Are Revitalizing American Religion*. Berkeley and Los Angeles: University of California Press, 2006.

Index